Robert C. Jenkins

Canterbury

Diocesan History

Robert C. Jenkins

Canterbury
Diocesan History

ISBN/EAN: 9783743368484

Manufactured in Europe, USA, Canada, Australia, Japa

Cover: Foto ©Lupo / pixelio.de

Manufactured and distributed by brebook publishing software (www.brebook.com)

Robert C. Jenkins

Canterbury

DIOCESAN HISTORIES.

CANTERBURY.

BY

ROBERT C. JENKINS, M.A.

RECTOR AND VICAR OF LYMINGE, HON. CANON OF CANTERBURY.

WITH MAP.

PUBLISHED UNDER THE DIRECTION OF THE TRACT COMMITTEE.

LONDON :
SOCIETY FOR PROMOTING CHRISTIAN KNOWLEDGE.
NORTHUMBERLAND AVENUE, CHARING CROSS ;
43, QUEEN VICTORIA STREET, E.C. ; AND 48, PICCADILLY, W.
NEW YORK : POTT, YOUNG, & CO.
1880.

DEDICATED, BY PERMISSION,

TO

THE RIGHT HON. AND MOST REVEREND

ARCHIBALD CAMPBELL,

LORD ARCHBISHOP OF CANTERBURY,

PRIMATE OF ALL ENGLAND AND METROPOLITAN.

CONTENTS.

CANTERBURY.

CHAPTER I.

THE ROMAN PERIOD.

In opening our retrospect of the history of the Diocese of Canterbury, it is necessary to bear in mind the fact that the diocesan system in its later and local meaning can in no case be traced up to an earlier period than that of the establishment of Christianity in the Empire, begun by Constantine in the fourth, but only fully completed by Justinian in the sixth century. Before this adoption of the Church by the civil power, that local organization of its government represented by the modern parish and diocese was absolutely impracticable. The divisions of the Church were then rather personal and congregational, than local or geographical. To this the titles of parish (παροικία) and diocese (διοίκησις) expressly point;[1] and here

---

[1] The word *diœcesis* in the Eastern Church, and at the period of the Councils, has an entirely different meaning from that which our later usage has assigned it. The same may be said of the *parœcia*. The latter is equivalent to our modern *diocese*, the former is the largest division of this ecclesiastical world, and includes not only the *parœcia*, but also the metropolitical

they stand in marked contrast with those which
belonged to a later age, when, coactive jurisdiction
having been conferred upon the Church by the
State, the titles of "*eparchia*" and "*exarchia*" were
applied to the ecclesiastical districts of the Empire as
they had hitherto been to its civil divisions.   In the
primitive Church, as a learned canonist observes, the
divisions were simply into the urban, suburban, or
rural districts, the bishop presiding over the former,
for which a single church was then sufficient,
while in the neighbouring villages and rural places
churches were built which the Greeks called παροι-
κίαι, the Latins "*parochiæ*," over which presbyters
or chorepiscopi were appointed.   When the cities had
so increased as to render it difficult for a single prelate to govern them, the people were divided into
"legions" and "centuriæ," and the districts of the
city defined by certain limits, so that every one should
possess its own priest or governor.[1]   This organization was derived from the ancient civil divisions of
Rome, for, as the same writer observes, "Antiquity
presented an early image of these 'Parishes.'   For
when Rome was divided into nineteen urban 'tribes,'
and every tribe again into ten 'curiæ,' to every one
of these its proper temple and proper priest was
assigned."[2]

sees which represented *eparchies* or provinces.   It was equivalent to the *Exarchate* of the civil divisions of the Empire, and
to the *Patriarchate* of the ecclesiastical system.

[1] Emanuel Tellez Gonzalez, ad c. 2. X. de Paroch. n. 9.

[2] St. Epiphanius (Hæres. 69, n. 1) says of the churches of
Alexandria that "they are subject to one archbishop, and a priest

So persistently did the Romans adhere to their original tribal forms, that notwithstanding the early establishment of Christianity throughout Italy, a learned writer has proved that no parochial boundaries existed even in Rome itself before the year 1000.[1] Thus the claim of Pope Evaristus (resting on the spurious decretal which goes by his name) to have first instituted local parochial divisions in Rome, falls to the ground; while the improbability that this delimitation of parishes took place at an earlier period in the more distant parts of the Empire than at its centre becomes apparent. If Rome in the tenth century had no such local parishes, it is very unlikely that Kent in the seventh (as some affirm) had substituted the local for the congregational system.

Churches were undoubtedly designated by the names of the places in which they were situated, as the Church of Jerusalem, of Alexandria, of Rome; but no idea of a local division of dioceses or of parishes could have been entertained, until the Church entered upon a much more advanced stage of her existence, and the principle of jurisdiction was

---

is appointed over every one of them to administer in spiritual things to those who live around the church "—(διὰ τὰς ἐκκλη- σιαστικὰς χρείας τῶν οἰκητόρων πλησίων ἐκάστης ἐκκλησίας αὐτῶν). These were called by the citizens ἀμφόδοι (districts within roads), or λαύραι (squares), and were probably the earliest approach we know of to a parochial subdivision in a modern sense.

[1] Mario Lupi, Arciprete di Bergamo, ap. Tamagna, "Origini e prerogative dei Cardinale della S. R. C."

introduced into her system—a change which the
new relations between the Church and the State
necessitated, and which the confusions that had
already arisen from the intrusions of bishops and
clergy into other dioceses and parishes made as
important to themselves as to the state. The first
three General Councils exhibit to us the disorders
which had arisen from the want of this local separation.[1] Yet, strange as it may appear, the confusion
and even absence of local boundaries existed in many
places in the West at the time of the Council of
Trent. For in its chapters on reformation (Sess. xxiv.
c. 13) it is enjoined, "In those cities or places where
parochial churches have no settled bounds, nor their
rectors a distinct congregation under their care, but
where they administer the sacraments promiscuously
to all who come, the holy synod orders a separation
of the people into their regular and proper parishes,
and the assignment to every one of his own regular
and separate priest," &c. And this arrangement is
in every sense a necessary one ; for when " jurisdiction " was added to " order," and the general right
of officiating everywhere and for every one became at
once limited in its scope and made absolute and
exclusive within its new limits, it became essential
that these limits should be accurately and locally
defined. "Without limiting the jurisdiction of its
different magistrates, no government would be possible. And to grant to bishops the unlimited and

---

[1] Concil. Nicæn. can. 15. 'C. Ptan. can. 2. Ephesin.
can. 8, &c.

universal exercise of their authority would be the same as to take away from the Church all order and peace." Such is the conclusion of the late Cardinal Nardi,[1] forgetful that his argument has a fatal bearing upon the "*jurisdictio præveniens et concurrens*," claimed by the See of Rome in every diocese alike.[2]

From the age of Constantine to that of Justinian the government of the Church was gradually but most effectually brought into a perfect corre-

---

[1] "Elementi di Diritto Eccles." Ven. 1846, p. i. pag. 241.

[2] To take a clear view of the origin of *jurisdiction*, we must remember that the first great separation in the Christian body was that of the *ordo* and the *plebs*, described by Tertullian, and corresponding to our *clergy* and *laity*. The second is that between *order* and *jurisdiction*, represented by the *clerus* and the *ordo*, indicated very clearly by St. Ambrose (in Eph. c. iv. v. 11). After describing the earliest period of the Church, in which all her ministrations were in common, he adds, "When she embraced every place, congregations (conventicula) were constituted, and rectors and other officers ordained in the churches, in order that none of the clergy (clerus) who was not *ordained* (ordinatus) should presume to take any office which was not entrusted to him, and thus the Church began to be governed in another order and providence." It may be mentioned here that the *ordination*, or appointment to a special charge, became, in consequence of this new system, identical with the ordination to the ministry itself—no one being made a priest, but on his appointment to, or "incardination into" a distinct cure—"Dopo fatti i beneficij (writes Sarpi), l' istessa cosa era ordinarlo e assegnargli l'ufficio da exercitare." * Hence the later practice of requiring a "title" (properly a parish) before ordination.

---

* Trattato delle M. Benefic. p. 54. Ed. Mirandola, 1676.

spondence, and even coincidence with that of the
State. Even in the time of the Council of Chalce-
don, the union was so complete that every change in
the civil government produced a corresponding one
in that of the Church, the Council decreeing that
"Wherever a city was privileged by the Emperors,
the order of ecclesiastical dioceses ($\pi a \rho o \iota \kappa i a \iota$)
should follow the political and civil arrangements."
As the power of the Exarchs, and the civil Gover-
nors under them, died out—which in the West was
comparatively early—the bishops became the promul-
gators of the imperial laws, as the letters of Gregory
the Great indicate, and the patriarchal authority
growing (as Socrates complains) into a vast political
system, the Empire failed gradually before it, so that
the canons of the Church superseded at last the code
of Justinian itself. It might be supposed that this
growth of the power of the Church was more rapid
in the more distant provinces of the Empire than in
its central points ; and that Gaul and Britain in the
extreme West would present a very marked instance
of this development of ecclesiastical power. The
very feeble hold which the Empire had retained
over its more remote dependencies after the removal
of the Emperors to Constantinople, rendered the
alliance of the Church with the State in the West a
very different thing from what it was in the East,
and the three provinces into which Britain was originally divided, viz., Britannia prima, containing all on
the south side of the Thames; Britannia secunda,
all on the farther side of the Severn ; and Maxima
Cæsariensis, all the rest of the island to the northern

borders, do not appear to have had more than the single metropolitan bishop by whom they were severally represented at Arles and Ariminum. London, which was the metropolis of the southern province, York, of the northern, and Caerleon, of the intermediate one—appear, from all we know, to have been the only episcopal sees in the island; two others being added at a later period,—Valentia, which extended to the Frith of Forth, but was still under the jurisdiction of York; and Flavia Cæsariensis, including the district between the Thames and the Humber, of which the Colonia Londinensis (whether it be identified with Maldon or Lincoln) mentioned in the subscriptions to the Council of Ariminum (in 314), was probably the metropolis. The present diocese of Canterbury must then have been a kind of " *ecclesia suburbicaria* " to the metropolis of London.

The letter of Gregory the Great to Augustine which enjoins the consecration of bishops for other sees, exempts London from the jurisdiction of his successors, and appears to regard London and York as having the same metropolitical rank which they enjoyed during the Roman occupation. There is no reference in this letter to any previous diocese as existing in Kent, which there could hardly fail to have been if Augustine had been merely restoring, instead of actually founding, an episcopal see.[1] The city of Canterbury itself had been scarcely recovered, during the later Roman period, from the marsh on the verge of which it stands, as Mr. Godfrey

[1] Greg. M. Reg. Epp. l. xii. Ind. vii. ep. xv.

Faussett has shown in his masterly sketch of its earlier history; and was little more than a Roman station founded on the site of a British fastness—a site which, but for military purposes, would never have been chosen, and which even in the Saxon period was exposed to constant danger both from warfare and inundation. But what rank it may have held in regard to our early Christianity must, in the absence of all documentary evidence, be left to conjecture.

Previous to the arrival of Augustine (A.D. 597) " we have," as Kemble writes, "no trustworthy record of any single event of English history. Whatever precedes this, by whomsoever, and at what period soever related, is nothing more than tradition, and liable to all the accidents by which tradition is affected."[1] This statement, though substantially true, is somewhat too general and broad. For there can be no doubt that Bede, and even Goscelinus at a later date, possessed documentary evidence of the events which they record which preceded the advent of the Saxons. And Gildas, whose writings have reached our time, and who lived more than a century before, quotes "ecclesiastical histories" as his authorities for the narrative of the Diocletian period and the martyrdom of St. Alban and the other victims of that great persecution. The often-quoted words of Tertullian, affirming the conquest by Christianity of places in Britain which had been inaccessible to Roman arms, are admitted by Bishop Kaye, in his admirable work

---

[1] Cod. Dipl. Ævi Saxon. Intra. p. v.

on Tertullian, to be "declamatory." "Yet such a representation" (he adds) "would not have been hazarded unless it had been realized to a considerable extent in the actual state of Christianity."[1]

But when Britain is spoken of in connection with "countries and islands scarce known to us by name, and which it is impossible for us to enumerate," we can hardly believe that Britain itself was known to the writer by much more than its mere name, or attach great weight to so vague a statement. Whatever may have been the success of Christianity in the earliest days of its plantation in Britain, which Gildas carries back to the time of Tiberius, its progress seems to have been slow and arduous here, as among all the Celtic nations. Gildas speaks of its "cold reception" by some, while by some "it was received more, and by others less perfectly," and mentions its continuance in this state until the time of the Diocletian persecution. Bede seems to attribute their preservation of the faith to the "quiet tranquillity" they enjoyed; but, perhaps, this was to be attributed rather to the indifference which Gildas hints at, than to the depth and activity of the faith which seems so completely to have died out after the arrival of the Saxon conquerors. It would appear, from the absence of any record of warfare or of the triumphs of the Roman arms in Kent, that this county enjoyed a large share of that "quiet tranquillity" whose reign until the Diocletian persecution is asserted by our earliest historian.[2] The

[1] Eccl. Hist. from Tertullian, p. 94.
[2] This has been often observed and well illustrated by my

works of defence, of Roman or British construction,
are confined almost entirely to the coasts, showing that their design was rather to protect than
to overawe the population, whose settlements and
villas are to be traced along the principal roads,
indicating a wide-spread prosperity and opulence,
though inferior in many of their features to the similar remains discovered in more distant parts of the
island.   The civilization of Rome, which had reached
Kent immediately from its numerous continental
colonists, had tended to give its inhabitants a more
settled life and a more established form of government.   Fewer military inscriptions or records relating
to the garrisoning of the country are to be found
here than in any of the northern counties ; records
which ever indicate a disturbed and unsettled history.
On the other hand, the remains of villas and private
residences are very numerous, and the objects of
art which have been discovered in connection with
the Roman period in various parts of Kent show a
progress in refinement and civilization, which has not
always been found even in places where the remains
of public buildings are grander and more remarkable.
The advice given by Gregory the Great to Augustine,
in his letter to Mellitus, leads us to believe that
some, at least, of the temples and public buildings
were of good construction and of considerable size.
He charges him not to destroy these temples, but to
throw down the idols, and build altars to God in

friend Mr. Roach Smith, the most eminent of our Roman
antiquaries.

their stead, " For if," he adds, " these temples are well built " (which Augustine had doubtless reported them to be), " it is necessary that they should be adapted to the worship of the true God instead of to the service of devils."[1] The remains of the ancient basilical buildings at Dover, Lyminge, Reculver, and other places, justify this wise advice ; that it was acted upon afterwards is proved by the successive surrender of all these buildings to the Church, recorded in the Anglo-Saxon Chartulary.

On the history of the parish churches in the rural districts of Kent we have nothing to guide us before the mention of their existence in the Domesday Survey, except in those cases in which the Saxon charters give proofs of their still earlier foundation. At this point we may derive a reflected light from the contemporary history of the Gallican Church, as it is given us by St. Gregory of Tours. After giving us a more detailed description of the larger and costlier foundations which the great Gallican bishops had built in their principal cities, he enumerates the various village churches which were founded by St. Martin of Tours, and his successors, Briccius, Eustochius, Perpetuus, and Volusianus.[2]

It is not unreasonable to believe that our rural churches were thus founded as suburbicary appendages to the larger towns or monasteries in their immediate vicinity, and that the accession of Constantine produced here, as in Gaul, a great revival of church-

---

[1] Reg. Epp. l. ix. Ind. iv. ep. 71.
[2] Greg. Turon. Historia Franc. l. x. c. 31.

building, as well as of Christian art in general. We see the same zeal illustrated in a later day by the building of churches on their several manors and dependencies by the archbishops and monastic bodies of Kent, while the Roman materials frequently found in rebuilding the parish churches of the county indicate some primitive structures of a like kind as preceding them. One of the relics of this earlier stage of Christianity was the little church in Canterbury, in which Bertha is said to have worshipped before the arrival of Augustine in Kent.

The descriptions of Gildas and Bede of the great reaction which followed the persecution of Diocletian lead to the belief that a vast number of churches and oratories had been founded or restored at that period; though this sudden return of the Christian worshippers from the caves and crypts, or in some favoured cases the private houses of their more powerful brethren, is less to be attributed to the relaxation of the Diocletian persecution than to the accession of Constantine a few years after. De Caumont, a very competent authority on such a subject, affirms that "in Gaul up to the reign of Constantine there were no churches properly so called, and the mysteries were celebrated in the houses of the new converts, in crypts and in secret places. After the accession of this prince, Christianity prodigiously increased in the provinces as well as in Italy, and churches were multiplied."[1]

The state of religion, and the causes of its revival, could not have been very different in countries so

[1] Cours d'Antiquités Monumentales, p. iv. pag. 61.

closely connected as France and England. The Council of Arles had brought their Churches together as early as A.D. 314; while the connection of Arles with the Church of Kent in the injunctions of Gregory the Great, points clearly to an earlier and, probably, even closer bond. In the absence, however, of documentary proof, we are led to appeal to the monumental remains we still possess, which, however scant and fragmentary, are yet of the greatest interest and importance as indicating the state of the Church in Kent in its earliest age.

The Roman-Saxon church within the precincts of the castle at Dover, so admirably restored by Sir Gilbert Scott, and so graphically illustrated by him in the "Archæologia Cantiana," is the most important and conspicuous of these ancient remains. Roman churches existed also at Lyminge, Folkesstone, Reculver, and other places, while the cruciform foundation at Richborough may possibly have had a Christian origin.

From the mention of the principal churches during the Roman occupation, we shall now pass on to the consideration of the kindred subject of their endowment and sustentation at this early period. Here the external aid derived from archæological facts necessarily fails us, and we have to fall back upon the history of the general state of church endowment before and after the period of Constantine. This history, admirably shadowed forth in the "golden treatise" of Fra Paoli Sarpi "*delle Materie Beneficiarie*," has been clearly illustrated both by Roman Catholic and Protestant canonists, and by

C

none with greater learning or sounder judgment than by Böhmer in his "*Jus Ecclesiasticum*," and specially in his history of the Parochial system, which forms a separate portion of that great work. We have here to bear in mind that the endowment of the Church has three distinct stages, which are very clearly marked out in the history of the first six centuries. Before the time of Constantine it possessed only movable or personal property (*bona mobilia*), for no corporation could then hold real property (*bona immobilia*) without the permission of the Emperors and the licence of the Senate. During the confusion occasioned in the Empire after the imprisonment of Valerian, lands had been illegally left to the Church, especially in Africa, France, and Italy; but these were all confiscated by Diocletian and Maximian in 302, though it is said that this law was not carried out in France, through the influence of Constantius Chlorus, who was then governor. Probably the same toleration was extended to Britain, and the first traces of the second period of the history of endowment may thus ascend upward to the close of the third century. But it must be remembered that this real estate, though legally secured to the Church from the time of Constantine, was alienable like any other property; nor was it until the reign of Justinian that the prohibition to alienate church lands, established at Constantinople as early as A.D. 470, was extended to the whole Church.[1] This law was

---

[1] Böhmer, in tit. "de Rebus Eccl. alienandis vel non," tom. ii. pp. 686–89.

based originally on the principle of the *major utilitas* of the civil law, and not on any canonical or spiritual ground. Promulgated and carried out by the bishops, at least in the Western Church, it became gradually transferred from a civil to an ecclesiastical foundation.[1]

The endowment of the Church of Britain with real property was probably as early as that of any of the Western churches. The "*quieta pax*" which the Church is said to have enjoyed until the days of Diocletian, must have greatly facilitated this kind of dotation; and it is not unreasonable to believe that the appropriation to Christianity of the temples and even the basilicas of the older worship, carried with it the possession of the lands connected with them, which on the Saxon conquest were reoccupied by a new form of idolatry, and became for the most part the residences of the Kentish kings. The remarkable surrender of all these residences one after another to the Church, made from the time of Æthelbert, would stand almost alone in history, were it not for the supposition that it was rather a restitution of what had originally belonged to the Church than an actual endowment *de novo*. From the incidental light which falls upon our Church history from that of France, with which it was so early and closely connected, we gather that until the Saxon invasion (in 449 or 450), land as well as other property had accrued to the Church, and that the power of making testamentary gifts in its favour was exercised in

---

[1] Gregorii M. ad Episc. Panorm. Epp. l. ii. ep. 49.

Britain as in Gaul. We read of St. Perpetuus, Bishop of Tours, in 450, as "a very rich man having possessions in many cities," and "leaving by will, to the churches which he had founded, his property in these several cities, the Church of Tours itself coming in for a considerable inheritance."[1] We are led to conclude that the churches founded both by his predecessors and successors were in like manner endowed with houses and lands, and that the new security which was thus given to the property of the Church was enjoyed generally through the West at this period. All this public property in Kent must have fallen into the hands of the Saxon conquerors of the country, who seem, from Pope Gregory's letter to Mellitus, to have taken possession of many of the churches and public buildings, as temples of their idolatrous worship, the well-built structures he refers to being doubtless of Roman origin.

Another consideration of great importance to us, as we approach the history of the diocese, is the great change, which was effected by the gradual growth of the parochial system, in the form of the endowment of the clergy. Up to the year 500 the clergy appear to have lived in community, and the endowments of the principal churches were divided between them, the possessions of the Church being held in common. The income from these possessions was divided into three portions, that of the clergy, of

[1] Ingoberga, the mother of Queen Bertha, and widow of Charibert, left her chief property in the same manner to the churches of Tours and Le Mans.—(Gregor. Turon. Historia Franc. l. x. c. 31, and l. ix. c. 26.)

the fabric, and of the poor; but the proportions between them, equal in the beginning, became very unequal in the end, the first object almost absorbing the two last.[1] So undivided was the patrimony of the churches originally, that their several properties became designated as those of the saint to whom they were dedicated; that of Ravenna being called from St. Apollinaris; of Milan, from St. Ambrose; of Rome, from St. Peter. The local divisions of parishes and the gradual growth of an independent jurisdiction in them, led to a division of the endowment, which, beginning in the country churches, was at last carried on into the collegiate and capitular bodies by the separation of their property, hitherto held in common, into *præbendæ;* a change which Lanfranc introduced into England, and which had already been matured in France. By this scheme separate estates were attached not only to the several officers of the monastery or capitular body, but to the different departments of conventual life—to the table of the monks, their clothing, and other similar objects. The vast endowment of the Church of Canterbury was first divided between Lanfranc and the monks of Christchurch, while the portion of the latter was again divided according to the special needs of the community, one manor being assigned to one object of necessity and another to another, as we shall see more fully when we approach the period of the great Survey of Domesday. These preliminary considerations, though the period to which they relate is, from

[1] Sarpi, ut supra.

the absence of documentary evidence, the obscurest of our history, and only capable of illustration from the incidental and reflected lights which fall upon it from more distant lands, are yet necessary to the clear apprehension of the facts which we meet with during the Saxon period, when Christianity was re-established among us in a new form, and under singularly altered conditions. The first chapter in the actual history of the Diocese of Canterbury opens upon us at this point, and to this we will now proceed.

PEDIGREE OF THE ROYAL FOUNDERS

OF THE

SAXON CHURCHES AND MONASTERIES OF KENT.

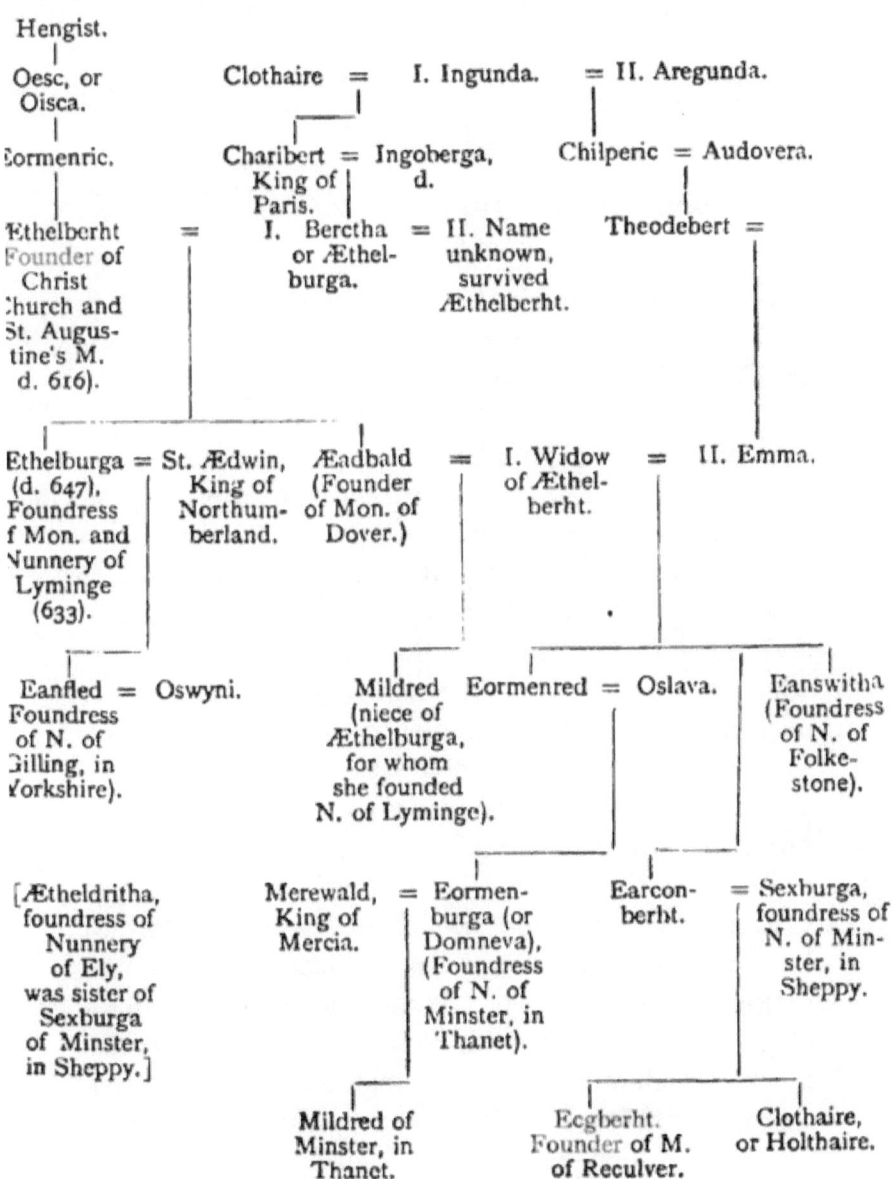

Hengist.

Oesc, or Oisca.

Clothaire = I. Ingunda. = II. Aregunda.

Eormenric.

Charibert = Ingoberga, King of d. Paris.

Chilperic = Audovera.

Ethelberht Founder of Christ Church and St. Augustine's M. d. 616).

= I. Berctha or Æthelburga. = II. Name unknown, survived Æthelberht.

Theodebert =

Ethelburga (d. 647), Foundress of Mon. and Nunnery of Lyminge (633).

= St. Ædwin, King of Northumberland.

Æadbald (Founder of Mon. of Dover.)

= I. Widow of Æthelberht. = II. Emma.

Eanfled = Oswyni. Foundress of N. of Gilling, in Yorkshire).

Mildred (niece of Æthelburga, for whom she founded N. of Lyminge).

Eormenred = Oslava.

Eanswitha (Foundress of N. of Folkestone).

[Ætheldritha, foundress of Nunnery of Ely, was sister of Sexburga of Minster, in Sheppy.]

Merewald, King of Mercia. = Eormenburga (or Domneva), (Foundress of N. of Minster, in Thanet).

Earconberht. = Sexburga, foundress of N. of Minster, in Sheppy.

Mildred of Minster, in Thanet.

Ecgberht. Founder of M. of Reculver.

Clothaire, or Holthaire.

CHAPTER II.

THE FORMATION OF THE DIOCESE AND THE SAXON PERIOD.

THE period which elapsed between the Roman occupation of Kent and the landing of St. Augustine in Thanet belongs rather to the domain of tradition and conjecture than to that of positive history. Whatever occasional gleams of light fall upon the more distant scenes of Roman conquest in Britain, here, at least, there is almost total darkness. Insulated in a manner from the rest of the country—for the great Andred forest and the woods on the east of London and Surrey, extending together from the sea to the Thames, completed the line of separation,—it was shut off from those great settlements which were so early formed in the more central districts of England and on the north of its river boundary. While the northern kingdom had a resident historian in Bede, and the western an illustrator (though hardly an historian) in Gildas, Kent possessed no chronicler, and its earliest history can only be vaguely conjectured from the various relics which have from time to time been recovered from the ground, from its structural monuments, which still take so conspicuous a place among the antiquities of England, and, lastly, from its local names, of which so many of purely British origin may still be recognised in its eastern districts. The effects of those great events which influenced the whole of the Roman Empire must have been here first felt, and the description given by Gildas (and transferred often in the very same words to the narrative of Bede) of the persecution of Diocletian and the revival of Christianity at its close; of the introduction of Arianism and the irruption of the Picts and Scots, must have been (excepting in the last case, in which the isolation of Kent gave it a partial relief) as true of Kent as of the rest of Britain. It is difficult perhaps to determine whether both the writers we have mentioned did not derive their narrative from some common source, from which many passages, which are word for word the same, may have been taken, the rest being filled up independently. To this source, possibly, the *historia ecclesiastica* mentioned by Gildas may refer.[1] In any case, Kent must be held to be included in their descriptions, and to have shared in that great revival of Christianity after the persecution of Diocletian to which the building of the ancient church at Dover has been attributed. The words of Gildas and Bede which

---

[1] There is a singular discrepancy in one place between the two writers, as will be seen by this collation :—

GILDAS.—"Jussit construere inter maria murum . . . . quia vulgò irrationabili absque rectore factus non tam lapidibus quam cespitibus non profuit."

BEDE.—"At insulari murum quem jussi fuerant, non tam lapidibus quam cespitibus construentes . . . . ad nihil utilem statuunt."

Bede evidently misunderstood his predecessor, as the Roman wall itself most clearly proves.

are here identical run thus: "They rebuild the churches levelled to the ground, they found, build, perfect, and unfold everywhere as banners of victory, the Basilicas of martyrs, they celebrate the feast-days, they perform the sacred rites with pure heart and mouth."

Of the effects of the Arian controversy in Kent, to which both Gildas and Bede pass on, we know even less than of the revival of Christianity after the death of Diocletian. Forming as it did a mere out-lying portion of the bishopric of London, and hence having no mention in the subscriptions to the councils of Arles or Ariminum, the state of the present diocese of Canterbury in this earliest period must be left to conjecture. One remarkable fact must appear to the reader of our Church historians, viz., that in the great conflict between the Celtic and Saxon Christians in regard to the keeping of Easter and the difference between the Roman and Oriental ritual, the adherents of Christianity in Kent, who must have been numerous even then, appear to have taken no part. A change which in the north and centre of England, and above all in Wales, occasioned so violent a warfare, here seems to have been regarded with comparative in-difference. It cannot be supposed that Christianity was altogether extinct in the scene of its earliest plan-tation in Britain, or that it was in a state of persecution wherever it had survived, for the perfect toleration which Æthelberht gave to all his subjects in regard to those who hesitated to receive the new religion must have been granted to all who differed with him in the retention of the older one. This ready acquiescence in the Roman forms must, I think, rather be attributed to that devotion to Imperial Rome as the centre of government which was so easily transferred to the Bishops of Rome as its spiritual representatives. The unfortunate Britons had appealed in vain to the failing power of Rome as a civil power; they would be therefore led to regard the revival of that power in a spiritual form as their best protection against their Saxon conquerors, as it had been anciently against their more distant invaders. But had any been even disposed to take part with the adversaries of the Roman rite, the influence of the Saxon converts, whose absolute devotion to Rome is testified in all the charters of their kings, and who received as a part of the Gospel itself the popular interpretation which had been assigned to the passage conveying the so-called " Petrine Privilege," would have prevented any effectual resistance.[1] It was left for a later and more enlightened age to remove the veil which centuries of exegetical ignorance had drawn over this assumption of an imperial authority in the spiritual household, and the theses of Wyclif and the protest of Bishop Hallam of Salisbury, at Constance, were among the first utterances which broke the spell of ages. Rome herself, as we shall see presently,

---

[1] Recent Roman Catholic writers have drawn unfavourable contrasts between the simple devotion which the Anglo-Saxon Church exhibited towards the Papacy and the vigorous independence asserted by its Norman successor. The real contrast is, however, between the Rome of Gregory the Great and the Rome of Hildebrand—the Rome of Augustine's age and the Rome of the day of Lanfranc.

brought about this great deliverance by the conflict she created in the Church between the regular and secular clergy, between the ordinary jurisdiction and that which *a Romanâ urbe directa est.*[1]

But we pass on to the consideration of the circumstances under which the direct and exclusive influence of the see of Rome was first introduced into Kent, a subject which involves the narrative of the conversion of England, a narrative so well known in its results, but perhaps too little regarded in the light of its origin and causes. It must be remembered that when Christianity was accepted by Æthelberht and his court, the Kentish kingdom founded by his ancestors was already in the first stage of its decadence. His alliance with the daughter of Charibert, king of Paris, and that of his son with another Gallic princess, were successive attempts to strengthen the failing dynasty by means of external ties. The same motive we may discern in the subsequent marriage of Æthelburga with the Northumbrian Æadwin. Indeed, when the religious gloss of Bede's narrative of the conversion of England is removed, we are led to the conclusion that political necessities had as much influence in bringing about this great change as religious convictions, and that the material aid of France, though the powerful Queen Brunichildis, the sister-in-law of Charibert, was one at least of the motives which led Æthelberht to choose a foreign bride, and afterwards to accept her religion. To this extraordinary woman, whose life is so beautiful in its beginning and so

---

[1] Chart. Anglos. c. xxx. an. 689.

repulsive in its close, St. Gregory the Great attributes a large share in the conversion of England.[1]   Bertha (or Æthelburga, for this latter is her true name) had been brought up in the greatest seclusion by her saintly mother Ingoberga,[2] whose name indicates so clearly her Scandinavian origin.[3]   Deserted by Chari-bert who, in defiance of his marriage vows, had formed an alliance successively with two of her attendants, Marcovefa and Merofleda, Ingoberga lived in retirement at Le Mans, where in her devoted friend and counsellor, St. Gregory of Tours, she found her greatest comfort.   It was from this scene of the highest Christian life that her only daughter who had shared her seclusion and inherited her faith was called to reign over a heathen kingdom, encouraged, doubtless, by her mother and aunt, as well as by St. Gregory himself, to introduce Christianity among her new subjects, in the observation of which she had the fullest freedom.

The history of this great work, for which her example and influence so well prepared the way, has been too often and too well told to need any repetition here.   It belongs, indeed, rather to the history of the country than to that of the mere diocese which formed its scene.   But there is some reason to believe that the description of Bede from which every subsequent picture of it is derived, received not a

---

[1] Greg. M. Epp. l. ix. ; Indict. iv. Ep. 56.

[2] Greg. Turon. "Hist. Franc." l. iv. c. 26, and l. ix. c. 26.

[3] It will be remembered as, in a slightly modified form, the name of the heroine, Ingeborg, in the "Frithiof's Saga."

little filling up and colouring, either from his own hand or from that of his authority on all points of Kentish history, the abbot Albinus, of St. Augustine's. The ignorance of the king of the nature and doctrines of Christianity could not possibly have been so profound as it is described to be; for the relations between France and England were too close and intimate, and the residence of English females in continental convents, which Bede himself describes, too early and frequent, to make such ignorance possible; to say nothing of the knowledge which must have been acquired through Bertha herself and her chaplain, Luidhart. In any case, however, the great and good work was crowned with complete success, and the spirit of Christianity was no less triumphant than the doctrine. For the gentle piety of Bertha and the wise toleration of Æthelberht presented such a picture of primitive Christianity as has never perhaps been altogether reproduced in our land.

The peculiarity of the position of the Kentish kingdom, and its moderate extent, pointed it out as fitted no less for an ecclesiastical than a political organization, and thus the diocese of Canterbury (then including also that of Rochester) was constituted. But we must not forget that but a very small portion of this large tract of country was then really settled. The great Andred forest covered the larger portion of West Kent, and spurs from this vast tract of woodland extended irregularly towards the Roman road from Canterbury to Lymne,—not only the "Weald of Kent," but the names of villages

much farther west giving evidence of their earlier
state. The great woods, now represented by the
Blean, spread beyond Canterbury to the north, and
dense woods appear to have fringed the borders of
Romney Marsh (then only partially redeemed from
the sea), extending to Lydd and the borders of
Sussex. These are clearly indicated in several of the
earliest of the Saxon charters, and lead us to see how
slow and gradual was the settlement of the country
in its ecclesiastical aspect, and that the process of
cultivating the land and opening up the forests
necessarily retarded the progress of the Church in its
new inheritance. The Domesday Survey of Kent
shows how little of the now most populous district of
the country, that of west, and especially south-west
Kent, had been even then occupied, either civilly or
ecclesiastically, and the recently-published " History
of the Weald of Kent," by Mr. Furley, shows how
late was the colonization of this vast tract of woodland
in comparison with the settlement of East Kent, that
" open country" which gave name to the county when
first discovered by the Romans.[1] The reduction of
the vast forests which covered the western district, so
as to bring about their occupation for purposes of
husbandry, was very slow and gradual, and the
spiritual followed the temporal settlement. The
process by which this reclamation of land, both for
the Church and the State, was carried on was by
attaching " dennes," or wooded allotments, in the

[1] " Caint" is still the word for an " open country " in modern
Welsh.

Weald of Kent to the grants of land in East Kent, which had been given to the Church by the Saxon kings or nobles, and which are represented in the aggregate by the great ecclesiastical manors described in Domesday. To these were added also large tracts of land in Romney Marsh, and other similar districts, for the pasture of sheep, which led to the recovery and protection of the marshes from the inroads of the sea, and to the formation of parishes and the foundation of churches in places hitherto uninhabitable. The clearance of that portion of the great forest which skirted the marsh and the sea was effected by the grants of waggon-loads of wood in the " Andred," for the purpose of carrying on the preparation of salt, and in this manner both the habitable part of the county became extended, and the diocese assumed its present proportions, no longer being, as it was at first, a mere "geographical expression," but a " diocese " in its truest meaning. But in order to see how this great change was brought about, we must fall back on that element in the history of the conversion of England which is ever the least considered, though it was the more important and influential than any other, the monastic system, which Augustine, rather monk than archbishop, adopted as the very ground-plan of all his work. We should do well to bear in mind the fact that it is not to Canterbury as the seat of the episcopate, or even of the primacy, that the conversion of the diocese is to be assigned,[1] but to Canterbury as the

[1] In the case of Tours the village church appears to have

scene of the two most powerful and richly-endowed
monasteries in Kent; and to the great and then
almost co-ordinate foundations of Dover, Lyminge,
Folkestone, Minster in Sheppy, Minster in Thanet,
and Reculver, all founded within the first century of
the establishment of Christianity in England. The
Cathedral of Canterbury is one of the "new foundation"—that is, was created out of the monastery
(afterwards more often termed the priory) of Christ
Church, one of the two grand institutions which
Augustine had established through the concessions of
Æthelberht in his principal city. Though the estates
of the archbishops and the monks appear in a separate form in Domesday, the fee-simple of them was
held by both in common: nor could the archbishops
make any important change even in regard to the
manors specially assigned to them without the permission and concurrence of the chapter, as appears in
the day of the successive surrenders of the principal
manors to the Crown by Cranmer, in which the confirmation of the chapter was uniformly given,[1] and,
still more remarkably, in the decree by which Arch-

been founded through the influence of the successive bishops
and the secular clergy—as Gregory of Tours indicates (l. x.
c. 31). In Kent it was the regular and not the secular clergy
who carried the preaching of Christianity into the rural districts
(see Bede, l. iii. cc. 3, 5).

[1] In the surrender of the church of Lyminge by Cranmer to
Henry VIII., of which the original is in the possession of the
writer, the concurrence of the then newly-formed chapter is
given in a formal manner with their seal attached. Yet this
was one of the "separate estates" of the archbishops from the
time of Lanfranc.

bishop Courtenay sanctioned the demolition of several of his manor-houses in order to build the grand baronial residence of Saltwood.[1] From these proofs of the power of the monastery, even in its later history, we fall back upon the influence exercised by the system of which it formed a part, upon the conversion of Kent, and the formation and settlement of the diocese, which, until the creation of that of Rochester, included the entire county.

The founder of the monastic system in the West, as is well known, was Benedict of Nursia, who by a rule which Gregory the Great describes as "*discretione præcipuam sermone luculentam,*"[2] so mitigated the severity of the monastic laws of St. Basil as to adapt them to the different character of the climate, position, and social circumstances of the people of the West. He founded in 515 the monastery of Montecassino, and in 527 that of Subiaco. "Literature, science, agriculture, in a word, the entire civilization of Europe owe to the Benedictine monks everlasting gratitude."[3] English Protestants will not fail to echo these words of the recent ultramontane writer, for they represent a great historical truth, and one which the history of the diocese of Canterbury, perhaps, more than any other has witnessed and recorded up to the days of the Reformation.[4] Up to the year 960, when the

---

[1] See the Register of Abp. Courtenay.

[2] Dial. i. 2, c. 36.

[3] Nardi, "Elementi di diritto Ecclesiastico," tom. ii. p. 3.

[4] While agriculture in all its branches received from the monks of Europe its greatest impulse, the cultivation of the vine, of which there are so many illustrations in Domesday,

deplorable ninth and tenth centuries had corrupted every part of Christendom, and the ancient rule of St. Benedict was found unequal to carry out the objects of its first institution, no one had ventured to introduce any change in so venerable a code. A number of reformations of the order began after this period, which at first assumed the form of " congregations " of the order, and at last became proper and distinctive orders, though still retaining the Benedictine rule as their foundation.[1] Such were the Cluniac monks, whose name so often appears in English and Scottish nomenclature, the Camaldules (1023), the Cistercians (1098), the Bernardines (1153), and the Carthusians (1084). These were the later branches of the great Benedictine family, which, it will be observed, retained during the whole of the Saxon period its original and simpler form.[2] Gregory the

---

would seem to have been introduced into England by the foreign monks who had settled in our early monasteries. The vast collection of fragments of pottery and the refuse of its manufacture which covers the site of the monastery of Lyminge, proves that the monks of that place were actively engaged in making the ruder kinds of vessels then in popular use.

[1] "The new Orders," observes Wessenberg ("Grossen Kirchenversammlungen," tom. i. p. 347), "were themselves mere attempts to reform the Benedictine Order when it had degenerated." But instead of reforming they simply divided the original order, for he adds, "they had the injurious effect of producing a jealous disunion among the monastic orders, when even in the beginning of the 13th century the new orders had become infected with the corruption of the old."

[2] Nardi, tom. ii. p. 4, who cites Marrier et Querectanus, "Biblioth. Cluniac." Paris, 1614; Mittarelli et Costadoni,

Great was himself a member of the order,[1] as was also Augustine; and the bishops in England, including those of Canterbury, assumed the monastic habit and professed the Benedictine rule before their consecration.[2] Lanfranc drew up a special form of that rule for his own church, and it was at the altar of St. Benedict that Becket received his mortal wound. In the Saxon period the archbishops were less regarded in the light of prelates or heads of a secular clergy, than as the priors and superiors of that grand foundation which even yet is called throughout East Kent "the great Church," and in which in process of time many of the earlier monasteries, almost coeval and coequal with it, were merged. As the great centres from which the work of building up and forming the diocese of Canterbury was carried on, our attention is therefore first directed to the seven greater monasteries in East Kent, by means of which the evangelization of the entire country was effected. The singular unity and connection between these (in some cases even their property being held in common) gave to the monastic system in Kent a missionary influence which it is not easy for us to overestimate in our consideration of the formation of the diocese. " Founded as they were by the members of the same family, belonging to the same religious order, and springing from the same impulse of zeal, they present

"Annales Camaldul. Venet. 1755"; Miraeus, "Origines Carthusian. Monaster. per orbem, Col. 1610."

[1] Luc. Dacherii Not. in Lanfranci Epp. p. 569 (Migne, tom. cl. 569).

[2] Ibid. p. 574.

a marked contrast to the foundations of a later age,
which discover no such features of early and intimate
union."[1]

Let us briefly describe these foundations in their
chronological order. We begin with the great monastery of Christ Church, the foundation of Augustine
himself. "When Augustine, the first Archbishop
of Canterbury," are the words of Bede, "assumed
the episcopal throne in that royal city, he recovered
therein, by the king's assistance, a church which,
as he was told, had been constructed by the original
labour of Roman believers. This church he consecrated in the name of the Saviour, our God and
Lord Jesus Christ, and there he established an habi-
tation for himself and all his successors."[2] "This
was that very church," writes Eadmer (or rather
Gervase, adopting his narrative), "which had been
built by Romans (as Bede bears witness in his history),
and which was duly arranged in some parts in imitation of the Church of the Blessed Prince of the
Apostles, Peter."[3] The knowledge which we possess
of the plan of the original basilica of St. Peter in
Rome enabled Professor Willis to verify exactly the
description given of its imitation at Canterbury. Like
most of the ancient basilicas, there was in both
churches not only an eastern apse, but a western one

---

[1] See my remarks, "On the Connection between the Monasteries of Kent in the Saxon Period," in the "Arch. Cantiana,"
vol. iii. p. 19.

[2] Bed. "Ecc. Hist." l. i. c. 33.

[3] Prof. Willis, "Hist. of C.C." pp. 9, 10.

of very large diameter.   This feature is also visible in
the foundations of the basilical church at Lyminge,
founded (as it is supposed) at about the beginning of
the fifth century.   There were no transepts either in
the Roman church or its British representative at
Canterbury, the ancient basilical type, which was a
simple parallelogram, having been adhered to in
both.   This church, as Professor Willis conjectures,
was rather restored than rebuilt by Augustine, who,
acting under the advice of Pope Gregory even in
regard to heathen temples, would have naturally been
specially conservative in his preservation of Christian
buildings.   Added to and altered by several of the
Saxon archbishops (Odo, 940; Egilnoth, 1023), this
first basilica was utterly destroyed by fire in 1067,
which led to its rebuilding from the foundations by
Lanfranc (1070).

As, however, that calamitous event belongs to a
later period of our history, we will pass on to enumerate the successive stages of the endowment of
the monastery with those ample lands which are
represented to us in an aggregate form in the Domesday Survey, and in the contemporary schedule of the
manors belonging to it which is given by Somner.
This is a necessary preliminary to our consideration
of the formation of the diocese, inasmuch as the
foundation of the churches in the large tract which
was then bestowed upon the Church, and which
spreads itself throughout the country, followed necessarily the preaching of the monks, who were the first
cultivators of the soil and builders of churches.   "For
the monks," as Bede writes, " were the principal of

those who came to the work of preaching."[1]   Of their work as church builders we have many remarkable instances in later as well as earlier periods.   The *monachi cæmentarii*, as Ivo of Chartres (a contemporary of Lanfranc) terms them, seem to have acquired even then almost the form of a distinct guild. [2]

To follow up the stages of the endowment of Christ Church and the great rival foundation of St. Peter and St. Paul (St. Augustine's), through the course of the Saxon charters, would need a larger space and a greater degree of the reader's patience than can be expected for a narrative so limited in its object as the present.   It will suffice, therefore, to give the sum of the possessions of Christ Church as we find it in the Domesday Survey, premising that the separation of the lands between the archbishop and the monks, introduced by Lanfranc, after the præbendal system of Normandy, did not affect the integrity of the title to the whole property as originally granted to the monastery :—

In the city of Canterbury there were 12 burgesses, and 32 " mansuræ," or dwellings, held by the clergy of the town, rendering 35s. yearly, and a mill of 5s.

The town of Sandwich (appropriated to the clothing and table of the monks) was worth £50 a year—

---

[1] " Hist. Eccl." l. iii. cc. 3, 5.

[2] Ivonis Carnot. Ep. · 266, "ascivit quosdam monachos cæmentarios "; Goffridus Vindoc. in Ep. ad Ildebert. Ceno. Mann. Ep., " Johannem cæmentarium Ecclesiæ Nostræ."

	£	s.	d.		£	s.	d.
Darenth equal to	18	o	o	Burnes equal to	30	o	o
Otford ,,	60	o	o	(Bishopsburn)			
Sundridge ,,	23	o	o	Charing ,,	60	o	o
Bexley ,,	30	8	o	Pluckley ,,	20	o	o
Erith ,,	21	o	o	Wingham ,,	77	o	o
Malling ,,	15	o	o	Merstham ,,	20	o	o
Northfleet ,,	37	10	o	Aldington ,,	122	o	o
Wrotham ,,	15	o	o	St. Martin's			
Maidstone ,,	20	o	o	(Canterbury),,	4	o	o
Gillingham ,,	26	o	o	Lyminge ,,	78	3	o
Reculver ,,	7	o	o	Newenden ,,	18	o	o
Norton ,,	14	6	o	Northwood ,,	17	o	o
Petham ,,	9	o	o	Seasalter ,,	20	5	o
Estursete ,,	49	o	o	Preston ,,	15	o	o
(Westgate)				Chartham ,,	30	o	o
Bolton ,,	30	16	o				

HELD BY THE MONKS.

	£	s.	d.		£	s.	d.
Orpington ,,	28	o	o	Great Chart ,,	27	o	o
Peckham ,,	8	o	o	Little Chart ,,	8	8	o
Hollingbourne	30	o	o	Welle ,,	40	o	o
Meopham ,,	18	o	o	Eastry ,,	36	10	o
Farleigh ,,	41	o	o	Adisham ,,	46	16	o
Cliffe at Hoo ,,	7	o	o	Wareborne ,,	3	10	o
Monkton ,,	40	o	o	Appledon ,,	16	17	o
Ickham ,,	32	o	o	Wye ,,	4	o	o
Godmersham ,,	30	o	o				

The great abbey, dedicated to St. Peter and St.
Paul, without the ancient walls of Canterbury, and
founded by St. Augustine so shortly after his first
work was accomplished, was hardly inferior in the extent of its endowment to its ancient and inveterate
rival. Its rent-roll fills nearly four columns of the
contracted pages of Domesday, and its growth from
age to age corresponded with that of the foundation
with which it had been placed in such dangerous

contiguity.   Founded almost together (for Augustine apparently had in view the separation of the purely monastic part of his plan and the secular work of the episcopate) the contention began even on the point of their relative antiquity as well as on the exemptions from ordinary jurisdiction to which the Augustinians laid claim.   One of the foundations of this claim was laid in a charter of King Oswyn, in 689, granting certain lands [1] adjoining the ancient park, or chace, in Lyminge, to the Abbot Adrian, of St. Augustine's, " *qui a Romanâ urbe directus est.*" [2] But, as even Nardi affirms, monastic exemptions from ordinary jurisdiction are of a comparatively recent date, a fact which it will be necessary to bear in mind in approaching that conflict between the regular and secular clergy which developed itself so early in this diocese.   " All monks remained at first subject to the bishops, like the rest of the faithful.   Ecclesiastical laws (Conc. Chalced.) ordered and confirmed by the civil power (Justinian, Nov. 67), enforced this entire subjection, which, approved of by the Greeks and Latins (Conc. Aurel. et Epaon.), was maintained for a long period.   In the Middle Ages, as the monastic life gradually rose to a higher importance, the Church and the State began to protect it by granting it special privileges.   Towards the year 1000 monks became free from the contributions due to the parochial clergy and the bishops, but still continued

[1] The endowment amounted to 11,680 acres of land (see Preface to Thomas de Elmham's " Hist. Monast. St. Augustini," p. iv.).

[2] "Ch. Anglo.," xxx., Kemble, vol. i. p. 33.

subject to the bishops." . . . " Finally, new privileges
removed them effectually from their obedience to the
bishops, and placed them entirely under the Holy
See." This was called the *exemptio plena*, or *totalis
emancipatio*. The long struggle of the monks of St.
Augustine with those of Christ Church, and even with
the archbishops, arose out of this claim of exemption,
and the bitter controversies it awakened lasted in some
of their many phases until the very day of the Reformation.[1] But other monasteries had sprung up in the
meantime, scarcely less venerable in their antiquity,
and almost rivalling the two first foundations in the
rapidity of their earlier endowment. The melancholy
relapse of Ædbald into idolatry, after the death of
Æthelberht (616), and his marriage with his father's
widow, produced in its violent reaction, through
the remonstrances of Archbishop Laurence, the
successor of Augustine, a new harvest of endowment for the Church, and the foundation of
the monastery of Dover, whose venerable church
was among the firstfruits of this profound repentance. The endowment of the monastery does not
seem to have been considerable, though it shared
with Canterbury, Lyminge, and Folkestone, in the

---

[1] The earliest Papal grant exempting a monastery from all
episcopal control is believed to be that granted to the monks of
Fulda at the instance of St. Boniface in 751. On the lofty
pretensions of the monks of St. Augustine's and the spurious
documents by which they were supported, the reader is referred
to the Preface to the " Historia Monast. St. Augustini," supposed to be by Thomas of Elmham, published in the " Rolls "
series (Lond. 1858, Introd. pp. 7 and 28).

estate of the Duke Oswulf and his wife, Beornthrytha
—a gift which was confirmed in the Synod of Aclea
(Oakley?), in 844,[1] whose acts are recited in one of
the most interesting of the charters of the Anglo-Saxon
series.

The foundation of the monastery of Dover was
succeeded, in about 630, by the foundation of the
monastery and nunnery of Folkestone, of the remains
of which (destroyed as it was by the inroads of the
sea within the Saxon period) not a vestige has survived to our day. The foundations of an ancient
church in a field nearly adjoining the present railway
(junction) station, now unfortunately destroyed, might
possibly form a portion of the original building, while
the discovery of a Roman hypocaust, within a few
yards of it, indicated the remote antiquity of the site.[2]
The dotation of this monastery, which appears to
have been annexed to Canterbury in 927,[3] occupies
seven of the earliest of the Saxon Charters. Its
founder was Æadbald, who established and endowed
it in behalf of his daughter, Æanswitha, who became
its first abbess. Very little is known of its history,
though undoubtedly it became, with the neighbouring
monastery of Dover, the principal means of the
evangelization of that south-eastern portion of Kent
over which its lands extended. This and Lyminge
constituted the two earliest nunneries ever founded in
England, whose object, according to Bede's account,
was to supply those educational advantages to females

---

[1] "Ch. Anglo Sax." n. 256.
[2] See the "Arch. Cantiana," vol. x. p. 173.
[3] Cart. Anglo-Sax. n. 1100.

in England which before could only be enjoyed by a residence at one of the great convents which had been so early established in France. The foundation of the nunnery and monastery of Lyminge, the second of those double foundations which, though now so strictly forbidden, were in the earliest period so characteristic a feature of the Benedictine system, followed within three years. It carries up its origin to the memorable year 633, in which Æthelburga, the only daughter of Æthelberht and Berctha, returning into Kent with Paulinus and a few faithful followers, after the fatal battle of Heathfield, in which her husband, Eadwin, the sainted Northumbrian king, had perished, obtained from her brother Æadbald the gift of the lands of Lyminge, formerly a royal residence, and described by monastic writers as the "villa," or the "villa maxima de Lyminge." The relics of this extensive building, which yet remain, were considered by the members of the Archæological Institute to represent a Roman residence, including a Christian church, and to belong to the close of the fourth or the beginning of the fifth century.[1] The interest of this site in its connection with the early Church history of England, could scarcely be surpassed. The residence of Æthelberht and Bertha—the scene of the early life and widowhood of Æthelburga—the place in which her daughter Eanfled was brought up—the starting-point of the two great missions by which the conversion of the whole of northern England was brought about ; from which, first Paulinus, and then the Pres-

[1] See the "Arch. Cant." vol. ix. p. 205.

byter Romanus went forth, as chaplains of Æthelburga and Eanfled, as Luithard had been of Bertha
in a still earlier day—few ecclesiastical sites could
possess memories of such singular interest as Lyminge—which, as the burial-place of Æthelburga (or
as she was afterwards called Æadburg),[1] and, as the
"*locus beatissimæ Virginis Mariæ*" of the Saxon
Charters, retained, during the whole of this period, the
reputation of a peculiar sanctity.   But it is chiefly to
the influence of this double foundation on the formation of the diocese that our attention is now directed.
The endowment of the monastery, which is recorded
in no less than fourteen charters of the earliest period,
ranging from 689 to 965, conveyed a large district of
southern and south-western Kent to the monks, and
to them, doubtless, the foundation of the principal of
its churches is to be attributed.   The Presbyter
Romanus, to whom a large tract of land in Romney
Marsh,[2] covering the site of the present town and
extending to the borders of Sussex, had been granted
in the middle of the seventh century, accompanied
Eanfled to the Synod of Whitby (or Stroneshalch),
where the Roman period for keeping Easter was
finally settled, and where he became a strenuous advocate for the Roman observance.   The lands granted
him were bestowed by a subsequent charter (no. 86,
an. 740) on the Monastery of Lyminge ; but his name
remains in that of the ancient Cinque-Port, still the

---

[1] V. Goscelin, " Contra inanes B. Mildrethæ usurpatores."
[2] This district is described in the Charter of Wihtraed in 700
as Rumening-seta (the settlement of Romanus).

principal settlement in "the Marsh."[1]   To these first foundations were added, towards the close of the same century, the monastery, or rather nunnery, of Minster, in Sheppy, the foundation of Sexburga, the wife of Earconberht, and niece by marriage of Æthelburga; and somewhat later the famous nunnery of Minster, in Thanet, founded by Eormenburga, the grand-niece of Æthelburga, though chiefly celebrated as the scene of the wonder-working life of her daughter, St. Mildred.   The identity of her name, with that of an earlier Mildred, the niece of Æthelburga,[2] and inmate of the Nunnery of Lyminge, led to the long controversy between the monks of St. Augustine and those of St. Gregory, which lasted from the death of Lanfranc until the dawn of the Reformation.[3]

The surrender to the Church of almost the last of the residences of the Kentish kings, the Palace of

---

[1] Previously it had no distinctive title, being merely termed "the Marsh," and its inhabitants "merscwara" men (see the Saxon Charters and Chronicle, passim).

[2] Lyminge is said by the monkish historians to have been "founded by Æthelburga, in favour of her niece Mildred." There can be little question that as no niece is to be found in the legitimate pedigree, Mildred was the daughter of that first and fatal marriage of Æadbald which the Church had set aside, and that the king in the gift of Lyminge made provision not only for his sister but for this even more unfortunate daughter ("Arch. Cant." vol. iii. p. 27).

[3] See Goscelinus (1095) "Contra inanes B. Mildrethæ Usurpatores" (in MSS. Cotton. et Harleian, in Mus. Brit.; see also the paper "On St. Mary's Minster and St. Mildred" in the "Arch. Cant." vol. xii. p. 177).

Reculver, a Roman foundation of the highest antiquity and interest, and its transformation into a monastery, in 669, completed the unexampled sacrifices
which the descendants of the first convert had made
to the new faith.   This also received from time to
time a considerable endowment, and is mentioned in
several of the Saxon charters.   For somewhat more
than a century the progress of the establishment of
Christianity in Kent met with little or very slight
obstruction.   The building of churches and temples
for Christian worship succeeded the missionary work
and the temporary stations of the monks ; and although the evidence of the foundation of secular
churches (for they could be hardly yet called parochial) during the earliest period is necessarily very
limited and imperfect, we know that such churches
were even then existing in Thanet, through the influence of the great nunnery of Minster, in South
Kent, through the agency of the monastery of Lyminge, and on the estates of the other religious houses,
every one of which formed the centre of those church-
building operations which necessarily followed the
evangelization of the county.[1]   It is of course difficult, from the absence of topographical informa-
tion, which fails so completely at this period, and is
only preserved (as in the Saxon charters) in connection with secular and territorial boundaries, to

---

[1] In the course of the ravages of the Danes, we find that
they spared these secular churches ; and the ancient chapelries
attached to the churches of Minster and Lyminge, as well as to
other principal churches of the district, indicate the gradual
formation of the parochial system round its first centres.

determine how many of the churches which are indicated in Domesday to have existed in the days of the Confessor (for very few could have been added by Lanfranc, however diligently he may have assisted in their restoration), belong to the seventh or eighth centuries. The law of King Edmund, in 944, which required the bishop and the king to restore the houses of God on their respective domains,[1] a law which evidently had respect to the ruin occasioned by the Danish invasions, which had led to the suppression of some of the earliest monasteries, and their transfer to the archbishops or to the Crown, leads to the belief that many churches had been built at the earliest period in Kent, though the portion of it now known as the weald, and a considerable part of the marsh, must have been yet unoccupied. The Danish ravages, which began in 787, have destroyed almost every direct evidence in regard to the previous state of the diocese and its earliest churches; but the fragments of Roman and Saxon building which are found from time to time in churches where they might be least expected, lead at least to the supposition that the first great impulse in diocesan church-building was more fruitful in its results than it is generally believed to have been.[2]

"It is probable," observes Mr. Roach Smith, "that many of our old churches are of Saxon origin, although in consequence of enlargements and repara-

---

[1] Spelman, "Concilia," tom. i. pp. 421, 424.
[2] Even in the walls of the church of Frittenden, within the limits of the weald of Kent, lumps of Roman concrete were found during its recent restoration.

tions, only a very few can be referred to with masonry positively assignable to so early a period. That many occupy the sites of Roman buildings is demonstrated from the intermixture, among other materials, of stone and mortar that had previously been used in Roman structures. A long list of such churches could easily be enumerated."[1] Passing away from the consideration of this early period, which rather presents to us problems than facts—problems which can only be solved by the careful scrutiny of the structural remains still existing, assisted by a more perfect knowledge of the criteria of Saxon building than we even now possess, we arrive at one of the most important epochs in the first part of our history —that of the Danish invasions, or rather raids—for they seldom assumed the proportions of a carefully-projected invasion. The first landing of these piratical adventurers in England is assigned by Florence of Worcester to the year 787. The chronological system (adopted by Kemble), of Simeon of Durham, however, would place it two years later. From this year till the accession of Knut, in 1017, a period of nearly a hundred and thirty years, they continued at intervals to make descents upon the coasts of Kent, carrying their ravages from sea to sea, and directing their principal attacks upon the religious houses, the members of which seem ever to have offered them the most organized though unsuccessful resistance, and to have been regarded by them with the most special and determined hostility. On this subject I

---

[1] "Lyminge in Kent," Collectan. vol. v. p. 185.

have observed elsewhere,[1] that the "exclusive attention
we have given to our English chroniclers, almost
always monks, or at least identified in interest with
monastic foundations, has led us to form a very
inaccurate and one-sided opinion on the nature and
tendency of these piratical raids. It is always assumed by these chroniclers, and too readily admitted
by their copyists of a later day, that the Danes were
heathens as well as barbarians, and the most virulent
haters and persecutors of Christianity in all its forms.
On the other hand, the Danish writers maintain that
they were the converters of East Anglia, and the in-
troducers of a purer form of Christianity than had
hitherto been propagated in England. Those who
imagine the Danes, at least of the later Anglo-Saxon
period, to have been idolaters, should remember that
the conversion of the whole of Denmark to Christianity took place in 858, and that in 880 the Danes
are asserted by their ancient chroniclers to have introduced Christianity into East Anglia on the occasion of their re-conquest of that kingdom. Anscha-
rius, bishop of Hamburg, had spread Christianity in
Denmark in the beginning of the ninth century, and
we are told by the Saxon historian, Albert Krantz,
that it was handed down from father to son among
the common people, even in the days when it suffered
persecution from the rulers. The conduct of the
Danes at Minster in Thanet, seems to me to establish the fact that it was not against the religion but
the religious orders, on account of their implacable

---

[1] "Arch. Cant." vol. xii. p. 188.

enmity to the Danish settlers, that their hostility was directed; for when they utterly destroyed the conventual buildings at Minster, they spared the chapels of St. Mary, and St. Peter and St. Paul"—which were the places of parochial worship[1]—"and in the battle which is recorded as having occurred at Lyminge, where the monks gave them a most vigorous and partially successful resistance, the only one of their number who is said to have escaped was the secular priest of the place—an incredible statement, unless his life had been actually spared by the enemy." The whole of these invasions look like an anticipation of the Bohemian warfare in the Hussite period, which was a crusade against the monastic orders by those who professed a simpler form of Christianity, and regarded them as carrying on an organized conspiracy against their rights and even existence as a nation. . . . . " The mythical statements of the monks, in regard to the first piratical invasion of the Northmen, might well lead us to receive with caution their descriptions of the events of this period. The story of Hyngwar and Hubba, and their descent from a bear, must prepare us for narratives scarcely less mythical." But whatever character we may assign to these piratical

---

[1] The tower of the church of Ospringe in North Kent was by some supposed to be actually a Danish building, by which it was probably meant a building of the time of Knut. It was of flints and of a circular form, a kind of building very common in Norfolk, but almost without another example in Kent. It fell down in 1695, having been fatally shaken by the bell-ringing to celebrate the return of William III. from the campaign in Flanders — (Ducarel's " Repertory of the Endowments of Vicarages in the Diocese of Canterbury," p. 135).

attacks or to their leaders, their immediate results to
the ecclesiastical interests of the diocese were most
fatal and irreparable.   Everyone of those great centres from which religious instruction had gone forth
to the yet unsettled districts of the county was destroyed in sad succession.   The suppression of the
nunneries of Folkestone and Lyminge, and the incorporation of the monasteries connected with them,
with the great foundation of Christ Church, and
the total destruction of the abbey and nunnery of
St. Mildred in Thanet, and St. Sexburga in Sheppy—
these were among the firstfruits of the Danish inroads ;
and though in the end the Church was strengthened by
the process of centralization which was thus effected,
and which afterwards gave so vast an endowment to
the archbishops, it was long, indeed, and not until
the accession of Knut, that it in any degree recovered
from the shock of the Danish invasions.   While the
endowments of Lyminge, Folkestone, Dover, and
Reculver thus passed to the "Great Church," those
of Minster in Thanet devolved, by the gift of Knut
himself, to the rival foundation of St. Augustine's.
This centralization of the monastic system is generally believed to have been brought about by Dunstan, whose zeal in the cause of monachism, and in
the building and restoration of churches is celebrated
by all the chroniclers of this period.[1]   Immense
power was given to the archbishopric by this incor-

---

[1] " Tu mihi Pater Dunstane, tu mihi de construendis Monas-
teriis, de Ecclesiis aedificandis consilium salubre dedisti "
(Oratio Regis Edgari, ap. Spelman, tom. 1. p. 478).

poration of the lesser into the greater houses, while greater force and virulence were given to the rivalry between the monasteries of Christ Church and St. Augustine's, the latter of which received so rich an income in the possession of the ruined nunnery of Minster, in Thanet.[1]   The results of the Danish invasions to the actual fabrics of the churches of Kent cannot but appear to the careful inquirer to have been much less serious than they are described to have been by the monkish historians.   Except where they were built of wood, or any perishable material, the stay of the piratical hordes, in every one of the scenes of their attack, was too brief to enable them to do more than pillage and set fire to the churches ; and where the latter were built of stone, which must have been the case wherever that material abounded, they could not have been so completely destroyed as the popular histories and legends describe them to have been.   It is not therefore improbable that many relics of actual Saxon work remain in the churches of Kent, according to the suggestion of Roach Smith, hidden in many cases by later work, and probably refaced, as is the case in the work of Lanfranc at Caen.

But the history of the introduction of Christianity into Kent and its earlier fortunes would be but imperfectly seen were we not to inquire into those local and social conditions which rendered its reception so

---

[1] The Monastery of Lyminge "cum omnibus terris et consuetudinibus ejus" was incorporated with Christ Church in 965, Folkestone in 927, Reculver in 949 ; while Minster, in Thanet, was bestowed on St. Augustine's by Knut in 1025.

much easier and its establishment so much less interrupted than they were in other parts of the Heptarchy. To one feature of the Roman period we have already adverted, viz., the comparative freedom from warfare and political disturbance which the Kentish kingdom is proved, by the very absence of those military inscriptions so often found in other parts of England, to have enjoyed. Its population, recruited not only from the Roman settlers but from the colonists of the neighbouring coasts of France and Belgium, seem to have adapted themselves to the settled forms of Roman law and order, and this must have led to a degree of religious toleration most favourable to the cause of the Christian missionaries. The faith of the conquered Britons and its sanguinary rites were little likely to present an obstacle to the new faith; while the hold of the Saxon idolatry had been seriously weakened by the very loss of those special objects which had awakened it, the sacred groves, trees, and streams of their native country. Döllinger has well observed that " the religion of the ancient German peoples had a local character, and was identified with special sacred towns, springs, groves, and streams. By their wanderings from their former " gauen "[1] and their settlement in foreign lands their mode of religion lost its hold, and its foundation, and their dependence upon it was already greatly weakened, so that those German tribes were much more accessible to the Christian faith than they would have been had they remained in their original

[1] The "*gau*" was properly the "land held in common" under the tribal system of the Teutonic races.

settlements. This, in some measure, accounts for the perseverance with which the Saxons, who remained fixed in their older home, adhered to their ancient idolatry and opposed Christianity." [1]

But the institutions and traditions of Roman law and order, which the introduction of the Teutonic "tribal" or family system appears but little to have disturbed, contributed no less towards this great result. Kemble has justly remarked that "throughout Europe the documentary dispositions of the Latins prevailed. The conquerors readily adopted such portions of the law of the conquered as applied to those new relations of life which the conquest itself had created, and those social wants which had not been provided for in their own unwritten customary law. The formal study of the Roman law still survived in the seventh century." He proceeds to show that the clergy everywhere introduced and fostered the influence of the Roman law, " which was moreover the code of the orthodox, the German invaders being for the most part tainted with semi-Arian, if not Arian heresy." [2]

The Anglo-Saxon charters, even of the seventh century, bear testimony to the ease and rapidity with which the habits of the people of Kent became subject to all the civilizing influences of the Roman law, and probably the singular success and almost unexampled endowment of the monasteries, arose greatly from their resemblance to the tribal system of the

[1] Döllinger, "Geschichte der Christl. Kirche," b. i. abth. ii. pp. 139–140.

[2] Kemble, "Cod. Dipl. Ævi. Sax." Introd. p. 7.

Saxons, and the idea they presented of land held in community. Yet with all these facilities for the reception of Christianity, we must not too hastily conclude that its success was either complete or immediate during the earlier period of its history in Kent. Though exempted from those fatal reverses which it experienced in the west and north of England, its progress was gradual, and sometimes interrupted by the relapses of some of its highest converts into idolatry. There is reason to believe that the worship of Thor and Woden survived in parts of the county —the Thunor legend in Thanet, and the names of Woodesborough and Cold Friday, near Sandwich, still preserving the memories of Thor, Woden, and Freia, as is the case in the remoter parts of England, which Christianity less early penetrated.

It cannot but be further observed, that the form in which Christianity was first exhibited to the people of Kent, and the singular beauty and simplicity in which it was placed before them, contributed more than any other circumstance to its success. Without entering upon any subject of controversy, or raising any needless questions on the relative claims of the Celtic or Roman phases of the same faith and ritual, we cannot pass over an element of such vast importance in the history of the diocese and of its religious and social development.

We have already noted the singular absence in the Kentish kingdom of the controversies on the keeping of Easter, and on the other subjects of unreasonable division by which the Northumbrian Church was so early distracted. The Church in Kent had no con-

flicting traditions of this kind, inasmuch as it regarded
Rome as its sole model, and the reference of every
subject of difficulty to Gregory and his successors was
so easy and so immediate. It is hence that the
church of Canterbury, unlike many other churches
in England, had no particular "use" or distinctive
ritual order. The Roman office, as improved and
reformed by Gregory the Great, and the method of
chanting which he had brought to what was then
supposed to be a perfect musical state, were religiously
followed in Kent, and the doctrinal writings of its
first great teacher were studied with equal devotion.
The religious ideal of the Anglo-Saxon Church, as it
presents itself to us in the simple but most authentic
forms of its earliest charters, centres in the *quatuor
novissima*. Death, the judgment, the penalty, and the
reward, appear everywhere as the incentives to virtue
and holiness, and as giving the most awakening and
impressive motives to good works and a life of devoted
piety. Scarcely a single charter of the earlier periods
fails to urge the truth that "earthly goods are transitory, but things eternal are abiding; hence, that
things transitory ought to be freely given to purchase
things eternal"—that "we brought nothing into the
world, and can take nothing with us from the world"
—and "the duty of charity as enforced by the command, 'Date, et dabitur vobis.'" But the spirit of
the offering and the necessity of faith to make it an
acceptable one are no less clearly intimated.[1] The

[1] "Pius Deus non quantitatem muneris, sed devotionem
offerentium semper inquirit" (Æthelbald of Mercia, 748).

proem which describes the motive of the giver is very variously conceived: " for the remedy of my soul," —" for the absolution of my sins "—" for the love of my heavenly country "—" for my own soul and the souls of my predecessors "—" for the love of our Lord Jesus Christ "—" for the remedy and salvation of my soul and for the hope and love of a future and eternal recompense in heaven "—" for the love of Almighty God, and the veneration of the blessed Mary, the mother of God, and the authority of all the saints." [1]   These are among the many introductory sentences of the charters, the last being also the latest in time, and coming down to the tenth century. In the earliest period these donations do not seem to imply the condition of any masses or services for the souls of the donors; but in the very remarkable charter of the Duke Oswulf to the church of Lyminge in 798 he enjoins his anniversary to be kept by the monks there " with fastings and prayers, singing of psalms and celebrations of masses "—and " with the refection of the brethren in food and drink." [2]   In the charter of Wulfred a few years later, the condition is that " the brethren should chant in behalf of his soul the Lord's prayer, or else that short form of prayer which Dodda the monk used in his monastery." These directions by no means indicate the existence at this early period of any doctrine in regard to masses for the dead such as that which now prevails in the Roman Church, but the institution of services in which the names of these benefactors should be

[1] Kemble, Introd. pp. 10-18.
[2] Cart. 175, tom. i. p. 212.

read in the diptychs and prayers offered up for their souls. The simplicity of the early faith of the Anglo-Saxon population is indicated even in the laws of Knut which belong to its latest period, in which the Lord's Prayer and the Apostles' Creed are made the sum of necessary Christian doctrine and practice[1] a sufficient qualification for the reception of the Eucharist and the admission to Christian burial.[2] But perhaps the most precious of the traditions which the Anglo-Saxon Church derived from her great apostle was that intense and exclusive devotion to the authority and sufficiency of the Scriptures, which all who are acquainted with the writings of Gregory the Great must admit to be his distinctive doctrine. Nowhere it may be affirmed has this tradition been more unbroken than in England, and the very century which preceded the Reformation witnessed one of its strongest assertions in the petition presented by Bishop Hallam, of Salisbury, on the part of the clergy, to the Council of Constance demanding that the whole teaching of the Scriptures should not be made sub-servient to the forced interpretation of the single text which involves the so-called Petrine privilege, but

---

[1] Spelman, "Conc." tom. i. p. 549.

[2] The distinction between *necessary* doctrines and those which are either derivative or subordinate appears to be here clearly recognised. Even in the important Assembly of the Tuscan Bishops at Florence in 1787 this distinction was asserted by the Teologo Regio, Bianucci, and accepted by all the bishops, in the words, "Che bastando per esser Cattolici il trovarsi concordi negli articoli fondamentali era sufficiente il tener fermo e convenire nel solo *Credo*." (Istoria dell' Assemblea tenuta in Firenze, 1787 ; Sess. v. p. 81, Fir. 1788.)

that the whole law of God should be duly honoured
and observed by all alike.[1] From this brief glance
at the features of doctrinal simplicity which the
teaching of the Anglo-Saxon Church exhibits in all
its documentary forms, we proceed to take an
equally rapid view of its outward state, which was as
primitive, both in principle and structure. The Priesthood was held to be the highest order (properly so
called) in the Church, the Episcopate being rather the
highest grade of the priesthood than itself a separate
order.[2] Kemble has observed that "the Anglo-Saxon
clergymen appear to have been more thoroughly
national than any similar body of men in any part of
Europe. Hence, those among them who were most
imbued with the doctrines and feelings of the Tra-
montanes always indulge in a great deal of gratuitous
declamation on the state of slavery in which the
English Church was held—meaning only that by
becoming clergymen, the Anglo-Saxons had not
lost their nationality or their position under the
national law."[3] It may be reasonably conjectured
that the higher view which was entertained of the
equality of order as between the priesthood and the
episcopate, contributed to this feeling of independence and consciousness of a common citizenship.
It is not a little singular that while Lanfranc, an

---

[1] Von der Hardt, "Concil. Constant," tom. i. p. iv. pp. 1138–
41.

[2] "Ambo siquidem (Presbyter et Episcopus) unum tenent
eundemque ordinem, quamvis dignior sit illa pars Episcopi."—
"Canones Ælfrici," (Spelman, tom. i. p. 576).

[3] Introd. p. 52 (note).

Italian, was the greatest and earliest vindicator of the liberties of the English Church, Theodore, a Greek, was the most zealous and successful agent in merging its national character and individuality in rite and law.   The latter was accordingly the greatest promoter of English monachism, while the influence of the former was directed towards strengthening the position of the secular clergy.   At this point a most important element of the diocesan system forces itself upon our attention, viz., the parochial division of the diocese, whose origin and earliest history are lost in the obscurity of the mediæval period.   We have observed that the Roman divisions of the county were rather personal than local—rather regarded population and its centres, than mere local or topographical lines of division.   The larger divisions of lathes, hundreds, wapentakes, and sokes bear witness even in their names rather to divisions of number and population than geographical delimitations.[1]   It will be observed that while the hundreds and larger divisions of the county preserve with very few exceptions their natural form and compactness, the parishes, on the other hand, are of the most varied and irregular form, in many places having large detached portions belonging to them, and for the most part so inconveniently situated in regard to the

---

[1] A *hundred* came afterwards to designate a *local* division, as a *centuria* did in the Empire.   "Quis non contemnat unam centuriam," asks St. Augustine, "si illi promittatur quia possessurus est centum ?" "Sermo 45, de verbis Isaiæ," c. 57.) Here we have a clear proof that the *hundred* has a Roman, not a Saxon origin.

churches as to make it almost impossible to suppose
that their local boundaries were arranged in accordance with their ecclesiastical necessities. It is difficult
to avoid the conclusion that the local boundaries of
parishes were simply a civil division suggested by the
ancient boundaries of estates granted by the successive
kings and nobles—estates which in the Norman
period became manors. For these boundaries are so
carefully recorded in the Saxon charters as to make
them almost the only permanent lines of local separation. The lines already marked out would supply
also the boundary marks of the intermediate lands,
and thus by a gradual and natural process those
ancient and most capricious of all local divisions, the
parishes of England would be constituted in the
form in which we now find them. In the laws
of Knut this connection between the parochial
churches and the estates of the thanes is clearly
shown. "If a thane has a church on his bocland"
(*i.e.* his private estate) "to which a cemetery is
attached, he shall give to it a third part of his tithe." [1]
We see here in the early part of the eleventh century
the approach to that manorial system developed in
Domesday where there is no mention of parishes, but
the church appears as an appendage to the manor,
and the root of the parochial institution is traced
rather to the feudal estate than to any ecclesiastical
origin. As the manor (or secular estate) created the
parish, so the subdivisions of the estate created in
their turn subordinate manors and dependent parishes.

---

[1] Spelman, tom. i. p. 545.

This is clearly seen by an examination of the outlying
manors in Domesday in connection with their parishes
as now constituted, and of the various forms in which
subordinate manors have been created within larger
manors through the separation of the original feudal
estate.[1]   This view is sustained by the authority of
the learned canonist Zypæus, who in answering the
inquiry how the boundaries of parishes are to be
ascertained, replies that "the boundaries of villages
and of secular jurisdictions are a strong presumptive
evidence of the bounds of parishes.   For patriarch-
ates, primacies, archbishoprics, bishoprics, dioceses,
and parishes were arranged according to the places
and limits of provinces, towns, and villages, wherefore
it was rigidly forbidden to confound or change these
already-constituted boundaries in any degree."[2]   The
Church divisions followed those of the State, and these
latter were in the rural districts constituted for the
most part out of the ancient estates of the kings and
nobles which were granted to the Church or to the
greater thanes in the early period of the Saxon occupation, and represented that subordinate kind of
jurisdiction which was afterwards developed in the
manorial system of Domesday.[3]   According to the view
here suggested, the estate of the thane or principal lord
formed the original unit of the parochial system.   This
was made chargeable with a tithe to the church,
which the thane was required by law to provide

[1] See for the whole of this subject Böhmer's exhaustive treatise, "Jus Parochiale," c. iii.

[2] "Responsa de Jure Canon." Antv. 1645, p. 122.

[3] Kemble, "Cod. Dipl." Introd. p. 43-50.

for it. This tithing became the foundation of the
new parochial division, while the church was built
by the lord near his own residence instead of
placed in that part of the parish or manorial property
which was most central or convenient for the tenants
on the estate. This is the only view upon which the
extraordinary irregularities of boundary in parishes
can be accounted for, and the location of their
churches often at the very extremity of their districts
be explained. An observation of Prebendary Jones
on the "Wiltshire Domesday" tends to corroborate
this theory. He says that " having gone in several instances over the boundaries of manors with an ancient
charter, and the Ordnance map divided into parishes
or rather tithe districts as his guides, most striking
has been the way in which boundaries described now
some thousand years ago may still be accurately
traced." [1] The history of the Tithe institution is
closely connected with that of the Parochial system.
Before the time of Constantine, as is admitted by all
who have given to the subject a legal and critical
examination, this kind of payment was unknown. [2]
The support of the clergy rested previously on landed
and personal property held by the permission or connivance of the State, and on the offerings of the
faithful, which were of a personal and voluntary
character. In the towns these voluntary offerings,
after the establishment of Christianity, became com-
pulsory, and laid the foundation of what are called

[1] "Wiltshire Domesday," Introd. p. 27.
[2] Böhmer, "Jus. Paroch." p. 394.

personal tithes, charged on the *bona mobilia* of the parishioners; while in the rural districts, where the land was cultivated by a servile class (the *villeins* and *servi* of the Domesday book), the charge fell like the charges of the *trinoda necessitas*, the reparation of bridges, fortresses, and military service, upon the feudal owner. In the Western Church in the close of the fifth century[1] the income of the churches was divided into four portions; the first for the bishop, the second for the ministers, the third for the fabric of the church and the clergy, and the fourth for the poor—not, however, in an equal proportion, but by a fair apportionment.[2] The idea so early propagated by the clergy that their portion represented the tithe paid to the priesthood in the Jewish Church, led to the assertion for the clergy of the actual tithe as of Divine right, and the recognition of it as such by the early Anglo-Saxon laws gave it that civil sanction upon which it now so securely rests. It would lead us far beyond our present limits were we to trace the progress of these laws, or the gradual stages by which the property of the English Church attained the vast proportions which it exhibited in the day when the great confiscations of the Augmentation Office reduced it to such comparatively modest dimensions. It will be enough for the reader to glance at the possessions of the Church in Kent as they are presented in the Domesday-book, which we shall have occasion at a

---

[1] "Circa il 470," Sarpi, "Trattato delle Materie Beneficiarie."
[2] " Non in 4 parti arithmetici e uguali ma con proporzione." Id. ibid.

later period to describe more fully. We pass on to consider the influence of the lives and characters of the archbishops upon the history of the diocese ; and here we must make the preliminary observation, that we are apt to take no account of the immense accessions of power which each successive arch-bishop acquired from the increasing endowment of the Church. It is less from the personal qualifications, or influence even of the greater prelates, than from the almost irresistible power which their property and position gave them in the history of their age that the see acquired that supremacy which excited the envy even of the popes, and led to the somewhat bitter controversy between Archbishop Chicheley and Pope Eugenius IV. on the legatine powers he had conferred upon Cardinal Beaufort. This is an element too much neglected in estimating the progress even of the Papacy itself to its almost world-wide supremacy. The immense accretions of the wealth of the Roman Church, so well described in the great work of Sarpi, constituted a far more solid foundation of its authority than the comparatively recent production of the forged decretals, or the doctrine of the Petrine Privilege. The growth of the power of the English primates resembled on a smaller scale that of the Papacy itself. A vast patrimony which under the solemn adjurations of its royal founders could ever be increased but never alienated, gave to the church of Canterbury, augmented as it was so largely by the incorporation into it of nearly all the earliest founda-tions of Kent, an influence which can hardly be too highly estimated. Characters of signal power

and marked talent, such as were many of the Saxon
archbishops, might give to the primacy a temporary
accession of authority which weaker men could not
confer upon it, but the vast resources of the primacy,
even before the prebendal division of Lanfranc, ought
never to be put out of view, especially in contem-
plating the history of the diocese itself, out of which
the revenues of the archbishops chiefly arose, and in
which up to the time of the Reformation so much of
those revenues was spent. In regarding the lives of
the Anglo-Saxon bishops and archbishops, for the
latter name did not extend to those of the earliest
period, our point of view is necessarily confined to
their influence upon the Church with which they were
more immediately connected. The bearing of their
lives upon the history of the Church generally belongs
to a much larger plan, which has been recently most
successfully carried out. It may be observed, as a
preliminary consideration, that the connection of the
archbishops with the diocese was much closer and
more immediate at the period when Kent constituted
a kingdom as well as a diocese than at any other;
that when the kingdom was merged into that of
Mercia, the connection though still most intimate was
very much weakened; and that the development of
the primacy, and the acquisition of Lambeth as its
principal centre in 1197 (through an exchange with
the Bishop of Rochester), rendered the tie gradually
weaker and weaker, until the surrender of the Palace
at Canterbury, and the great residences of Saltwood,
Aldington, Knowle, and other manorial houses in East
and West Kent, to King Henry VIII. by Cranmer

almost entirely severed the local bond which connected the archbishop with the diocese. In this point the Church of Rome had a great advantage over the filial church of Canterbury, inasmuch as the centre of the diocese in her case was identical with the centre of the primacy. In the Anglo-Saxon period, the cathedral city was the residence of the archbishop, the centre of his personal and local influence, the place of his constant preaching, especially on the greater festivals and during the Lent and Advent seasons. In a word, the "residence of the bishops as of Divine right" was assumed as a necessary condition of the episcopate, without whose fulfilment the office itself would cease to have a real and practical existence. This rule, so severely inculcated by Pius IV. in the celebrated bull, "*In supremâ militantis ecclesiæ speculâ*," needed then no assertion, far less any penalties to enforce it. The seat of the Episcopate was fixed by Augustine and Æthelberht at Canterbury, and the functions of the archbishops as Abbots of the great monastery of Christ Church rendered non-residence a virtual impossibility. The law of the Church referred to in the letter of St. Boniface of Mentz to Archbishop Cuthberht, that every year the bishop should make a visitation of his diocese was then very easily, and doubtless very punctually fulfilled. The lives of the earlier archbishops, mostly chosen as they were from the heads of the more important monasteries, belong therefore in a peculiar manner to the history of the diocese. Though Archbishop Theodore (668–93) is said in a certain sense to have built up the diocesan system in

England, acting under the strong impulse of the see
of Rome, the close connection of the primate with
the diocese was very little disturbed by the new
arrangement, for the ties of the cathedral city and
the headship of the monastery were still unbroken.
Nor was this firm bond loosened until the time of
Lanfranc, when the foundation of residence-houses
on all his principal manors led that great primate
to divide his time between the cathedral city
and a number of subordinate places ; a plan which
led his successors gradually farther and farther
towards London as the real metropolis, and induced them by exchanging their manor of Darenth
for Lambeth to make the latter place their principal residence. This broke up the union between the monastic and secular life of the archbishops, and led to the transfer to an elected
prior of that authority which they had originally
combined with the episcopal one in their own
persons. Up to the period when Lanfranc introduced the prebendal system at Canterbury, and
the estates till then held in common were divided
between himself and the monks, the archbishops
retained that mixed character which they had
in their first institution by Augustine, and the
Benedictine rule was as far as possible carried
out in their ordinary life. In modifying this
rule so as to adapt it to the altered circumstances of the church of Canterbury, Lanfranc
implies that he still retains the position of
abbot, and doubtless carried out when in

his cathedral the order and ritual he here lays down.[1]

The first five Bishops of Canterbury were immediately connected with Gregory the Great and his work of the conversion of England, and their lives in connection with the diocese had necessarily a somewhat missionary character. Laurentius was nominated by Augustine as his successor, and extended his missionary labours far beyond the limits of the diocese. Mellitus, another of the companions of the Apostle of England, having been appointed to the bishopric of London, and exiled from his diocese, succeeded Laurentius in the Kentish see, and was followed by Justus, the first occupant of the see of Rochester, which had been formed out of the north-western portion of Kent, having as its centre the important Roman station called by Bede "Rhof," or "Rhofescestre"—probably a corruption of the common Latin name of Rufus. Honorius was also a Roman, a disciple of the great pope whose death in 604 broke the earliest of those links of connection with Rome, which in the Anglo-Saxon Church had been so greatly strengthened by the immediate and personal relations of the first Bishops of Canterbury with the Roman see. The twenty-six years of Honorius's bishopric enabled him to extend and establish the influence of the primacy more than any of his predecessors; while his successor, Deusdedit, is

[1] "Inde nemo turbetur quod in tractatu earum consuetudinum nomen abbatis tantum non episcopi vel archiepiscopi ponitur—ordo quippe monachorum describitur," &c. (Decreta pro Ordine S. Benedicti. Lanfranci Opp. Migne, p. 445).

chiefly celebrated as having been the first native of England who filled the see. But the real history of the Primacy itself may be said to begin with Theodore, who was consecrated in 668, and was the first to obtain the recognition of his authority over the whole of the Bishops of England, and to exercise that legatine power over the whole country which the popes had attached to his office. In proportion, however, as his labours became extended over the province his connection with the diocese itself became less intimate, though the foundation of schools and the introduction both of Eastern and Western learning (for he was a Greek by birth and education) gave his episcopate a more general and influential character than that of any who preceded him. As a man of singular learning and great powers of organization he may well be regarded as the chief founder of the primatial power of Canterbury and the introducer of the synodical system into the English Church. Nor is his name less celebrated in connection with the penitential discipline of the Church which he may be said to have first reduced to a regular system—a task for which his Eastern education peculiarly fitted him. The assertion that he introduced and established that division of parishes which we now see, has already been shown to be without solid foundation. After him came almost an unbroken succession of monastic primates ; Brihtwald, who had been Abbot of Reculver, Tatwyn, who had been a priest in a monastery of Mercia, Nothelm, Cuthberht, who had been Abbot of Lyminge, Bregwyn, Lambert or Janberht, previously abbot of St. Augustine, Athelard, abbot of Malmesbury, Wilfrid, a monk of Canterbury, Ceolnoth, Æthelred, a monk of Christ Church,—bishops of whom little but their name survives, but whose influence was from their origin and position far more felt in the diocese than in the primacy. The Danish invasions had seriously crippled the power of the see at this period ; and the long incumbency of Plegmund, the first to break the monastic succession, though favourable to learning (for he had been King Alfred's instructor) appears to have been fatally influenced by the unsettled state of the country and the destruction of its inhabitants and ruin of their property which these sudden descents upon so unprotected a coast brought with them. From this time we find bishops of other sees elevated to the primacy, bringing with them more extended views, and less of the mere diocesan character than the monks of the great monasteries of England would naturally exhibit. Athelm, and Wlfelm—both bishops of Wells ; Odo, bishop of Sherborne ; Elsin, bishop of Winchester, were successively elevated to the primatial see—and well prepared it for the reign of the much greater Dunstan, who passed on to it from the bishopric of London. The life of this eminent man forms an epoch, not only in the history of the Church and State of England, but in that of the diocese itself, in which it well prepared the way for the work of the still greater Lanfranc. Dunstan, like Becket and Laud, has suffered as much from indiscriminate praise as he has from unqualified detraction. That he was the most devoted friend and patron of the monachism of his day, is simply equivalent to the statement that he was an admirer of learning, as well as himself in advance of the learning of the age, and that as an ecclesiastic he naturally supported the only institution which enabled the Church to extend and to organize itself—for we must remember that the monastic system was the sole society "for the propagation of the Gospel" and for "national education," which existed in this early period. But he was eminently a great church builder and friend of the secular as well as the regular clergy, as we have observed already; while by incorporating the smaller monasteries of Kent with the great foundation of which he was the head, he gave to the archbishopric the most substantial part of its power and influence. His twenty-eight years' primacy had therefore as important results in the diocese as it had upon the Church at large. The examination of the numerous charters of Eádgar and other Saxon kings, confirmed and sometimes originated by the great archbishop, prove the extent of his influence, exercised not only in behalf of his own diocese but in every part of England. The immense accession of power which this steady flow of monastic endowment gave to the Church, disturbed from time to time by the ruinous inroads of the Danes, was perpetuated and increased on the establishment of a settled kingdom by Knut, to whom more than to any of his predecessors the English Church is indebted for its development and stability. He carried on the policy of Dunstan in regard to the incorporation of the property of the lesser monasteries with the greater foundations at Canterbury, and to him the Monastery of St. Augustine was indebted for its rich inheritance in the Isle of Thanet, the spoils of the venerable Nunnery of Minster. The constitution of the diocese in its present form, and the organization of its parochial system as we see it in Domesday, which we must ever remember represents the earlier survey under Edward the Confessor in an enlarged and amended form—ever referring to that survey and to the previous state of the churches and their revenues, and describing the change they had undergone in the intermediate period—could not have been completed earlier than the reign of Knut, when the peace and order of the kingdom were finally settled, and there is no evidence of any material change occurring between this and the Domesday record. This leads us to the conclusion that those parochial churches which are mentioned in Domesday existed in the days of the Confessor, and to the reasonable conjecture that many of them were restored, if not actually founded, by Knut; who was the first to reduce into a systematic order the ancient laws of the Anglo-Saxon Church,[1] and by securing the temporal rights of the clergy, and defining the duties of the thanes and nobles in regard to the churches on their estates, to promote the building and endowment of the churches in Kent, and to prepare the diocese for the munificent operations of Lanfranc. But it is time that we should present to the reader a general view of the state of the diocese and the character of its population, as it must have appeared in the latter part of its Anglo-Saxon history. The absorption of the kingdom

[1] These laws in Anglo-Saxon and Latin are given at length by Spelman, tom. i. p. 538.

of Kent, first into that of Mercia in the time of Cœnulf, and later into that of Ecgberht (A.D. 823), and its complete incorporation into the empire of Knut (A.D. 1017), in the final settlement of the country, while they extended the power of the primacy, naturally reduced in the same proportion that of the diocese itself. The archbishopric gravitated more and more towards the centre of civil government, and had it not been for the Becket murder in a later century, Canterbury itself would have lost its place among the more important cities of England, and the city and diocese would have been almost swallowed up in the primacy. As we fall back upon the earliest period when the Kentish kingdom still existed, we observe that the diocese consisted mainly of three great districts ; 1st, the settled country of East Kent, the scene of its great monasteries and secular and ecclesiastical estates, and also of its ancient churches ; 2nd, the wild district of the weald of Kent, forming a kind of missionary region, gradually occupied by the Church as the woods were felled and cultivated places obtained ; and lastly the district of the Marsh, large tracts of which, as well as woodland in the Weald of Kent, had been attached to the estates of the clergy and nobles in East Kent, by successive grants of the Kentish kings. In the Domesday period, and consequently in that immediately preceding it, the 360 manors in Kent had only 183 churches.[1] " Benenden, Hadlow, Palster and Tudely were the only four places in the Weald returned in the Survey as possessing

---

[1] Furley, " History of the Weald," vol. i. p. 397.

churches." [1] Tonbridge, Tenterden, Cranbrook, and other of the now principal parishes in West Kent, were in the Saxon period occupied only by colonists from the more settled districts, and not till the twelfth or thirteenth centuries did the great " Andred forest " in its Kentish portion become in the proper sense an ecclesiastical possession. The absence of mention of most of the churches in Romney Marsh in the same great Survey leads to the same conclusion in regard to them, and we can only conceive the district as sparsely inhabited by tenants or servants of the greater manors of East Kent to which they were attached, one of these (Aldington) covering a vast district, both of the Weald and of the Marsh, while another (Lyminge) extended anciently through several of the parishes, both of the Marsh and of the Weald— the monks of Lyminge having been probably the first missionaries in the district, while those of Christ Church, in whom both these estates were ultimately vested, completed the work of evangelization. Towards the close of the thirteenth century, Mr. Furley conceives that " a complete parochial division had come to be established, with churches and appendant chapels." The boundaries of these parishes were probably conterminous with those of the outlying districts attached to the several manors, called in the Weald, *dennes*, and in the Marsh, *culets*. [2] It is most probable that long before churches were built in these

---

[1] Furley, " History of the Weald," vol. i. p. 397.

[2] From *culata* (from which the French *queue* and *culotte*), indicating an irregular stretch of land lying apart from the main parish or district.

districts, missionary stations existed, built of less solid materials. In one of the earliest charters relating to the Marsh, the "oratory of St. Martin's with the houses of the fishermen" are mentioned, clearly pointing to a mission-house and a missionary work which was being carried on in the district. But while this was naturally the work of the monks of the period, there is clear evidence that the establishment of a secular clergy was very early and general. A secular priest, called the *presbyter loci*, is described as having escaped during the Danish attack of a monastery in the ninth century. The Church of St. Mary which the same invaders spared at Minster was evidently served by seculars—and in all the monastic records and legends we have ample proofs that the settlement of a secular clergy invariably succeeded the missionary work of the regular orders. In Domesday (which reflects the earlier period of Edward the Confessor and his predecessors), "the usual title given to ministers is *presbyter*. In other parts of the record we meet with *capellanus* and *diaconus*."[1] A *clericolus* is mentioned in the Wiltshire Domesday who might have belonged to one of the lesser orders. The position of the clergy during the earlier Saxon period, as we have observed already, was one of comparative dignity and independence, their spiritual office never absorbing their temporal rights, or leading them to renounce their civil status in order to obtain a higher degree of ecclesiastical power. But this independence

[1] "Domesday for Wiltshire," edited by W. H. Jones, prebendary of Sarum, 1865 (Introd. p. 68).

was much disturbed in the later history of the Anglo-
Saxon Church, from the destructive inroads of the
Danes, which involved the property of the Church in
confusion and ruin, and led to the transfer to the
laity of much of its patrimony, not excepting tithes,
which even in the closing days of the Saxon rule in
England had been in many cases alienated from the
Church and held by laymen,[1] while a principal portion
of them was still held by the monasteries and other
religious foundations.   This led to the establishment
of vicarages, and to the office of vicar ; a title multiplied greatly in later centuries through the evil of
non-residence, which compelled the bishops to form
vicarages in churches which were properly rectories,
resulting in the still greater evil of sinecure rectories.
But a still more important change was effected in the
ecclesiastical framework of a diocese by the establishment of the order of *canons,* a title descriptive of a
body of clergy permanently attached to a particular
church, but devoted (like the monks of whose system
they were a kind of secular adaptation) to a common
life—" matriculated " as it were to that church—that
is, entered into the register (*matricula, album, tabula
clericorum,* κάνων, *concil. Nic. c.i.*).   In like manner the
office and name of Cardinal has its derivation from
those who were *incardinati* into the canonical system
of the Churches of Rome, Milan, Ravenna and other
principal cities of the West.   Without tracing the
origin of this institution into its earliest history and

---

[1] "Domesday for Wiltshire," edited by W. H. Jones, prebendary of Sarum, 1865 (Introd. p. 68).

first type, it will suffice to say that originating with the great St. Augustine of Hippo, and Eusebius of Vercelli, it passed into France, and became organised and established by Chrodegangus, bishop of Metz, in 760. He first drew up the rule and formed the order of canons regular, whose time was divided between the instruction of the young, the celebration of divine offices at different periods of the day (whence come the *canonical hours*), and the exercise of the higher acts of charity. The method of their life was like that of the Benedictines, but differed chiefly in this, that instead of dividing the goods of the Church between the clergy and the bishop, it left to each member of the body his separate estate. Out of this plan arose the division of the property of cathedral chapters into *præbendæ*, portions or allotments assigned to particular individuals.[1] This is the origin of our cathedral chapters; and Lanfranc by introducing the præbendal system into the chapter of Canterbury revolutionized in a manner its ancient monastic constitution, and placed it in more direct hostility than ever with the rival foundation of St. Augustine's. There are various references to this change in Domesday. Thus, of the canons of St. Martin's in Dover it is said, " In the time of King Edward the præbends of these (lands) were held in common. . . . Now they are divided by the Bishop of Bayeux into separate estates."

Such was the state of the clerical order during the

[1] Nardi, "Elementi di Diritto Ecclesiastico," p. i. c. x. secs. 194-7.

Saxon period, but at the time of the Conquest the whole of the clergy had reached a state of corruption and degeneration which Sir F. Palgrave has thus described. "The tenth century may be emphatically denoted the '*sæculum obscurum.*' The attempts of Alfred failed, and the clergy were settled on their lees. . . . Learning altogether decayed, and he who could read Latin was accounted a prodigy. Morals declined fearfully. The English clergy were viciously corrupted. Very many of the bishops and abbots had obtained their dignities by simony. The bishop was a judge, bound to attend to the reformation of manners, but he had *bought* his office, and so would *sell* immunity to the opulent transgressor. There were some holy men among the (clergy), but they were not sufficient to avert the destiny of the people, and all were involved in one common ruin. The empire seemed to exist under Edward the Confessor, but it was really on the verge of dissolution." [1]

In Kent the great influence of Dunstan had the effect of at least checking, if not altogether moderating, the worst features of this description. So great a degeneracy might excite greater wonder were we to forget the state of the Roman Church itself during the ninth and tenth centuries. Baronius tells us that he "only enumerates" the popes of these darker ages, admitting that "during them the only head remaining to the Church was Christ"—a very sufficient Head, if the popes had been content to be His members instead of claiming the headship themselves;

[1] "History of Normandy and England," III. 334, 637.

and an equally sufficient proof that a human supremacy is no security against the grievous errors of doctrine and failures of practice which prevailed most during those very periods in which the Papal supremacy was most complete. We pass on, however, with a sense of relief to the Second great Epoch of the Diocese of Canterbury, the reign (if we may so term it) of the illustrious Lanfranc, and to the revival under the Norman rule of the life and influence of the Church in Kent, aided as it was by the increasing power of the primatial see.

CHAPTER III.

LANFRANC AND THE NORMAN PERIOD.

HISTORY, like architecture, has its periods of "transition," periods, not unfrequently, of long duration, and always of the greatest importance. We are too apt to neglect these, and the popular habit of drawing "hard and fast lines" between the chapters of our national and ecclesiastical history has led us to break up our annals into abrupt and disjointed portions, instead of regarding them as presenting throughout a course of continuous development, often accelerated by events, which, however sudden in their fulfilment, may themselves have been as slowly developed.

This is eminently true of the transition period, which extends between the two closing centuries of the Saxon rule and the Norman Conquest, periods of history which we are singularly prone to separate, and on no ground more absolutely and abruptly than on that of the Feudal system, by which the Conqueror is so erroneously supposed to have set aside the ancient Roman and Saxon laws, and to have framed at once a new legal system and a new society adapted to this complete and even revolutionary change. A single glance at the Domesday Survey, and especially at that of Kent, must convince the most sceptical that the principles of the feudal system, which extended throughout Europe, and was first developed in Lombardy, to whose forms of law and of government the later Saxon kings were indebted so largely, were early sown in England, and very well developed in the days of Edward the Confessor. For the Norman survey, as we see throughout, is founded upon the earlier survey of Edward, and is, as it were, a second rent-roll of the kingdom, differing from the first, rather in the increased value of the manorial lands it describes, and in their transfer to other tenants in chief, than in any other feature. To see this truth in its clearest form, we have only to trace the gradual manner in which the Teutonic law, based, as we have seen it to be, upon the family bond, and represented by the *gau*, or land held in common, is neutralized and superseded by the Roman law, which regarded land as a personal and individual possession, a law which is the real parent of the whole of the feudal system, and which, by centering in the king the whole land of the country, enabled him to grant it absolutely or exclusively (in regard to its usufruct), to his nobles or retainers.[1] Some of the greatest legists have traced up the feudal system into the imperial laws of Rome, but it is enough for us to begin the pedigree with the Lombardic Kingdom, where the learned Marquis Scipio Maffei, in his historical work on the city of Verona, has fixed its earliest development. The idea of holding land on the condition of military

---

[1] Kemble has marked some of the earliest stages of this transition, Introd. pp. 43 and 53, in which latter place he shows how the rights conferred by the *gau* were first invaded.

service was developed in that kingdom by the dukes, who held as vassals under the king at Capua, Spoleto, and Trent, as early as 591. The same kind of tenure passed into Germany on the formation of the new Roman Empire there, and was represented in its grandest form in the Germanic Empire of the Mediæval period. Senckenberg, in his learned introduction to the Feudal Law, defines a "feud" as "a contract, in virtue of which a vassal hires his military services to a lord for a certain reward" (or stipend).[1]

The first element of feudalism is therefore clearly seen in that condition upon which land is universally granted in the Saxon charters, the "*trinoda necessitas*," *i.e.*, the obligation of repairing bridges and fortifications, and performing military service.[2] Even the grants to the clergy did not exempt them from these duties, though, as Kemble observes, it does not distinctly appear whether they involved the personal service (the *corvée* of the French feudists), or were capable of composition or commutation. From the period of Augustine, which brought in the Roman law and civilisation, or perhaps it might be more strictly said from the reign of Wihtraed, in 690, these obligations rest upon every grant of land, and though they are not identical with the more perfect feudal forms of knight-service, and infeudation in its later sense, it is impossible to escape the conclusion that they contain in them the germ of the feudal system. Spelman, accordingly, and Bishop Nicholson after

---

[1] Senckenberg, "Juris Feudalis Primæ Lineæ." Götting., 1736, c. vii. sec. 153.
[2] Kemble, Introd., p. 51.

him,[1] attributes the introduction of the feudal system to the Saxons, while Senckenberg gives it also a Teutonic origin. Böhmer, in his learned observations upon it, in connection with the Canon Law and the præbendal system, holds that it was originally simply a payment in land instead of money for military service, the only means by which Germany, a country destitute of money, and only able to pay in land, could provide for the support of an army, whose officers, under the Roman Empire, were paid by a salary out of the public chest.[2] Feuds were therefore called "*beneficia*," and the ecclesiastical law adopted this name as a special description of its own feudal estate, which thus became a benefice, held under the bishops for life under conditions of spiritual service, and requiring, like a military *feud*, a formal institution and investiture. Thomassinus and Van Espen here agree with the great Protestant jurist, the words of the latter being suggestive and significant :—" As princes were wont to give their property by a beneficiary right to those who yielded them military service or other offices of obedience, in like manner the bishops gave the goods of the Church to be held or used, or rather gave the right of receiving their usufruct to the clergy, in order that they might war for the Church, or give service to it, each according to his proper vocation."[3]   Like the ancient military *feud*,

---

[1] Spelman, "Leges Anglo-Sax., Dissert. de Jure Feud. Vet. Sax., G. Nicolson, Episc. Derrensis," &c., Lond. 1721.

[2] Böhmer, tom. ii. p. 298, ed. Halae, 1732 ("de Præbendis et Dign.").

[3] Van Espen, "J. E." p. 2, tit. 18, c. i. sec. 2.

the ecclesiastical benefice was originally dependent on the will of the lord, and might be resumed by him at pleasure. Like its first type it then became permanent, and held for life, a perpetual service being annexed to it. Hence the common definition of a benefice is "a perpetual right of receiving fruits out of the goods of the Church on account of an ecclesiastical office or ministry constituted by the authority of the Church itself."[1]

A clear view of the beneficiary system in this earlier stage is essentially necessary to the full understanding of the state of the diocese of Canterbury when its government passed into the hands of the great Norman primate. The Domesday Survey, as we are often told by its commentators, was not strictly or necessarily an ecclesiastical survey, nor did it exhibit the state of the diocese in the same manner in which the surveys of the popes at a later period represent it. But whether through the influence of Lanfranc, or from the greater accuracy of the Kentish commissioners, to which causes might perhaps be added the special importance of the county and its rank as the residence of the primacy, the mention of the churches is here more frequently and carefully made than in many other portions of the same great survey. We turn therefore to the Domesday of Kent, which opens this great compilation, as conveying to us the clearest view we are able to obtain of the state of the diocese in the reign of the Confessor, and its development between this and the year 1085. It is diffi-

---

[1] Böhmer, ut supr. p. 299.

cult to realize the vast extent of the property and the influence of the church of Canterbury at this period, without filling up an outline map of the county as Mr. Furley has done,[1] with the ecclesiastical manors, and thus presenting at a single glance the relations of the church with the county generally. The great feudal holders under the Crown are only twelve in number—the archbishop (for his separate estates), the monks of Christ Church and their tenants, the Bishop of Rochester, the Bishop of Bayeux, the Abbey of Battel, the Abbey of St. Augustine, the Abbey of Ghent, Hugo de Montfort, the Count Eustace, Richard de Tonbridge, Haimo the Viscount, and Albert the chaplain. There are thus only six private holders, for the Bishop of Bayeux held as a private person, and his estates very shortly fell into other hands by forfeiture, but the five remaining lay-holders represent but a small district of the county compared with the property of the Church; and the manors held by the Bishop of Bayeux, though very numerous, are none of them so valuable as the ecclesiastical holdings. In the descriptions of several of the manors we find four distinct classes of tenants or occupiers: first, the immediate tenants holding under the Church, who only occur as the "milites archiepiscopi" (the military tenants holding land by a subinfeudation). Under these are the *villani* (villeins), the *bondarii* (borderers), and the *servi* (servants in the higher meaning, according to some ; according to others, slaves in the proper sense of that term).

[1] "Weald of Kent," vol. i. p. 275.

Priests and ecclesiastics are sometimes mentioned as tenants, as in the case of the seven priests, holding land in Limne of the archbishop's manor in Aldington. In all the chief manors in which churches are mentioned there is also mention of servants or ministers. There can be little question that these represent the lesser orders of clergy who took part in the services of the Church, and were doubtless permitted to carry on some occupation of an agricultural or mechanical kind. For the "priests," who are mentioned under "Limne," were evidently farmers and cultivators, and no church, or at least no principal church, appears to have existed in that subordinate manor. The servants of the manors appear also to have been Lanfranc's workmen and assistants in his building of churches and manors, resembling the "*Monachi cœmentarii*," who are described by his contemporary, Ivo of Chartres. For in the "Dies Obitualis," which was read on the anniversary of the archbishop, it is said that "he built many and fair houses in his manors, which were not only for his own pleasure and honour, but also might be a benefit to the poor men who used to work in the building of his houses."[1] The position of the *villani* has been subject of a great variety of opinion, and even of controversy. They were certainly (as the learned editor of the "Wiltshire Domesday" observes), "no bondsmen." He concludes, after a careful examination of authentic documents, that the *villani* represented "the principal of the subordinate tenants or

---

[1] "Anglia Sacra," p. i. p. 55, apud Opp. Lanfranci, ed. Migne, p. 101.

cultivators of the land."[1]   The *bordarius* he shows to
be the same kind of servant of the manor who is
elsewhere in Domesday called a *cottar*, the name
arising out of the duty of supplying the table (or
bord) of the lord.   The meaning of the word *servi*
has led to much more serious differences of opinion ;
in many places we can hardly translate it but by the
term *serfs* or *slaves*.   But wherever it immediately
follows a church, as " *ibi ecclesia et vi. servi*," I think
it must be taken to mean (as several learned commentators have held), those ministers of the Church,
or persons in the lesser order who, though of servile
origin, and fulfilling many of the duties of labourers,
possessed, from their very connection with the principal churches, a higher position than an ordinary
servus.   Having thus briefly sketched the different
classes of residents in the several parishes of the diocese at the Domesday period, we proceed to a question yet more directly affecting its ecclesiastical state,
viz., the nature and number of the churches recorded
in the Survey, and the difficult problem how far we
have in it the entire list of the churches existing in
the age of the Confessor.

We may fairly admit that the absence of the mention of a church in any manor described in Domesday
does not necessarily imply that no church whatever
existed.   But it is a strong presumptive evidence that
no church of the highest order, the " *ædes primariæ* " of
the laws of Knut, existed at the time of the survey.
Four kinds of churches are described in this law :—
The " head church " (Þeaꝼoᵹ cýꞋueum), the secondary

[1] " Wiltshire Domesday," by Jones, Introd. pp. 57, 58.

church, the lesser church, and the rural church
(*Ecclesia campestris*). The third kind of church is
described as having less frequent services, but as
having a burial-ground, while the fourth is destitute
even of a burial-place. Probably only the first and
second kind of church, to which a competent number
of ministers was attached, is described in the Survey,
and the subordinate manors had attached to them
some one of the lesser rank. It is certainly unlikely
that at Limne (for instance) no church should have
existed of any kind, though seven priests are mentioned as holding land there. I am inclined to think
that we must here take a middle ground, and hold
that only those churches which were founded in the
greater manors, and represent what were termed later
"advowsons appendant," are mentioned in Domesday;
the churches in towns which rather represent "advowsons in gross," being either unmentioned or only alluded to where they paid some rent or due to the manor.
In one or two rare instances "lesser churches" and
"chapels" are mentioned ; as the "*ecclesiolæ*" of Postling, and the "three chapels" of Dartford. These
were the "secondary churches of the laws of Knut,
some of which, or at least some of the two last forms
of church, must have existed in every place in which
a settled population is described to have been resident. A hundred and seventy-seven churches are
actually mentioned in the Domesday Survey of Kent.
In the following cases more than one church existed.
Hoo, near Rochester, had as many as six; Folkestone
(the entire town and hundred), as many as eight ;
Dover and Lyminge, three each ; Dartford, a church

and three chapels ; Aylesford, Orpington, Monkton, Eastchurch (in Sheppey), Sellinge, Orlestone, and Halling, two each ; Postling, two "*ecclesiolæ*" ; Poulton, only a chapel ; while Oare is described as having "half a church," by which we can only understand that the manor had only half of the dues which arose out of the church—unless an alternate right of patronage, such as we so often see in later periods, is here indicated.

How many of the churches mentioned in Domesday and still represented in our own age, retain any features of architecture or masonry of a pre-Norman character, is a question as difficult as it is interesting. The subject, at least in regard to the masonry and mortars which form the truest criteria of the pre-Norman period, has been hitherto treated too superficially and imperfectly to enable us to determine whether any portions of the Domesday churches (representing, we must remember, rather those of the age of the Confessor than of Lanfranc), are still to be detected in the ancient fabrics of the diocese ; recent rebuildings and so-called "restorations" have greatly limited the field of this inquiry, and it is difficult to estimate the losses which we have experienced in what must have formed the richest materials for it.

A still more important question presents itself at this point—the state at this period of the parochial or secular clergy, those who were permanently attached (*incardinati*) to the principal churches. The creation of "*jurisdiction*," and the limit which was thus given to the exercise of the powers of "*order*," until then general and uncircumscribed, necessarily

involved the establishment of the parochial system
and a parochial priesthood; and this was followed up
in the ninth century in France, and subsequently in
England by the institution of Rural Deans, whose
origin is thus briefly described by the learned
canonist Rauttenstrauch :—" As the custom prevailed about the ninth century for the rural clergy to
hold monthly chapters in their several districts, in
which the parish priests assembled on the first day
of every month, in order to consult in common in
regard to their duties and scruples of conscience, it
was necessary to elect some of their number as presi-
dents of these chapters, and these were termed rural
deans. These officers were elected by the clergy
themselves, not from any qualification of locality or
standing, but from their knowledge, skill, and prudence, and were confirmed by the bishop, being
irremovable afterwards except on the ground of mis-
conduct."[1]

Hincmar of Rheims endeavoured to reform this
institution, which in his day had become too con-
vivial in its character. It was utterly unknown in
Italy; and the rural deans were succeeded generally
in later times by the *vicarii foranei*, the deaneries
becoming, as they even now are legally, a mere
geographical expression. The original diocese of
Canterbury had eleven of these subdivisions, viz., the
deaneries of Bridge, Canterbury, Charing, Dover,
Elham, Limne, Ospringe, Sandwich, Sittingbourne,
Sutton, and Westbere. In regard to the office and

---

[1] " Instit. Juris Eccl." sec. II. c. xv. sec. DCVI.

status of the parochial clergy, so much obscured by
Hammond[1] and other writers, whose absorption of
all the powers of the second order into the episcopate
is perhaps as injurious in its results as the absorption
of the episcopate itself into the papacy, Rauttenstrauch observes : " Since the parochial clergy hold
their jurisdiction by divine right, they are not to be
considered mere vicars of the bishops, having powers
only vicarious and delegated.   Rather they enjoy an
ordinary jurisdiction, and carry on their care of their
flock, together with the bishop, in their own right "[2]
(*jure gerunt proprio*).   We have already seen that the
English parochial clergy from even the Saxon period
maintained an ecclesiastical and social independence
which was outwardly blamed, but doubtless secretly
envied by those of other lands.   It was this which
made the struggle between the secular and regular
clergy, represented in some sense by the perpetual
warfare between the rival foundations of Christ Church
and St. Augustine's, so violent and protracted.   Nothing tended so much to intensify this hostility as the
introduction by Lanfranc and Odo, bishop of Bayeux
of the præbendal system both at Canterbury and
Dover ; by means of which that plan so essential to
the first idea of monachism, of a tenure in common,
was entirely abandoned, and a separate estate was
attached to the members of the conventual body, or
assigned to some special purpose of its support.

[1] The theological faculty of Paris condemned Jean Sarazin in
1429, and Jacques de Vernant in 1654, for denying the divine
right and *ordinary* and proper jurisdiction of the parochial clergy.

[2] Instit. Juris. Eccl.

The institution of "regular canons" was perhaps the severest blow which the monastic system proper has ever received. For out of the separate estate thus created, an individual power was conferred upon the several members holding it, and they had a direct interest in increasing it, and thus passed from the mere religious community in which their personality was merged and lost, into a new and secular life, which connected them in all its relations rather with the people with whom they mixed, than with the regular clergy, who, except through the farmers and managers of their common estates, knew but little of the outer world.

Nor was the clergy of the second order alone emancipated from the monastic rule by this great and momentous change. The episcopate, which during the Saxon period had been so closely identified with the monastic system, was now made entirely independent of it ; and Lanfranc had no sooner vindicated the rights of his see against the insatiable Bishop of Bayeux, and recovered twenty-five manors of which the church of Canterbury had been unjustly deprived,[1] than he carried out the plan which had long been adopted at Caen, and in other parts of Normandy, and divided the manors and lands of Christ Church between himself, the monks, and their respective feudal tenants, a division which the Domesday Survey at once recorded and ratified.

[1] It is extremely difficult to identify the manors thus recovered out of those (nearly fifty in number) which are described as belonging to Christ Church (or as it is there termed, the Church of the Holy Trinity) in Canterbury.

At this point we cannot but fall back upon the life of this great prelate, as it is given us by his contemporary biographer, Milo Crispinus. After describing the great Council of Windsor, at which the Primate Stigand was deposed, held in the year 1070, he writes: —" While the king was considering the matter, and consulting with the nobles of the kingdom, by a most happy result he rested at last in Lanfranc . . . . and sent legates accordingly into Normandy to carry out this design . . . . The Abbot of Caen being overcome as much by the will of God as by the apostolic authority . . . . passed over into England, and undertook the government of the church of Canterbury, which enjoys the primacy of the islands. . . . . After his translation into England, Lanfranc, not forgetful of the object for which he had come, directed all his endeavours to the correction of the manners of his people, and settling the state of the Church. And first he laboured to renew the church of Canterbury, the mother church of the kingdom. And because some years before it had been burnt, he strove to rebuild it from the foundations,—a great and extensive work. He built also necessary offices for the use of the monks ; and (which is very remarkable) he caused to be brought over the sea in swift-sailing vessels squared stones from Caen, where he had been abbot, in order to build with. He built also a house for his own dwelling near the church, and surrounded all these buildings with a vast and lofty wall. Having duly arranged all that was necessary for the table and clothing of the monks, he enriched the church with many precious ornaments. The dignities of the

church of Canterbury, which had fallen into abeyance
through age or neglect, or had been lessened in importance, he re-formed and renewed. Many lands
which had been taken away he brought back into the
property of the Church, and restored to it twenty-five
manors. He built two hospitals for strangers and for
the poor without the city—one on the north, the other
on the west, with all necessary buildings, to which he
assigned such annual payments as seemed good to
him out of his own income. He founded præbends
in his manors to be given to the poor yearly. On
many of his manors he built houses of stone for his
dwelling." [1]

The hospitals are those of St. John without Northgate, and of St. Nicholas, Harbledown; while the
manors in which he built houses are indicated to us
by those described in Domesday as held by the archbishop himself in demesne. [2] The principal of these
are—Otford (said to have been in a later day the
favourite residence of Becket), Charing, Aldington,
and Lyminge, with Darenth (exchanged in the subsequent century for Lambeth), Malling, Northfleet,
Bolton, Pluckley, and Mersham. [3] Whether the five

---

[1] Opp. Lanfranci, ed. Migne, pp. 40–46.

[2] In a letter addressed to a friend, whose name is not mentioned, the archbishop writes : "You know that in those counties
the charge of inquiring into which has been entrusted to you, I
have nothing in demesne, but that all the lands in those parts of
your church belong to the support of the monks altogether"
(Ep. liv. p. 516).

[3] Besides these, the archbishops held in demesne at the time
of the survey, Pagham in Sussex, Harrow in Middlesex, and
Croydon and Mortlake in Surrey. These with Canterbury

last places were actual residences of the archbishop cannot be easily determined.   Otford, Charing, Aldington, and Lyminge continued to be archiepiscopal abodes till a much later period.   The two last-named places had extensive parks, that of Lyminge being probably the most ancient enclosure of this kind in England, as it is mentioned in a charter of Oswini in 689.   The secular life upon which the archbishops thus entered, carried on as it was by a constant alternation of residence between their manors in Kent, Sussex, Surrey, and Middlesex, detached them effectually from the old monastic life which they had led at Canterbury.   Although the palace there was still their more central and official residence, and they continued to fulfil their duties in their cathedral, the ties which connected them with the diocese gave way before the stronger influence of the primacy.   It may be safely affirmed that the forged Donation of Constantine scarcely gave the Papacy a greater comparative power than the separate endowment which Lanfranc secured to the primatial see, conferred upon himself and his successors.   Hitherto the see of Canterbury had been rather the shadow of a great name than the reality.   The inheritor of great titles and venerable traditions, it had never till now secured that great secular and political influence which the union of temporal and spiritual power in Lanfranc conveyed to it in later ages.   For the first time in its history the arch-

would give at least eight residential houses at this early period. Lambeth, Knole, Ford, Wrotham, and other places were of later occupation.

bishopric was detached from the monastic bond in
which it had sprung up, and entered into the great
feudal system. The Monastery of Christ Church
assumed at the same time a new and more secular
form. A prior now took the place of the archbishop
as abbot, and the new and relaxed rule which Lanfranc drew up for the house tended greatly to promote
the secular tendencies it had shown from the first ;[1]
while the foundation of the Abbey of St. Gregory for
regular canons weakened still more the influence of
the regular clergy, which was so early and powerfully
maintained by the Monastery of St. Augustine. That
house founded all its claims upon the exemptions
which had been granted, or at least were asserted to
have been granted, by the popes at different times,
the germ of which is to be seen in the Saxon
charters. But its truest claim of authority rested on
the immense extent of its endowment, which rivalled,
as we have seen, that of the metropolitical church.
Its church was until the time of Archbishop Cuthberht (A.D. 741–58) the burial-place of the archbishops,
and the licence he procured for the transfer of this
right to his own church was among the earliest causes
of that virulent animosity which grew up in later ages
between the rival foundations. This was greatly
increased by the controversy which sprang up immediately after the death of Lanfranc between the
Monastery of St. Gregory, so closely allied to Christ
Church in its origin and government, and that of

[1] In the "Decreta pro ordine S. Benedicti" he describes
these as "gathered" by himself "out of the customs of the
greater monasteries of his age."

St. Augustine, on the possession of the relics of St. Mildred. The archbishop on founding St. Gregory's had endowed it with the relics of St. Ethelburga and her niece, St. Mildred, which till then had rested undisturbed at Lyminge. By an anachronism very unaccountable at a period in which Saxon hagiology must have been best known, this early Mildred had been confounded with her relative and namesake who two generations later had founded the great nunnery of Minster in Thanet, and as the latter had been gifted with extraordinary and miraculous powers, the Gregorians at once claimed her as their own, while the Augustinians with equal energy repudiated a claim which would have deprived them of their most sacred and wonderworking shrine. It is strange to reflect that up to the period of the Reformation, when both the rival houses fell in the common ruin of the monastic system in England, this controversy still survived in all its bitterness.[1]

Of the architectural works of Lanfranc it is believed by the most competent judges that scarcely a fragment remains. A careful and scientific comparison of his work at Caen with the earliest portions of Canterbury Cathedral led Mr. Parker to the conclusion that no portion of that great fabric can be attributed to Lanfranc.[2]

[1] See the tract of Goscelinus, the Augustinian monk (A.D. 1090), "*Contra inanes B. Mildrethæ usurpatores*" (in MSS. Cotton.).

[2] "It must be borne in mind," he writes, "that every one of our cathedrals was rebuilt in the twelfth century ; there is not a vestige of Saxon work in any one of them. Lanfranc's cathedral at Canterbury was entirely pulled down and rebuilt

The destruction of the previous building is described to have been complete ; and even the lengthening of the choir, attributed by Milo Crispinus to St. Anselm, could not have extended the building to that portion of the crypt which is sometimes erroneously assigned to his great predecessor. The chancel of the church at Lyminge, which was certainly built between 965 and 1086,[1] and finished when Lanfranc removed the body of Ethelburga, is built in the rudest imitation of the Roman work which preceded it, and represents the masonry of the Saxon servants of the manor rather than the squared stones which Milo describes Lanfranc to have obtained for his building from Caen.[2] The work of Lanfranc still remaining in the two magnificent abbeys at Caen, either of which might vie with the Cathedral of Canterbury, is marked by that peculiarity which has since become the criterion of buildings anterior to 1100, an extremely wide joint between every stone, indicating a reliance on mortars derived from the Roman period, and continued even when the Roman skill in their manufacture had long ceased to exist. Mr. Parker was the first to discover this important clue to the study of mediæval building, suggested by the undoubted work of Lanfranc, almost entirely hidden from view in the great churches of

by Ernulf and Conrad in the time of Henry I." ("Gentleman's Mag." Jan. 1863, p. 85.)

[1] See Goscelinus ut supr. and Leland's "Collect." tom. ii. p. 54, ed. Hearne, 1770.

[2] It is not a little remarkable that not a single piece of Caen stone is found in the church of Lyminge. In the dependent chapel of Paddlesworth (pre-Norman in its general features) Caen stone is largely employed.

his foundation at Caen.   Fragments belonging to
the period of Lanfranc may be found in the lower
portion of Malling Abbey, in the chancel and south
wall of Lyminge, and in a portion of the little church
of Paddlesworth ; probably also in a small chamber
attached to the church at Aldington, and in the
singular turret into which a corner of the tower of
Minster in Thanet is in a manner inserted.   The
tower of Limne belongs more probably to the time
of Anselm, and exhibits an instance of the Transition
period, marked by a rude massiveness which was probably its chief characteristic.   But far higher and more
fruitful in its results was the doctrinal work of the
great Norman primate, which has come down to our
day in his exegetical and controversial writings.   A
history of the diocese would be indeed imperfect if it
failed to mark at least the primary features and
character of the teaching which was thus fixed and
developed in every one of those churches over which
he ruled.   Unlike his architectural labours, these
works of the great master-builder are permanent and
imperishable.   The writings of Lanfranc, though not
numerous, are clear and comprehensive.   His controversy with Berengarius on the Eucharist, though
probably the best known, is the least valuable, and
does not exhibit him as in any degree equal to his
adversary, whose arguments he passes by with the
levity and impatience which betray his great inferiority
as a controversialist to the remarkable man whom he
endeavours to refute.   The treatise is from beginning
to the end a continuous *petitio principii* in its most

undisguised form.[1] When, however, we take up his
commentary on St. Paul's Epistles, in which he has
founded upon a paraphrastic text a kind of tesselated
gloss formed from the writings of St. Ambrose and
St. Augustine, supplemented and connected by his
own observations, we see at once that his exegetical
powers greatly exceeded his controversial ones, and
that his qualifications as a pastoral divine were of a
high order. It is not too much to say—and the fact
is an interesting one to the Church of England, which
he may be said to have moulded into its present form
as a national Church, giving it thus its distinctive and
individual character—that there is no part of this
commentary which could not be used to this day in
the sermons of our English divines and in the metropolitical cathedral itself. The entire work is a signal
proof of the continuity of the teaching of our Church,
and of its independence of those Italian influences
which were grafted upon it at a later period, but which
never assimilated themselves to the mind of the nation.
The most interesting features of this commentary

[1] The views of Lanfranc on the Eucharist, when they are not
expressed controversially or in connection with the Berengarian
doctrine which represented the opposite extreme, were singularly
clear and spiritual. In his commentary on the 1st of Corinthians
(c. xi.), and in his letter to Donaldus, an Irish bishop (Ep. 33),
this is very remarkably shown. Of the Sacrifice of the Mass
he observes in his commentary on the Hebrews, "Melchisedech
panem et vinum sacrificare Deo constituit quem ritum Dominus
Jesus Christus observavit et in ecclesiâ suâ observari præcepit"
(c. v. ver. 4). This rather represents the doctrine of the High
Churchmen of the days of Laud, than that of the modern
Church of Rome.

in connection with our diocesan history are those
in which the constitution of the Church is referred
to, which give an insight into Lanfranc's government
of the diocese and his views of the pastoral office.
On Eph. iv. 11, he writes : " Christ hath given different gifts to different persons, that every one might
be perfectly exercised in that work of ministry which
he has received. For if one had received all these
offices he could not attend to them separately." In
his rebuke to Berengarius for speaking slightingly of
the Roman Church, he suggestively remarks on the
passage of Matthew xvi. 16, that the words to Peter,
" *though they are believed to have been addressed to all
the pastors of the holy Church, and are so expounded by
certain Catholics*, are declared *by the holy canons and
the decrees of the popes* to be specially understood of
the Roman Church."[1] In his commentary on the
Galatians (c. ii. 12) he indicates the equality in rank
and power of Peter, John, and James ; while in his
speech asserting the claims of his see against those
of York he makes use of the popular interpretation of
the so-called Petrine Privilege in a somewhat curious
manner. Arguing against the advocates of the York
primacy, who had very justly alleged that Gregory
the Great had not extended the privilege of Augustine
to his successors, Lanfranc retorts that the same might
be said of the Church of Rome, in which Christ did
not extend the gift bestowed on the great Apostle to
his successors. His doctrine on the perfect individuality and integrity of every separate Church, notwith-

[1] " De Corpore et Sanguine Domini," c. xvi.

standing its union with Rome, is, however, here as
ever most jealously guarded.[1]　"As," he affirms "in
every human individual there is every property of
the perfect man, so in every Church of the whole
Christian faith there is the same integrity and completeness."[2]　It is easy to see that these principles,
carried out in his own diocese, must have largely
contributed to that independence of character which
exhibited itself from the Norman times in the English
clergy, and conspicuously in those of Kent. Notwithstanding the Roman tendencies of the Monastery
of St. Augustine, and the increase of those exemptions
of persons and places from ordinary jurisdiction, by
which, under the specious pretext of conferring upon
them "the liberties of the Roman Church," the
Papacy so largely extended its power at this period,
the great Norman archbishop left an inheritance of
freedom to his diocese and to the whole Church of
England of which it was never but during a few
stormy intervals of its history deprived. It must
be remembered that his primacy extended over the
whole of the tempestuous reign of Pope Gregory VII.,
preceding it by three years, and exceeding it by

[1] With St. Augustine Lanfranc holds that the future Antichrist would "sit in the temple of God, *tanquam ipse sit templum
Dei quod est Ecclesia*" (in 2 Thess. ii.); that is, that he
would destroy the liberties and even the individuality of the
separate Churches by absorbing their rights and powers in himself. It would appear from this that he did not regard with
favour the new theory of the Papacy then just put forth by
Gregory VII. in his famous "*Dictatus*."

[2] Opp. p. 623.

four.[1]   His independent spirit led him to resist the
frequent importunities of Gregory to do homage to him
in Rome, the king with true Norman chivalry supporting
the archbishop in his refusal.   In one of his letters the
pope expresses his wonder that Lanfranc from the
time he was elected has never journeyed to Rome,
alleging that he ought not " through fear of the king,"
or any "superstitious affection" to him, to withdraw
himself from the papal presence.[2]   In another he
adds threats to persuasions, and menaces him with
suspension unless within four months he fulfils his
journey.[3]   But perhaps the most interesting to us
of the writings of Lanfranc in regard to his diocese is
his adaptation of the Benedictine rule addressed to
the Prior of Christchurch, which gives us a perfect
picture of the ritual of the cathedral during the whole
year, and of the *modus vivendi* of the inmates of the
monastery, both lay and cleric.   The laxity of discipline and general morality which the archbishop found
in England on his arrival rendered the compilation
of a practicable rule of monastic observance a necessary work.   He complains in a letter to St. Anselm

---

[1] Gregory VII. held the Papacy from 1073 till 1085. Lanfranc
the Primacy from 1070 to 1089.

[2] Greg. VII. "Epp." l. vi. ep. 30.

[3] See the letters of Gregory VII. l. ix. ep. 20. It appears
from the 43rd letter of Lanfranc that this journey was at last
fulfilled, "In Anglorum enim terram veniens, *sive Romam profi-
ciscens*, omnia sanctitati vestræ reseravi," &c.   Possibly, as
Lucas Dacher affirms, this passage may allude to his journey
to Rome in 1071, which would be in the time of Gregory's
predecessor.

that " the land in which he is, is daily shaken with so
many and so great tribulations, is stained with so
many adulteries and other impurities, that no order
of men consults for the benefit of his soul, or even
desires to hear the salutary doctrine of God for his
increase in holiness."[1]   In his adaptation of the
Benedictine rule, he says that " he has added a few
things, and changed others, specially in regard to
certain festivals, which " he considers "ought to be
observed in our Church with a greater degree of importance on account of the primatial see."   Among
the most interesting of these directions is that relating
to the library of the monastery and the studies of the
monks.   In the first week in Lent the librarian has
to place in the chapter-house all those books which
had not been delivered to the monks for study during
the preceding year.   These latter are brought in by
those to whom they were entrusted, and the librarian
reads the list of them.   Then they are returned in
regular order, and those who have not fulfilled their
year's task by reading them through, prostrate themselves to confess their fault, and to obtain pardon.
The librarian then delivers another book a-piece to
all the brethren, and takes a list of those lent and
those returned.   It does not appear that any inquiry
or examination was made to see whether the reading
of the past year had been profitable, it being apparently assumed that the character of each of the
brethren was a sufficient guarantee of his honour and
truthfulness.   Mention is made in another place of

---

[1] Ep. 43, p. 539.

the *altare matutinale* and the *altare majus*, the former
being probably used for lesser celebrations.   The
five greatest festivals of the Church are defined to be
these : Christmas-day, Easter-day, Whit-Sunday, the
Assumption-day, and the Feast-day of the place (*i.e.*,
that of the patron saint).   Those of the second class
are the Epiphany, the Purification, the Feast of St.
Gregory, the Annunciation, the Sunday after Easter,
the Feast of St. Alphage the Martyr, Ascension-day,
the Feast of St. Augustine, archbishop of the English,
Trinity Sunday (octava Pentecostes), the Nativity of
St. John the Baptist, the Martyrdom of St. Peter and
St. Paul, the Translation of St. Benedict, the Nativity
of the Virgin Mary, the Feast of St. Michael, All
Saints'-day, the Feast of St. Andrew, and that of the
dedication of the Church.   Those of the third class
are the Feast of St. Vincent, the Conversion of St.
Paul, St. Philip, and St. James, the "Invention of
the Cross," St. James, St. Peter's Chains, St. Laurence,
the octave of the Assumption, St. Bartholomew, St.
Augustine (of Hippo), the Beheading of St. John the
Baptist, the "Exaltation of the Cross," St. Matthew,
St. Simon, and St. Jude, St. Martin, St. Thomas the
Apostle, and any others which may thereafter be
appointed.   It will be observed here, with not a little
surprise, that the "Assumption" is placed above the
Ascension, not only being in the first class, while the
latter is in the second, but also having its octave
observed by a distinct celebration.   That this order
of feasts was adopted also throughout the diocese
there can be little doubt, and the elevated rank
assigned to the Assumption-day in the cathedral may

have arisen from the commemoration of benefactors, who mention that day specially in their bequests to the monastery.[1] The place, however, assigned to the Ascension-day is singular in any case, and not a little significant.

The letters of Lanfranc are of peculiar interest, especially those addressed to St. Anselm, his dearest friend and most illustrious successor. The influence of this great prelate and divine on both those who preceded and who succeeded him, is one of the most remarkable features of this period of our diocesan history. Far beyond him as Lanfranc undoubtedly was in every kind of practical ability, though greatly inferior as a divine and theoretical writer, this influence seems to have prevailed during all his episcopate, and continually reveals itself in his writings. Though Anselm had been a pupil of Lanfranc, the great archbishop yielded to his advice and direction in all his spiritual conduct. Coming to England to consult his predecessor in the Abbey of Bec, he rather gave, than received counsel. An instance of this occurred in the case of the festivals observed by the Church of Canterbury. Lanfranc complained to him that certain saints were commemorated in England who were not properly in the calendar, and especially Archbishop Elphege, who perished in the Danish attack on Canterbury, and who was regarded as a martyr, though his death was less a martyrdom than a murder. But Anselm pleaded the cause of

---

[1] See the charter of Lufa (A.D. 832) in which the Assumption-day is expressly mentioned (Kemble, tom. i. p. 299).

Elphege so eloquently that his name continued to
hold the high place which we have already seen assigned to it by Lanfranc's own appointment.   During
his visit at Canterbury Anselm is said to have found
a gold ring in his bed, which led Lanfranc to pro-
phesy that he would be his successor in the archbishopric.   "As he predicted," writes his biographer,
"so it came to pass."

Anselm, though he took up the church-building
work of his predecessor with great zeal, extending the choir of the cathedral and carrying on
the work of Lanfranc with becoming energy,[1] was
far less equal to the political requirements of the
see, and through his long monastic life had failed
to secure that independence of character which
Lanfranc had not only possessed in himself, but
had impressed upon the whole diocese.   He had
succeeded to the see under the most unfavourable
circumstances.   For four years it had been vacant,
while the miserable successor of the Conqueror had
turned its revenues to his own account, and but for a
sudden compunction on the supposed approach of
death, would have sold it to the highest bidder.   At
this moment he was led to bestow it upon Anselm,
then in England, but exacted from him so large a
tribute out of the already wasted patrimony of the
see, that the new archbishop, unable to satisfy the
extortions of the king, suffered from poverty and pri-

---

[1] The tower of the church of Limne (among others) is held
by competent judges to be the work of Anselm.   It exhibits a
peculiar Transition character, and is perhaps one of the earliest
instances of the pointed arch to be found in the diocese.

vation, as well as continual persecutions, which compelled him to live for three years in banishment.
Soon after his recall, in 1099, began the great warfare on the right of investiture, in which he took the
side of the Papacy with so much warmth and energy
that his subsequent life was one of repeated exile and
almost incessant conflict. The condition of the diocese,
of which we have few notices at this troubled period,
may easily be imagined from the various synods over
which Anselm presided, and whose invariable object
was to check the abuses and corruption of manners
which this long state of comparative anarchy had
brought with it. But notwithstanding the fatal effects
of the enforced absence of the archbishop, and the
breaking-up of the order and discipline which Lanfranc, supported by the vigorous arm of the Conqueror, had established in the diocese, the work of
the restoration and enlargement of the cathedral proceeded, and the two priors, Ernulf and Conrad,
whom Anselm had appointed, with the aid of the archbishop rebuilt the choir, to which the name of the
latter prior gave so great a celebrity, known as it was
thereafter as the "glorious choir of Conrad." The
course, however, of Anselm, in regard to his government
of the see, involved unhappily, both for his diocese
and the country itself, the complete reversal of the wise
and enlarged policy of Lanfranc, and the fatal break-up
of that perfect unity between Church and State which
his co-operation with the Conqueror had effected.[1]

[1] Lest this estimate of Anselm's policy should seem severe, I
may refer to that given by the Commission "for the reform of
public teaching" appointed by the Republic of Venice about

Up to this time the clergy of the diocese had not been forced to celibacy, and (as the learned Juretus observes[1]) like the French clergy, had been allowed the privilege of marriage.   Anselm, carrying out the rigid Hildebrandine policy which Lanfranc had resisted, enforced under the severest ban the surrender of those rights which had been hitherto allowed throughout all England.   His letter to the Prior Ernulf denounces privation of their benefices against all who fail in their obedience to this law, and excommunication if they persist in their resistance to it. In France, the prohibition was so difficult to carry out that a canon of Paris, in spite of it, was regularly married ("*matrimoniales tabulas sibi composuit*").[2]

the year 1770, which is embodied in these words, "Fu inserito ancora nel catalogo dei Santi Anselmo, Arcivescovo di Cantorberi, perchè sosteneva una superiorità assoluta dei Papi sopra i vescovi, e l'independenza di questi dei loro sovrani, ai quali non voleva che prestassero giuramento di fedeltà." (Collezione di scritture di regia giurisdizione. Firenze, 1770, n. 116, tom. 30.)   The greatest of our archbishops as a divine and pastoral teacher, in his political character he was among the least.

[1] "Licet Rex Angliæ præcepisset ut presbyteri ecclesias et fœminas haberent sicut tempore patris sui et Lanfranci Archiep. Anselmus contra per totam Angliam jussit omnes sacerdotes qui fœminas tenerent privari ecclesiis et omni ecclesiastico beneficio" (Not. in Ivon. Carnot. "Epp." p. 734). It must not be assumed that the clergy of this period lived in mere concubinage. This was the calumny of those who enforced the new prohibition.   For the Chronicles of Auxerre (at the year 1119) in describing the Council of Rome of that date affirms "*uxorum quoque* et concubinarum contubernia presbyteris, &c., ibi sunt penitus interdicta" (Id. ibid).

[2] Ivon. Carnot. "Ep." 218.

The bishop consults Ivo in regard to what is to be done in the case, who recommends, contrary to modern authorities, that "the marriage tie should remain valid, but that the offender should lose his stipend." We can readily imagine the confusion which the course thus pursued by Anselm must have occasioned in the diocese, though so little record of its results has remained. But far more serious and immediate in its issue was the great contest on the right of investiture, which proved him, however illustrious as philosopher and divine, to be wholly wanting in that patriotic and practical spirit which was so distinctive a characteristic of his great predecessor. This controversy was the inevitable result of the entrance of the episcopal and clerical body into the feudal system, in which "investiture" into the feud was the inalienable right of the supreme lord. We have only to look at the Domesday Survey to enable us to see at a glance that the claim of the Papacy involved the surrender by the Crown of the supreme temporal power over the greater portion of the lands of England. Anselm, from the first, had cast in his lot with the pope against the Crown, which Ivo of Chartres had in some degree done in the sister kingdom.

"Anselm," observes Juretus, "going forth as an exile from England, and for the most part taking up his abode at Rome, at length, through his pertinacious zeal, induced the king, from whom he had received the archbishopric, to depart from the inveterate custom of investing the bishops of his kingdom."[1]

[1] Not. in Ivon., p. 561.

" It was fitting and necessary," writes Waltram, bishop of Naumburg, in 1109, "after the churches were endowed by kings and emperors with feuds, and their rights were thus transferred to the power of the bishops, that homages, oaths, and pledges should be required of them, that in the event of the irruption of an enemy, they might know to whom the custody of their cities was entrusted."[1] Anselm, who had delivered himself over in soul and body to Paschalis, the then pope, thought little of the example of his predecessor, or the claims of the sovereign whose investiture of him into his own archbishopric he had so readily accepted. To the famous Gundulf he writes, "Let no threats, no promise, no cunning extort from you either homage, or oath, or bond of fealty. If any should ask from you any of these, let this be your answer, ' I am a Christian, I am a monk, I am a bishop, and therefore I wish to keep with everyone the faith I owe to everyone.'"[2] A very unworthy subterfuge for so great a man, reminding us of the excellent remark of the Senator Ruccellai in one of his memoirs, addressed to the Grand Duke Leopold of Tuscany, " In the days of religious purity there were always to be found good subjects—in the dark days of error wretched slaves."[3] The episcopate of Anselm, bright as it was in his doctrinal teaching, marks one of the earliest stages of the decadence of the clergy of the diocese, and the approaching subjugation to a foreign power of the spiritual liberties

---

[1] Not. in Ivon., p. 710.   [2] Ibid.
[3] "Vie de Scipion de' Ricci," par de Potter, tom. iv. p. 116.

of England. The question of investiture was at last
settled by means of a compromise, which gave but
scant satisfaction to Anselm himself. The delivery
of possession by the staff and ring was surrendered
to the pope, while the king retained the power
of exacting the accustomed homage and oath of
fidelity[1].

Of Anselm, in his connection with the diocese,
we know little indeed. The contrast which his whole
character presented to that of Lanfranc was here
most conspicuous. It is as a primate contending
against the Crown for temporal supremacy that his
memory lives in the history of the Church, while the
fame of his theological works has given him the
highest place in the long list of the archbishops as a
divine. His celebrated treatise, "Cur Deus homo,"
is a contribution to the study of the doctrine of the
Atonement which would do honour to the brightest
periods of the history of the Church. As a church-
builder and restorer we must attribute to his influence
and counsel, if not direction, that enlargement of the
choir by the Prior Conrad, so celebrated in the history of the cathedral, yet destined to be so short-
lived. Gervase, in his history of the rebuilding of
the cathedral after the fire of 1174, gives us a full
view of the "glorious choir of Conrad," and describes
so minutely, not only the architectural features, but
the ornamentation of the church, which was then so
utterly destroyed, that we cannot but transcribe, from
the work of Professor Willis, a portion of his careful

[1] See William of Malmesbury, "de Gestis Pontif. Angl." l. ii.

description of Anselm's magnificent work.   Proceeding to the east of the great tower of Lanfranc, which was placed in the centre of the whole church, he writes :—" The eastern pillars of the great tower projected as a solid wall, and were formed each into a round semi-pillar.   Hence in line and order were nine pillars on each side of the choir, nearly equidistant from each other; after these, six in a circuit were arranged circularly, that is, from the ninth on the south side to the ninth on the north, of which the two extreme ones were united by the same one arch. Upon these pillars, as well those in the straight line as those in the circuit, arches were turned from pillar to pillar; above these the solid wall was set with small blank windows.   This wall (on either side), bounding the choir, met the corresponding one at the head of the church in that circuit of pillars. Above the wall was the passage which is called *triforium* and the upper windows.   This was the termination upward of the interior wall.   Upon it rested the roof, and a ceiling decorated with excellent paintings.   At the bases of the pillars there was a wall built with marble slabs, which, surrounding the choir and the presbytery, divided the body of the church from its sides, which are called aisles (alæ)."[1]   This important addition to the church of Lanfranc was carried on by Priors Ernulf and Conrad between 1096 and 1116, and was dedicated in 1130.

The death of Anselm took place in 1109, almost contemporarily with the close of the great work which he had inaugurated in the Cathedral, in the

[1] " Archit. Hist. of C.C." p. 42.

nave of which he was interred near his predecessor Lanfranc.[1] A vacancy of five years in the primacy must have fatally increased the disorganization of the diocese which the repeated exiles of the archbishop and his ill-concealed conflict with the Crown, even during the period of his apparent reconciliation, occasioned. In 1114, Radulfus (de Turbine), bishop of Rochester, succeeded to the primacy, of whose incumbency in regard to the diocese itself we know but little. He bestowed upon the hospital which Lanfranc had founded at Harbledown a penny a day out of his manor of Lyminge, for the purpose of finding milk for the lepers of that house, and died in 1122. He was succeeded in the same year by William Corboil, prior of St. Osyth, in Essex, on whose elevation to the see the ancient controversy for precedence between Canterbury and York was revived at Rome, but without any very practical result. Foreseeing, probably, the contest for the throne, which so soon broke out on the accession of Stephen, he obtained of Henry I. the custody of the Castle of Rochester, which gave him a feudal position of supreme importance, and enabled him to take far too active a part in the conflict which so soon broke out. Though he had taken an oath of allegiance to the Empress Maude, he took the chief part in the coronation of King Stephen, and joined that prince

[1] Eadmer says, *majori ecclesiâ*, which Hasted believes to refer to the lesser church, which would be that of St. John the Baptist, in the infirmary. It would seem more natural to conclude that the words refer to the nave of the building, as contrasted with the choir which Anselm had so largely extended.

when the nobility of the kingdom acknowledged him. The anonymous, but contemporary and impartial writer of the *Gesta Stephani*,[1] writes : " Among others there was present William the Primate of Canterbury, a man of dove-like countenance, and truly religious bearing, but more greedy for the acquisition of money than liberal in dispensing it. For when at length he departed this life, the commissioners of the king found an infinite amount of money secretly stowed away in his treasuries." The evil results of the feudal system upon the episcopate were never more remarkably seen than during the reign of Stephen. In the long conflict for the crown the bishops ever came to the front as military leaders, and their spiritual character passes entirely out of view. They affected a royal pomp, " built castles, towers, and fortified structures ;" . . . . " furnished their castles with provisions and weapons, soldiers and bowmen, and while they were supposed to be restraining malefactors and church-robbers, were even more cruel and merciless than they in oppressing their neighbours and spoiling their goods."[2] It may be readily imagined that the diocese of Canterbury at this turbulent period, though less injuriously affected than the midland and western parts

[1] " Gesta Stephani Regis Anglorum" (English Historical Society's Publ., 1846, p. 6). The learned editor considers that this narrative should be read together with that of William of Malmesbury " page by page." The latter is the advocate of the Empress Matilda, and wrote under the patronage of the Earl of Gloucester, her most devoted adherent.

[2] " Gesta Stephani Regis Anglorum," pp. 47, 98.

of England, which were the more immediate scenes
of warfare, was in a state of decadence rather than
progress, and that the grand development of it by ·
Lanfranc was now seriously retarded. The king
having overcome the bishops by force of arms, proceeded at once to the confiscation of their castles
and military stores, but afterwards was compelled to do
penance for his severe treatment of them in a council
held under Theobald, the successor of Corboil, at
Winchester. The primacy of Corboil, was succeeded
by that of Theobald, abbot of Bec, that ancient and
remarkable house, the influence of whose traditions
and discipline in the diocese was so marked during
the incumbencies of Lanfranc and Anselm. He was
elected in 1138, after a two years' vacancy of the see,
and consecrated in the same year. His primacy was
marked with all the vicissitudes which had attended
those of his predecessors. Alternate quarrels and
reconciliations with King Stephen, which led him
sometimes into banishment, and at others into a
retirement into another part of the kingdom, now
almost in a state of chronic civil war, rendered his
primacy of twenty-two years a period of nearly constant warfare, during which he once interdicted the
whole realm, but he was in the end the means of recon-
ciling the King with the Empress Maud. Surviving the former, he had the fortune to crown Henry II.,
and to spend the last years of his life in a dignified
repose which contrasted strangely with its earlier
history. He is said by Gervase to have been a great
enemy to his own convent of Christ Church, which
can hardly be accounted for but on the supposition
that during the anarchy into which the diocese was

thrown by his absence or exile, the convent had
become unusually powerful, occasioning conflicts of
jurisdiction which even in more peaceful times were
not unfrequent. Our knowledge of the actual state
of the diocese during these years of almost continuous conflict is necessarily very slender, and the
absence of facts leaves us only such methods of
inference as may be derived from the incidental
notices of the chroniclers, or the side-lights of contemporary history. As we approach the period of
Becket, these become clearer and more definite,
though the great events of his history rather illustrate
that of the kingdom and of the Church generally than
of the diocese. It is not until the primacy of Archbishop Peckham, which began in 1279, that clear
and authentic materials for diocesan history present
themselves in the registers of the archbishops, whose
earlier volumes are still supposed to be at Rome,
though repeated and diligent searches have at various
times been vainly made for them at the Vatican.
We proceed to mention a few of the more prominent
examples of the architecture of the diocese in the period
intervening between Anselm and Becket. At Boughton
Aluph, Barfreston, Brabourne, Brook, St. Margaret at
Cliffe, St. Clement Sandwich, and Minster in Thanet,
examples of entire churches, more or less perfect,
are still remaining. Of towers of this age, we have
the stately one of New Romney, that of St. Mary in
Dover, the lower portion of that of Ruckinge, with
others of inferior note. Fragments of this period are
still more numerous in the aisles of churches, as at
Hythe, and St. Lawrence and Monkton in Thanet;

but these it will not be necessary further to indicate.
A curious incident which occurred during the early
part of the eleventh century shows us at once the
plans by which church-building or restoration were
assisted in this early day, and the influences which
were brought to bear upon the popular mind in order
to carry them out. In 1114-15, a pilgrimage of
canons and burghers of Laon, in France, visited Kent
for the purpose of collecting subscriptions for the
rebuilding of the Cathedral there, which had been
reduced to a state almost of demolition. In order
to raise sufficient collections for this purpose they
crossed the Channel from Wissant to Dover, bearing
with them the most precious of the relics of the Church
of Laon, which included the reliquary (*feretrum*)
of the Blessed Virgin, the sponge, napkin, and other
relics of the Crucifixion, together with some of the
hair of the Virgin, and other inestimable treasures.
By the exhibition of these, which (according to the
account of Helinandus, preserved for us by Vincent
of Beauvais) was attended with the most astonishing
miracles, they obtained a vast sum for their purpose
from the clergy and people of Kent. Visiting Canterbury first, they were honourably entertained by
the Archbishop (Ralph, and not William Corboil, as
the narrative describes him), who had himself been
a hearer of Anselm of Laon, and a guest of a former
bishop of that city. We are told that the miracles
wrought by the *feretrum* were specially limited to the
inhabitants of the dioceses through which the pilgrims
passed. Canterbury, which had then no relics to
compete with those of the Canons of Laon, was a
mine of wealth to the exhibitors, and the drinking of

water in which the relics had been washed was a
specific for every imaginable disease.   From Canterbury the precious charge was carried to Winchester,
thus traversing the whole of the county, and indicating by the singular success of the expedition the
decadence into which the public teaching of the
diocese must have fallen, after it had lost the manly
teachings of Lanfranc.[1]   In a letter to Bishop Gundulf, the great Norman archbishop prescribes to his
friend then seriously ill, not the recourse to relics, but
prayer to God and the application of a simple medicine
which he recommends : a " confection "[2] prescribed
by the physicians as useful in such a case.   (Ep. 46.)
Turning, in conclusion, to the monastic foundations
in the diocese, we find that they received an important
increase during the twelfth century.   In 1137, the
Hospital of St. Laurence, in Canterbury, was founded
by the Abbot Hugh, of St. Augustine's : in 1140,
the Cluniac Priory of Monks Horton, by Robert de
Vere.   Anselm himself is said to have founded the
nunnery of St. Sepulchre, near Canterbury, about the
year 1100 ; while King Stephen, whether as an act
of penance or propitiation, founded the important
Monastery of Faversham.

We cannot pass away from this period of our diocesan history without observing how greatly the life
and genius of Lanfranc contributed to the formation
of the national character of the Church of England,
which at a later period became so fatally deteriorated,

---

[1] The story is told in the " Speculum Historiale " of Vincent
of Beauvais, l. xxvii. cc. 12-15.

[2] *Diaprasium magnum*, which must, I think, be thus translated.

and sometimes even partially lost. It is memorable that while to Theodore, a Greek, the formation and consolidation of the primacy may be chiefly attributed, to Lanfranc, an Italian, and to his vigorous, independent policy, we owe the preservation of that national character, which up to the very dawn of the Reformation distinguished our Church. We have only to compare the treatise of Cardinal Pole, " de Concilio," with the " England and Christendom " of Cardinal Manning, to discover the extent of the contrast between the ancient doctrine of the Church of England and the Mediæval Roman theory in regard to the relations of the ecclesiastical and the civil powers. We have already noted the views of Lanfranc on this subject.[1] Pole advances even farther than his great predecessor when he affirms that the king represents the " Royal Headship of Christ," while the pope has only the " Sacerdotal Headship." The pope (he alleges) is not in such sense the Vicar of Christ as to leave no office for others, for all Christians hold a portion of this vicariate, inasmuch as they fulfil their work in the power of Christ. Hence he asserts that " the vicarious office of Christ as King in a General Council pertains to the supreme Civil Power."[2] The frequent and almost mortal conflicts between the Church and the State during the Primacies of Anselm, Becket, and other archbishops can only be accounted for by the strong vitality of the principle of the nationality of Churches as held from the days of Lanfranc.

[1] Opp. p. 625 and p. 298.
[2] Ad Cæsarem pertinere dicimus." Poli Lib. de Concil. Resp. 74.

CHAPTER IV.

FROM BECKET TO PECKHAM.

IT is a singular and significant fact that the grandest of the figures of the past which stands out in the history of the Primacy and of the country casts so faint a shadow on that of the diocese, and that Canterbury itself should have witnessed so far less of the life of the great St. Thomas who revived for so many centuries its fading glories, than the distant Abbey of Pontigny, which gave him refuge during his long exiles. But this will seem less strange when we consider that barely two years and a half of his primacy was spent in the diocese, and that every record which would have thrown light on his connection with it has either perished entirely or has yet to be discovered under the vaults of the Vatican Library. The history of this remarkable man in its fullest and largest bearing has been recovered with extraordinary penetration, and its disjointed features put together with the most elaborate care, by Canon Robertson in his biography of Becket, in which he has placed before us the life of the archbishop as it *really was*, relieved at once from the glowing colours and heavenly tints of the monastic artists, and from the disfigurements of that age of detraction which from the day of the Reformation until our own com-

pelled the perplexed student of history to apply to it
the words of the famous Dr. Owen in regard to the
pope himself:—"This is he of whom nothing not
great, nothing common, nothing not exceeding the
ordinary state of mankind, on the one hand or on
the other, is thought or spoken." We cannot however
admit his conclusion, after recapitulating the extreme
adulation of the flatterers and the unqualified abuse
of the detractors of the pope, that "there is no mean
between these—he is undoubtedly either the one or
the other." For Canon Robertson has drawn the
true historical mean between these excesses, and
shown that the history of the times fairly studied
leaves the illustrious "martyr" to the so-called
liberties of the Church, a position in the annals of his
country somewhat analogous to that which Gregory
VII. is now universally admitted to have held in that
of the Papacy, and which that pontiff, had he died a
violent death, like Becket, would have maintained in
the world-wide orbit in which his turbulent life
revolved. But the resemblance between the two
ecclesiastics is rather derived from the manifest effort
of the later one to imitate an example whose real
points of greatness he could not apprehend, than
from any similitude of mind or character which existed
between them. And this brings us to the influence
of the life of Becket upon the diocese, which, whenever and in whatever manner it was capable of
exercise, either during his residence or in the periods
of his exile, must have tended to increase in the
greatest degree the simony, the non-residence, the
pluralities and the almost undisguised immorality

which reigned at the time in almost every diocese in
England, and more signally perhaps than any, in the
diocese of Canterbury.   The pictures which are given
us of the state of the clergy in the twelfth century
throughout Europe, are so extremely drawn and so
deeply coloured that we might almost deem them to
be exaggerated, if it were not that they are the work
of devoted churchmen who, however, discordant at
other points are here in the most marked agreement.
None has more vigorously drawn them than Cardinal
Jacobus à Vitriaco (Vitry) in his description of the
state of the Eastern and Western Churches in his
day.[1]   Born in the close of the century which witnessed the death of Becket, he describes the clergy
of his age as " non pastores, sed dissipatores, non
Prælati, sed Pilati—non solum viso lupo veniente
fugiebant, sed cum ipsis lupis plerumque in detrimento
ovium pacem habebant ; nocte in lupanari, mane in
altari, Filium Dei conculcabant et sanguinem tes-
tamenti pollutum ducebant."   We cannot but conclude from such a picture as this, given by one who as
papal legate had studied both Eastern and Western
Christianity, that had Becket been less of a primate
and more of a diocesan, the conflict with the king
which ended so fatally for the interests both of the
" Pontificale " and the " Regale " would have been
avoided, and the state into which the diocese had
fallen at the period in which we have the first distinct
view of it—that, namely, of Archbishop Peckham,
just a century after the death of Becket—would not

[1] Jac à Vitr. "Histor. Occident." c. v., ed. Duaci, 1597, p. 271.

have been so miserable and almost hopeless. Of Becket, as a diocesan, we know much less than of his life as chancellor, or his posthumous claims as a martyr and worker of miracles. Of the last of these claims indeed we never lose sight, for the only picture which we have of him in his diocesan work represents him as working miracles of the highest order, and even raising the dead to life. On his last progress from London to Canterbury, " he confirmed great numbers of children, dismounting for that purpose wherever they were brought to him : and we are told that he performed many miraculous cures on the blind, the deaf, the dumb, and the lepers, nay, that he even recalled the dead to life." [1]

But the most important feature in the life of Becket, in its bearing on our diocesan history is undoubtedly the part he took in regard to the privileges and immunities of the clergy and the withdrawal of them even in criminal cases from the civil tribunals. The reader will see at a single glance the vast influence for evil which this claim, unhappily successfully urged, exercised upon the lives of the clergy and their moral and religious influence over the people. The " martyr for religious liberty " might have been more properly termed the " martyr for irreligious license," for by withdrawing the clergy in its most corrupt period from all the secular courts, while he encouraged their absolute secularization in life and conduct, he contributed in the most fatal degree to bring about the deplorable state of the Church, when it entered into

[1] Robertson, " Becket, a Biography," p. 261.

the anarchy of the great schism of the fourteenth century. "The defences which have been lately set up for the archbishop's conduct in this matter," observes Canon Robertson, "vary according to the views and position of their ingenious authors, who might perhaps be safely left to refute each other."[1] Archbishop Richard, Becket's successor, recognised that the result of this kind of ecclesiastical liberty was to withdraw clerical robbers and murderers, and also the robbers and murderers of the clergy, from all secular penalties—an effect signally instanced in Becket's own case—the murderer of an ecclesiastic being only subject to ecclesiastical penalties. He wrote a vigorous letter on the subject, in which he shows the utter inadequacy of Church censures and penalties for such offences. "The king," he writes, "claims the right of punishing them, but we of the clergy damnably reserve it to ourselves, and we deserve the consequences of our ambition in usurping a jurisdiction with which we have no rightful concern."[2] Yet it was this usurpation for which Becket died, and we can hardly wonder that even in his own day, when the terrible incidents of his death were most vividly impressed on the mind of the age, his claim to the crown of martyrdom was actually disputed. One of his biographers reports "that some persons regarded his pretence for justice as merely a covering for pride and vain-glory; that they held him to be lacking in that charity without which suffering was of no avail—to have been fond of pomp, haughty,

1 "Becket," p. 85.   2 Ib., p. 82.

rapacious, violent and cruel; that they argued that as it is not the pain of death which makes a martyr, so neither is it his cause alone, but that a good cause must be accompanied by graces of character and conduct in which Thomas of Canterbury was mainly deficient. There were even in his own monastery of Christ Church those who held that his obstinacy had deserved his fate."[1] Murders of prelates were not uncommon in those days and the French chronicler Robert de Thorigny (or de Monte) mentions the death of Becket in as brief and incidental a form as that in which Vincent of Beauvais records the similar murder of Waldric, bishop of Laon, some sixty years before. When we turn from the life of Becket as Primate to that of Becket as a Diocesan, we find that the same course of violence and wrong which marked his course in the one office signalized it as fatally in the other. Lanfranc in the endeavour to recover the manors of his see, of which it had been dispossessed by the Bishop of Bayeux and others, appealed to the assembly of the secular powers at Penenden Heath, and by his able and honest advocacy of his claim procured their entire restitution. But Becket, with his usual arbitrary and lawless spirit, proceeded to the violent seizure of the lands which he held to belong to his see, and dispossessed the tenants with a high hand. We can readily imagine the results to the diocese of this conduct on the part of a virtually non-resident prelate—who, unlike his predecessors or successors, neither came into the diocese to occupy

[1] "Becket," p. 311.

his manors from time to time, nor spent any of his income among his tenants. Except on the roads from London to Canterbury, and from the latter place to Sandwich, which were the scenes of his triumphant progresses on his return from exile, the diocese could have seen scarcely anything of him. Otford is said to have been his favourite residence when he was in Kent, but how rarely could it have been occupied. He chose his town of Romney, round which in right of his manors of Aldington and Lyminge he had a vast estate, for his place of transit on one of the occasions of his departure to France, where, it is said, he was delayed by a severe tempest. Perhaps the diocese suffered less from his absence than it must have done from the residence in it of one who used the terrible weapon of excommunication with such reckless haste and almost indiscriminate aim, that not only almost all the highest persons of the realm, but all who were in communion with them, fell under the inevitable ban. But the effects of the conflict between the Church and the Crown were bitterly felt in the diocese on the fatal morrow of the Christmas of 1164; on which the king issued orders for the confiscation of the revenues of the see of Canterbury, and for the banishment of all Becket's kindred, clerks and servants, with all who had harboured him in his flight. While Becket's previous excommunication of the king's tenants had been comparatively a *brutum fulmen*, we can easily imagine how terrible a reality the counter-blow of the king must have given to the diocese from which the greatest part of the revenues of the primacy was derived, and in which

K

so many of the friends of the primate were resident.

During the whole of the nine years in which he filled the see, he appears to have had that degree of popularity among all classes which usually attaches to the energetic opponent of a government of an arbitrary and despotic character, especially when he combines with that the rank of a powerful landlord and the office of a primate. The picture of the triumphant progress from Sandwich, and every other public appearance of Becket in his diocese, shows that he was regarded as the representative of the people as against the feudal nobility; while it is to be feared that his defence of the immunities of the clergy made him no less popular among too many of the ecclesiastics of an age in which simony, peculation, and non-residence had begun to bear their pernicious fruits. But whatever may have been the results of Becket's primacy to the diocese, and however unedifying the example of his tumultuous life, it is certain that his death had an influence upon the city and county which no other event either before or after it has ever produced. Canterbury had fallen at this time into the position of a mere provincial city lying on one of the great approaches to the metropolis; and the county itself was a mere place of transit, which, but for its containing the highway from the Continent to England, would have been almost as much a *terra incognita* as the marches of Wales or the border districts of the north. When the emissaries from Laon visited it with their unique collection of relics, the monks of Canterbury had little of this kind to show ; and the golden harvest which they reaped at what was afterwards the shrine of Becket was gathered and carried away to a distant scene by the enterprising canons. But the death of Becket and the possession of his inestimable relics made Canterbury a centre of the religious life of the day, second to no other place of pilgrimage and devotion ; and gifts and offerings of whose value the splendour of the shrine itself, as Erasmus has described it, was a very significant symbol, gave proof of the hold which the Becket *cultus* had upon every class, from Royalty downwards. Every route from the coast or the interior to the City became a pilgrim's way—specially the Watling-street along which Becket had so often passed from London to Canterbury, and the Stone-street which his murderers traversed on the terrible night of the " martyrdom " on their way to Saltwood. The picture drawn of the city by the French Jew in Richard of Devizes' chronicle is certainly not flattering, but his general invectives against England must render it more of a caricature than a portrait :—" If you should land near Canterbury you will waste your trouble even if you do but pass through it. It is nothing but a collection of wretches under their—I know not whom—whom they have lately defied, who had been Archbishop of Canterbury ; wretches who die everywhere throughout the streets at midday from want of bread and work."[1] It doubtless presented at this time all the vicissitudes which are described as having developed themselves in the rural districts

[1] Ric. Div. Chr., c. 79.

K 2

where periodical famines were the frequent result of
failing means and absent proprietors. The wealth of
the country was running in channels from which it
was little likely to reach the poorest class, still in a
state of serfdom ; and the rich offerings of Becket's
shrine stood in melancholy contrast to the sordid
misery which must have been witnessed daily at the
gates of the monastery. During the civil war in the
days of Stephen the property of the archbishopric
had suffered such irreparable losses, that the predecessors of Becket had to fall back upon that of the
monks already heavily charged with the claims of the
poor and mendicants. "The miserable monks were
reduced to the extremity of need, for nearly every
guest was expelled from their court, and the poor were
driven out."[1] The destitution of the city may be
regarded as the faithful index of that of the diocese,
covered as it was in every direction with the immense
estates of the Church and of the greater nobles. The
Becket pilgrimages may be therefore regarded as the
grandest endowment the diocese ever possessed, and
as supplying the means of rebuilding the magnificent
cathedral, which, by a strange kind of coincidence,
perished by fire less than four years after the murder
of the great primate. The fate of a building so
intimately connected with the history of the whole of
the diocese cannot but be given in the words of its
most authentic narrator Gervase, who thus records it :—

"In the aforesaid year (1174). . . during an extraor-
dinarily violent south wind, a fire broke out before the

[1] Gervase, " Life of Abp. Theobald."

gate of the church and outside the walls of the
monastery, by which three cottages were half-destroyed.
From thence, while the citizens were assembling and
subduing the fire, cinders and sparks carried aloft by
the high wind were deposited upon the church, and
being driven by the fury of the wind between the
joints of the lead, remained there amongst the half-
rotten planks, and shortly glowing with increasing
heat set fire to the rotten rafters ; from these the fire
was communicated to the larger beams and their
braces, no one yet perceiving or helping. . . .Meantime
the three cottages, whence the mischief had arisen,
being destroyed, and the popular excitement having
subsided, everybody went home again, while the
neglected church was consuming with internal fire
unknown to all.   But beams and braces burning, the
flames rose to the slopes of the roof, and the sheets of
lead yielded to the increasing heat and began to melt.
Thus the raging wind finding a freer entrance increased the fury of the fire ; and the flames beginning
to show themselves, a cry arose in the churchyard,
' See, see, the church is on fire !' Then the people
and the monks assembled in haste—they draw water,
they brandish their hatchets, they run up the stairs
full of eagerness to save the church, already, alas!
beyond their help. But when they reach the roof
and perceive the black smoke and scorching flames
that pervade it throughout, they abandon the attempt
in despair, and thinking only of their own safety,
make all haste to descend. And now that the fire
had loosened the beams from the pegs that bound
them together, the half-burnt timbers fell into the

choir below upon the seats of the monks ; the seats, consisting of a great mass of wood-work, caught fire, and thus the mischief grew worse and worse. And it was marvellous, though sad, to behold how that glorious choir itself fed and assisted the fire that was destroying it. For the flames, multiplied by this mass of timber, and extending upwards full fifteen cubits (about 25 ft.), scorched and burnt the walls, and more specially injured the columns of the church."[1] For a long time the monks cherished the hope that this glorious choir of Conrad, which had been to them what the Church of St. Sophia was to Eastern Christendom, and had received almost all the exaggerated epithets which Phranza bestows upon that temple " of the great wisdom of God,"[2] might be saved to form the nucleus of the restored church. But the wise master-builder whom they had engaged for this important work of rebuilding, William of Sens, gradually prepared them to recognise the impossibility of preserving anything whatever from this disastrous wreck, and under his judicious counsels the work of restoration began. After one year devoted to the task of preparation, four pillars, two on each side the choir, were re-erected, and thus gradually the work went on ; its progress being so carefully chronicled by Gervase, that we may fix the date of almost every column of the choir, and are thus provided with a typical building enabling us to fix within a few years the date of every similar erection in the kingdom.

[1] Gervase, ap. Wilkins, " Archit. History," p. 32.
[2] " τῆς μεγάλης τοῦ θεοῦ σοφίας."

Unhappily, an accident which befell the great architect
during his work disabled him from superintending it
in person, but for a time he was ably assisted by a
monk, who acted as his overseer under his directions.
At length William of Sens, crippled by the fall, whose
effects baffled all the skill of his physicians, returned
home, and was succeeded by a namesake, who is
called for distinction the English William—or, as
Gervase has it, " William by name, English by nation ;
small in body, but in workmanship of many kinds
acute and honest." He proceeded successfully with
the work, and " laid the foundation for the enlargement of the church at the eastern part, because a
chapel of St. Thomas was to be built there." " For
this," continues Gervase, " was the place assigned to
him, namely, the Chapel of the Holy Trinity, where
he celebrated his first mass, under whose crypt for so
many years he was buried."

The reader will recognise this as representing the
addition made by Anselm, when he extended the
church of Lanfranc so far eastward, and as the scene of
that magnificent shrine in which the relics of Becket
received for so many centuries the adoration of his
devotees and the worship of pilgrims from all parts
of Western Christendom. The close of the fifth year
of the restoration witnessed only the progress of the
columns of the choir and the foundation and walls of
the crypt under the Trinity Chapel up to the bases of
the windows. The sixth year was signalized by a
violent longing of the monks to prepare the choir for
the celebration of the Easter solemnities, which was
seconded by a corresponding zeal on the part of the

architect; and after the careful translation of the relics of the saints and bodies of the archbishops and royal personages, from their temporary resting place to their new depositories, the restored choir was joyfully occupied on Easter Eve, 1180.

The translation of Becket's relics was alone reserved until the completion of his chapel. Gervase carefully enumerates the successive works of the seventh, eighth, and tenth years, in the last of which Archbishop Baldwin's primacy began. At this point his narrative abruptly terminates. The vast expenses which were incurred in the rebuilding appear (as Professor Willis observes) to have been chiefly defrayed by the oblations at the tomb of Becket, which had now become a golden harvest to the monastery. The translation of the body of the great archbishop did not take place until the year 1220, when, with great pomp and solemnity, this crowning act of the restoration was fulfilled in the presence of the king and a magnificent assemblage of the clergy and laity of the kingdom.

Between the primacy of Becket and that of Baldwin, the peaceful and uneventful reign of Archbishop Richard formed a kind of transition period. His zeal for the interests of his church and for the monks calls forth the most unqualified praise of Gervase, and deservedly, for he restored to them all the churches which belonged to their villes—and appears to have been their advocate against the claims of the secular clergy, or, as Gervase terms them, "the slanders of the clerks,"—among which were the churches of Monkton (in Thanet), Eastry, Meopham

and Eynesford ; remitting also to the convent the
offerings of the villes, which had been hitherto (but
"unjustly") made to the archbishops.   We shall find
presently that this concession opened a serious controversy between the monks and the archbishops in
the days of his successor.   Richard, who had been
Prior of Dover, was rather the advocate of the
regular, than of the secular clergy ; and having been
a monk of Canterbury, leaned naturally to the interests of his earlier conventual abode.

Baldwin, his successor, on the other hand, though
brought up in a monastery, had held also the
episcopal office, and had learned the danger of
allowing that to be subordinated to the growing
power of the regular clergy, then daily more and
more insidiously withdrawn from the ordinary jurisdiction, and placed under the immediate protection
of the Papacy.   The immense endowment of the
monastic orders during this and the following century
had so crippled the condition of the secular clergy
that, as the provincial synod of Mayence declared
in 1261, " Most of the monks not putting any bounds
to their avarice, nor content with the stream of riches
which they are known to absorb, by accumulating to
themselves the largest farms and other copious means
of income, so that all Jordan flows into their mouth,
have contrived to unite with their foundations so
many parishes by their lust of wealth, and those for
the most part the best, that there are few churches to
be found in Germany which are able to give susten-
ance to the clergy. . . . These same (regular parish
priests) are so much more given to gain inasmuch as

they deem themselves exempt from ordinary jurisdiction by the claim of their religious order."[1] This description of the state of the Church in Germany, not a century after the death of Becket had turned towards Canterbury one of the most copious springs of this golden "Jordan," is doubtless as faithful a representation of the Church in the diocese as it is of the kindred Churches of continental Europe. It supplies the reason of the hostility awakened against the regular clergy from the day of Lanfranc until that of the Reformation, and explains the readiness with which the people acquiesced in the first great work of the latter epoch, the dissolution of the monasteries. To the bishops whose ordinary and ancient jurisdiction was set at nought by the claim of exemption and the immediate dependence of the religious orders on the pope, and who saw the destitution into which the parochial clergy had fallen from the appropriation of the tithes to the monastic houses, the only remedy seemed to be the establishment of an intermediate order, which, while giving its undivided allegiance to themselves, should rather aid than obstruct the work and influence of the parochial clergy. The foundation of the houses of "regular

---

[1] Of the immense wealth of the monastic bodies and their affected poverty St. Bernard exclaimed in the Council of Rheims,—"Hi sunt qui pauperes esse volunt, eo tamen facto ut nihil iis desit." Of their exemption from local jurisdiction, he says with equal force in his 42nd Letter, "O! libertas omni (ut ita loquar) servitute servilior. Patienter ab hujusmodi libertate abstineam, quæ me pessimæ addicat superbiæ servituti."

canons" both at Dover and Canterbury by the Bishop of Bayeux and Lanfranc was the first step in this direction in the diocese. But a second and a far bolder and more important step was that taken by Archbishop Baldwin, in his controversy with the monks of Christ Church, so bitterly and pathetically recounted by Gervase. After describing his expressions of devotion to the "brethren" of his monastery on his election, the chronicler proceeds :—" But amidst all these bright promises of so much religion and grace, as though it were he who was to have redeemed Israel, he was seduced by the clerks " (*i.e.*, the secular clergy) ; "and beginning his works of sacrilege even at the very sanctuary of the Lord, he plundered Christ Church of those offerings which for long had been usually offered from the villes of the monks."[1] After an enumeration of his various appropriations of the property of the monastery and their partial restitution, the chronicler describes his negotiations with Pope Urban, in order to obtain the papal authority for building a new cathedral, which was said to have been commenced by St. Thomas. This application succeeded both at the papal and royal court. For " when the king heard of the plan " we are told that he " was easily induced to agree to it. The bishops, too, gave their sanction." Then comes the solution of this mysterious

---

[1] These would appear to be the offerings made at the tomb of Becket, which for the eleven preceding years the monks had received during the incumbency of Archbishop Richard. Had they been of more ancient date it is hardly possible that Baldwin could have claimed them.

unanimity. " It was decided either by promise or oath that all those bishops who had monks under them should convert their cathedrals into conventual churches for secular clerks, to whom they should assign the churches and tithes belonging to the monks." Here the great cause of warfare between the secular and regular clergy reveals itself in all its force and magnitude, and we see the first pre-Reformation effort to free the Church of the crushing weight of the monastic orders, and of the absolute subjection of the ordinary and national jurisdiction to that of an illegitimate and foreign power. However injurious the rule of Baldwin must have seemed to the monks, to the parochial clergy he must have appeared a real deliverer ; while to the popes, whose devoted clients the monastic orders had been from the first, he was as dangerous a reformer as he was to the monks. The foundations of a new cathedral had been actually laid—a building 500 ft. in length, and this in spite of the protestations and appeal of the monks. They were suspended and deprived of their rents, and finally even of their villes. Urban ordered the restitution of all their property, and denounced as accursed the work of the archbishop ; notwithstanding which the building was continued, and the controversy carried on with almost increased bitterness. Meantime, Urban died, and Gregory, " who patronised the archbishop," succeeded him. Baldwin again triumphs ; he denounces the sub-prior and those who hold with him as excommunicate ; deprives the monks of all their possessions outside the gates of the monastery ; and, according to Gervase, proceeds to acts of violence and outrage, which in that day must have been regarded as in the highest degree sacrilegious. But now Pope Gregory dies, and is succeeded by Clement, who undoes the work of his predecessor, and returns to the policy of Urban. He commands that the work which had been commenced at Hackington, near Canterbury, shall be destroyed : that the property of the monks should be restored ; and that the archbishop should cease from the persecution of the monks. Unfortunately for the monastery, it lost at this moment not only its prior, but its best advocates at Rome, and was reduced again to the greatest straits in its conflict with the archbishop. But, at the same time, most opportunely for its present state, the king, " by whose instrumentality the Church of Canterbury had endured so many troubles " died, and was succeeded by his son Richard, under whom, after much altercation and many abortive conferences, a composition was at length arrived at by which it was stipulated that the property of the monks should be restored, that the new cathedral (or " chapel," as it is generally termed) should be left unserved or entirely demolished ; and that there should be a mutual forgiveness of mutual injuries. After a vain attempt to carry out his favourite building plan in London, the archbishop assumed in his own church at Canterbury the staff and scrip of a pilgrim to the Holy Land, and bidding a last farewell to the monks, crossed the sea, and reached Acre. There his health rapidly declined, and he died after a reign of nearly six years, and was buried in the place of his death.

After his decease the church of Canterbury was vacant for two years and a-half, during which period Pope Clement died, and was succeeded by Celestine III., by whose orders the "chapel" of Hackington was entirely destroyed, and all Baldwin's proceedings condemned. It is impossible for any Englishman not altogether divested of national and patriotic feeling to look upon this long controversy in the light in which the monkish historian regards it, and not rather to view it as an effort premature, indeed, but not without its after-fruits in the annals of his country, to vindicate the claims of the secular clergy, and to protect the Royal authority against the inroads of the Papacy so insidiously and successfully carried on through the exemptions of the monastic orders. We may well conceive, that notwithstanding the final issue of the conflict, the secular clergy of the diocese must have recovered through it a considerable measure of power and influence. And this is rendered more probable from the fact that the successor of Baldwin, Archbishop Hubert (Walter), who had sympathized with the monks of Canterbury during their conflict with his predecessor, began after his accession to take the side of the "clerks" (*i.e.*, the seculars), and actually entered upon the work of completing the church at Lambeth, which Baldwin had begun in the last days of his primacy. In vain the monks, who foresaw in the creation of a new church for the archbishopric, the almost extinction of their exclusive possession of the primates, both in life and death, entreated the new archbishop to desist from so fatal a work. The death of King Richard and the succession of John gave Archbishop Hubert an almost absolute power in the kingdom, of which he was now the chancellor, and led him to renew the dispute concerning the chapel. After a protracted litigation, a compromise was at last effected. This archbishop regained for his church many of its lost estates, including Saltwood, Hythe, Rochester Castle, the fee of Geoffry de Ros, the homage of Tunbridge Castle (due from the Clares, Earls of Gloucester), and other estates. During his primacy the work of the rebuilding of the cathedral made great progress. On the 29th of June, 1205, he came to Canterbury that he might survey the buildings and the convent; and foreseeing his death, which happened in the following month at Teynham, he took a touching and sorrowful leave of the brethren of the convent, reminding them that while he must die, they (in their corporate capacity) could not die, and therefore should devote all their energies to the promotion of the honour and usefulness of their church. Among his bequests to the church of Canterbury, after the mention of many and rare objects of ecclesiastical art, we find that he left to it a Bible containing the Old and New Testaments, and a Psalter, glossed; a clear indication that that devotion to the Word of God which had been urged in so many forms by the great teacher of England, Pope Gregory the Great, still reigned in the English Church, however it may have been dimmed from time to time by a too-superstitious reverence for trivial and ceremonial observances. The author of

the "Life of Stephen Langton," in the series of
"Lives of the English Saints," writing in the interest
and in the spirit of the Vatican, has used the life of
Hubert Walter as a kind of foil, to set off the devotion of the subject of his panegyric to the Court of
Rome.[1]   Hubert Walter committed, in his view, the
signal crime of being first an Englishman, and then
a spiritual subject of the Papacy; but the picture
given of him by the impartial Gervase in no degree
justifies the Roman advocate in his depreciation of
the archbishop.   As a diocesan bishop few of his
predecessors in the see can bear comparison with
Hubert Walter.   His last words were worthy of
a Christian bishop, which cannot be said of the last
words or the last acts of either Becket or St. Edmund
himself.[2]   The death of Hubert Walter was the signal
for the opening of that bitter warfare between King
John and Pope Innocent III. which belongs rather
to the history of the kingdom than to that of the
diocese, although it suffered from it more than any
other, inasmuch as it was most nearly involved in
those almost inevitable hostilities between the king
and the archbishop to which the precedent of Becket's
quarrel had given so fatal and chronic a tendency.
The immense income of the archbishopric presented
too ready a temptation to the successive kings to keep
it in their own hands as long as possible, and to ex-

[1] London, Toovey, 1845, p. 15.
[2] See Robertson's "Becket," and the "Life of St. Edmund
of Canterbury" ("Lives of the English Saints," no. xiv.
pp. 81, 82).

tend more and more the delay of filling up the vacancy. A conflict either with the Chapter, in whom the right of election (at least nominally) resided, or one with the Papacy, which almost always superseded with a high hand the nominees of the king or of the chapter, rendered the suspension of the primacy an ever-impending danger, and left the diocese constantly, for long periods, in a state of widowhood. The injury which this inflicted upon the Church can hardly now be fully measured, for the earlier records of the diocese have either perished or are still latent. But the picture we are able to derive from the earliest glimpses we have of diocesan history, in the close of the thirteenth century, enable us to see how fatally the interests both of the clergy and laity had been neglected, and how perfunctorily every office of the Church had been performed. Of the three great functions which an archbishop was held to combine in his own person, that of "born legate" of the Holy See, Primate of the English Church, and Diocesan in the see of Canterbury, the early archbishops appear to have regarded the first as absorbing every other, and the forced residence of Becket, Langton, and Edmund at Pontigny,[1] where so many precious years of their lives were spent, appear to have left in their minds no

---

[1] The extreme indiscretion of these successive retirements to a French convent must be obvious to every one who remembers the ever-doubtful relations between France and England, and the suspicion of treason (often justified by the overt acts of the exiles themselves), which the recourse to such an asylum must have awakened.

L

anxiety and no regret in regard to the diocese itself.
In the case of many of their successors, the primate
may be said to have swallowed up the diocesan, but
in theirs the legate absorbed both the one and the
other. The churches were occupied by those "*conductitii sacerdotes*," or temporary vicars, whom the
convents and chapters employed to do the work of a
hireling ; nor is it until the period when the archbishops were permanently resident that we trace the
foundation of the perpetual vicarages such as we now
see, or that indispensable residence of the rectors and
chaplains of churches by which alone the healthy
existence of the Church can be carried on. The
election of Stephen Langton to the archbishopric took
place in 1207, nearly two years after the death of
Archbishop Hubert. But between his election and
peaceable possession of the see a period of six years
was interposed, during which the mortal conflict between John and the see of Rome was carried on
without intermission. This culminated in the Interdict, which fell so cruelly and heavily upon the whole
kingdom; but most heavily upon the see of Canterbury, which drew upon itself, on account of the non-
submission of the chapter and the monks, the fullest
weight of the king's indignation. "The monks of
Canterbury were his first thought, and they were in
his power. They had committed treason, he said.
They had first made an election without his licence,
which prejudiced his prerogative, and now they . . .
had elected a known enemy of his own, Cardinal
Langton." The monastery soon experienced the

terrible results of an anger which is described by the chroniclers of the time to have been more like the outburst of a homicidal insanity than any mere human emotion. They were exiled without mercy, either for age or sickness, and but for the tender care of the Count of Gisnes must have perished from want and exposure. The effect of the Interdict upon the parishes and the clergy who might be resident in them must have been disastrous, not only in regard to their spiritual state, thus wantonly sacrificed in a conflict for temporal power with which they had nothing to do, but also to their outward condition, dependent as most of them still were upon a great conventual body whose income had been suddenly sequestrated to the king's use.

In the close of 1209 the fatal interdict fell on the kingdom. Various efforts at negotiation had been made without success, of one of which the neighbourhood of Canterbury was the scene. This may be introduced to the reader in the words in which the writer described it on the spot to the Archæological Society of Kent :[1]—" The terrors of excommunication, in addition to the Interdict, were impending over King John. The three months given him by the pope for repentance had closed upon him, and one reprieve after another had been granted in the vain hope of a settlement, until the octave of St. Michael was fixed upon as the limit of the papal forbearance. Stephen Langton, the archbishop, who was working the terrible instruments of spiritual tor-

[1] Lecture on Chilham Castle, "Arch. Cant.," vol. vii., page lv.

ture from the other side of the Channel, was invited to
meet the king at Dover, letters of safe conduct being
sent to him both by the king and the barons.   With
the Bishops of London and Ely he crossed to Dover
on the 2nd of October.   The king came to Chilham
Castle, and sent the Justiciary and the Bishop of
Winchester with certain articles which they were to
demand of the archbishop.   They were such as he
could not agree to, and he recrossed the sea.   If the
preceptory of Swingfield,[1] in which John surrendered
his crown to the legate, must ever be the scene of
humiliating reflection to those who feel that the
honour of England is involved in that of her Crown,
the Castle of Chilham must ever be associated with
the better traditions of our unceasing, though then unsuccessful, struggle against the only power which has
ever trampled on the liberties of England.   We may
imagine the arrival of the king among his barons ; his
entertainment by the heiress of the great Fulbert de
Dover, to whom the very key of the kingdom had
been entrusted ; his bold resolution not to proceed to
Dover, lest he should seem to give way at such a
juncture as this ; the stern patience in which he
awaited the return of his commissioners ; the proud
thoughts which filled his mind, and which live in
the lines of one who alone could worthily retrace
them.”

[1] Our learned local antiquary, Mr. Knocker, has brought
considerable evidence to prove that the scene of this humiliating
surrender was the now-destroyed church of the Knights Templars on the west cliff at Dover.   The popular belief points to
Swingfiel[1].

" Thou canst not, cardinal, devise a name,
    So slight, unworthy, and ridiculous,
    To charge me to an answer, as the Pope—
    Tell him this tale, and from the mouth of England
    Add thus much more—that no Italian priest
    Shall tithe or toll in our dominions."

The failure of this attempt to negotiate hastened the fatal act of the Papacy, one which, in spite of the most specious representation of its defenders, is as absolutely opposed to the genius of Christianity as the most barbarous retaliations of heathenism, a kind of "murder of the innocents," in order to destroy the single victim who could not be reached but by a general act of destruction. The impartial reader of the life of Langton cannot but perceive that it represents a series of coalitions, the object of which was the establishment of his personal power, rather than the interests of his diocese and its unfortunate inhabitants. First, we find him siding with the pope against the king, then with the king against the pope, then with the barons against both pope and king. As the writer of his life admits, " Innocent, who so firmly carried through the struggle in behalf of Langton against the king, is now found supporting the king, and condemning the archbishop and barons;" and naturally, for the king by his unkingly surrender of his crown to the Papacy had made him one of the lowest of his vassals, while Langton, who saw in the first article of the great charter the surest defence of his own authority, sided, as might be expected, with those who were maintaining it. His refusal to publish the Bull of excommunication against the barons was at once the worthiest and most patriotic of the acts of his life, while his subsequent submission to the pope in the matter of his suspension again exhibited the weaker side of his nature.

The death of the pope and of the king introduced a state of peace into the kingdom and the diocese it had not known since the death of Hubert, and the twelve peaceful years which followed, and which completed the primacy of Langton, we may well conclude were years of recovery and progress in the Church of Canterbury. " Two actions by which he illustrated this period of peace and repose " were—

I. The translation of St. Thomas à Becket in 1220; and

II. The celebration of the Synod of Osney in 1222.

Alexander III. having canonized the murdered archbishop, called on his successor to provide a more fitting place for his relics than the undercroft in which they had so long mouldered. His successor, Honorius III., exhorted accordingly " the English of every condition " to prepare themselves by every kind of religious exercise and act of charity to show due honour to their saint in this crowning celebration. The day fixed for it was Tuesday, the 7th of July, and Langton, who had at the same period in the previous year officiated at the coronation of Henry, was now called upon to take the principal part in this spiritual act of coronation. " Never before in England had such a multitude been gathered into one spot ; from every shire's end in England, from every corner of Christendom, of all sexes, and of all ranks, abbots, priors, barons, and clergy. There were twenty-four bishops present. The Archbishop of Rheims said mass, and the holy remains were transferred from the unadorned stone coffin to a sumptuous chapel at the back of the high altar. . . . For the entertainment of this vast crowd of pilgrims all the resources at the archbishop's command were put in action. His manors and houses in Canterbury and the neighbour hood were opened for their reception; wine flowed in every part of the city, free entertainment and forage were provided all the way from London, ' and though all he could do could not provide for anything like all who came, yet it showed his generous will.' Langton's princely hospitality, indeed, was not only to his power, but beyond his power, for the revenues of the see did not recover this outlay under himself and three of his successors." Thus far the able advocate of the archbishop, written under the inspiration of a recent conversion to Rome. He has not, however, added the fact that on many of the archbishop's manors, and notably upon those of Lyminge and Wrotham, the tenants were in a starving condition not many years after, and that the inability of Archbishop Boniface to repair his churches and houses, which left his successor in a state of the greatest embarrassment, arose out of this wicked and wilful expenditure at a time when the country was prostrate under the shock of the civil war, and the cruel effects of the Interdict.

The Synod of Osney, at which Langton presided, in 1222, occupies a very important place in the history of the English councils. A number of laws affecting the discipline and government of the Church

were here drawn up, and they form some of the
earliest of the provincial canons upon which our
ancient and even our present ecclesiastical laws are
founded.   But it was easier to make the most perfect
system of canon law than to carry into execution
the very lightest portion of it; a truth which was
singularly illustrated in the fruitless labours of the
successors of Langton, and especially in those of
St. Edmund of Canterbury, next but one in succession to the primacy.   His immediate successor
was Richard Wethershede,[1] whose residence in the
see was even shorter than his brief tenure of it,
dying, as he did, on his way from Rome, after filling
the see for the brief period of three years. A suspicion
of poison, too common in the case of those who have
ventured Romewards in every age, hangs over his
death, as several of his suite died at the same time.
He was succeeded by one of the most illustrious of
the holders of the primatial dignity, the sainted
Edmund, elected (after several rival candidates of the
chapter had been set aside) in 1283, and consecrated
in the following year.

If Langton had exhibited the political side of the
primacy in perhaps a higher aspect than any of his
predecessors, except Lanfranc, Edmund of Abingdon,
whose surname of Rich or Le Rich indicated the
opulence, if not the nobility, of his ancestors, and
made his name a singular contrast to the extreme

---

[1] This appears to have been his true name, though by some
he is called Richard Grand, or the Great.   It is probable that
this was merely an epithet, and that he is more properly called
from the name of his birthplace.

humility and simplicity of his life, presented in a high degree the features of a diocesan bishop. The multiplied abuses which had sprung up in the diocese during the previous primacies, and which developed all the evils which we have seen so forcibly summed up by Cardinal de Vitry, called for all the energies and all the zeal of the Church reformer of that age of degeneracy; an age which at the same time by a strange and sad con- trast bore such wonderful material fruits in art and refinement, and which is now recognised as the classic age of church architecture, with all its adjuncts of painting, sculpture, and every artistic triumph of skill and genius. It is sadly to be noted that the highest periods of Christian art have been frequently also the periods of the most fatal spiritual decadence. Edmund of Canterbury was a Church- builder in the highest sense, but not in that of the builders of his great cathedral. In the long suc- cession of primates it is not easy to find one who surpasses him in the perfections of the Christian character, or in the attributes of a Christian bishop. What the diocese might have become had it preserved the light of such an example and the influence of such a ruler it is difficult now to determine. But every effort made by the archbishop to reform the corruptions of the clergy and the multiplied evils of an age of spiritual degeneracy, both in Church and State, was frustrated by the intrigues of the court and the connivance of the pope. His biographer, to whom we have already referred, is here at least an impartial witness. The peculiar trial of St. Edmund was, as he affirms, "the secular spirit which had invaded the Church ;" but the resistance he met with, not only in his diocese, but throughout the country, not only at the court of Henry, but in the court of Rome, was inveterate, and in the end irresistible. "That the king, the barons, the lay people, some or all of them should be in opposition to him might neither surprise nor grieve him, but the bishops were unfriendly, his own chapter disliked his asceticism, the legate went against him in everything, and, worst desolation of all, the very occupant of the Holy See seemed little inclined to support him, if the king or the Crown party were to be in anything offended or resisted. At first the archbishop seemed to make great progress in arranging matters which had long been subjects of contention. For example, the long-standing disputes with the Convent of St. Augustine were set at rest by a composition, both parties abating something from their claims for the love of peace. . . . The archbishop's difficulties with his own con-vent were of a graver nature."[1] Here he had to con-tend against the luxury and secularity which had made the Benedictine rule a mere cloak to hide its daily practical infraction. Unhappily the support which the archbishop might have looked for from the court had been withdrawn, partly through the influence of the nobility, who regarded him with suspicion, if not repugnance, and partly through the difference he had with King Henry on the occasion of the marriage of his sister with Simon de Montfort. This princess on

---

[1] "Life of St. Edmund," pp. 48, 49.

the death of her first husband, the Earl of Pembroke, had bound herself before the archbishop himself to a life of continence, from which the pope had dispensed her.   The archbishop, who had in every way opposed the alliance, which he held under the circumstances to involve a sacrilege, fell naturally under the displeasure of the king; who, in order to frustrate his plans of reform, invited the visitation of a legate from the pope, without the consent either of the archbishop or of the states of the kingdom.   The legate appointed to this ungrateful task was Cardinal Otho, whose constitutions make so important a figure in the ecclesiastical law of England.   Edmund complained to the king without effect of this inopportune and unwelcome intrusion.   The motive of the pope in authorizing it soon became as apparent as the object of the king in inviting it.   Otho claimed to fill up all the vacant preferments, and was not unfairly represented by a contemporary chronicler as " a poor Italian who was sent to England to make his own fortune and that of as many of his friends as possible, and to extort money under divers pretexts."   Edmund was met at every point and in every stage of his duty by a series of obstacles and affronts, which rendered his episcopate almost insupportable.   In every effort, either of reformation or vindication of himself, he found failure and disappointment.   The legate, eager to gain over the king and the nobles, brought over the pope to his views.   At last the tenure of the archbishopric seemed no longer possible to a man so exalted in mind and motive as Edmund, and he determined to retire from a position which he could no longer occupy with dignity or usefulness. "The archbishop was now thoroughly weary of his office. He saw that he could do nothing as he wished and as he knew he ought to do it. His reforms were merely ridiculed, set aside without question or even opposition. All men were agreed that they were fanciful, impracticable schemes." He resolved to retire to that scene which his predecessors had chosen as their retreat under circumstances of greater danger, but, perhaps, of less disappointment; Pontigny again received within its venerable cloister the saintly man, weary of the world, and worn out with its many trials. "His departure from London resembled a secret flight. On a rising ground, from which was a view of the city, he halted, and turning towards it he gave his solemn blessing to his country, and his curse on the sacrilegious marriage of the Countess de Montfort and its offspring."[1] This was in the year 1240. The two years that followed, while they were a season of perfect rest and peace to the saintly exile, were a season of loss, and even widowhood, to the diocese. A greater martyr than Becket had been lost to his people; and the wonders which are said to have been wrought at the tomb of the saint, and which occasioned his canonization only four years after, may have well led the monks of Canterbury to repent the course they had taken in resisting and accusing a prelate whose purity of life and doctrine should rather have provoked them to imitation than stimulated them to persecution. Pontigny soon rivalled

[1] "Life of St. Edmund," p. 74.

Canterbury as a place of pilgrimage, and the relics of
the saint, more fortunate than those of Becket, are
said to have escaped the destroying hands of the
Huguenots, when the venerable Abbey of Pontigny
was sacked by the Prince of Condé. It will be seen
from this brief sketch of the primacy of St. Edmund
that his life had but too little bearing upon the history
of the diocese, and left no trace of its influence upon
a corrupt and degenerate age. His successor was
Boniface, provost of Beverley, whose exalted birth,
for he was the son of the Duke of Savoy and uncle
to Queen Eleanor, wife of King Henry III., pointed
him out as a suitable representative of the spirit of
the age, and one who would best conciliate the
affections both of the court and of a clergy which
had become utterly secularized. Of the history of
the diocese during the twenty-six years and a half of
Archbishop Boniface's government of it we know
little indeed. To the foreign ecclesiastics with whom
Otho the legate had filled the chief benefices of the
land, he contributed some of his own countrymen to
swell the ranks of those fortunate adventurers whose
presence and influence were at once the scorn and
disgrace of the Church, and whose memory was fresh
even in the days of Shakespeare. Some of these,
conscious of their unpopularity, resided abroad, and
left their place to be filled by the itinerant preachers
who have been already mentioned as employed by
the monasteries to officiate in their dependent
churches. Thus Petrus de Albi, a Savoyard, and
afterwards executor to the archbishop's will, held the
sinecure rectories of Lyminge and Wrotham, leaving

the people, as Archbishop Peckham wrote, in both
"temporal and spiritual destitution." Archbishop
Boniface appears to have resided at his various manor-
houses, as his successors did,[1] and to have been a
munificent benefactor to the see in his contributions to
its buildings, already inconveniently multiplied, for he
built a hospital (afterwards converted into a college)
at Maidstone. He perfected the stately hall of the
archbishop's palace at Canterbury, and what is better
than all, paid off the great debts which his predecessors had charged on the see, affirming that "as
they had built their palaces with borrowed money, he
might be more justly regarded as the builder of them,
because he had paid their debts."[2] But notwithstanding these works of princely munificence, which
probably belonged to the earlier years of his long
term of diocesan rule, the state of the manor-houses
and buildings of the see was so dilapidated and
almost ruinous on the accession of Archbishop
Peckham in 1279 that that primate had to remonstrate with the executors of Boniface, especially with
Petrus de Albi, the Savoyard pluralist, who held the
sinecure rectories of Lyminge and Wrotham, on his
failure to pay the sums for the dilapidations which
had been left in the will of the archbishop. As the
most conspicuous of those foreigners who had preyed
for so long a time on the richest benefices of England,
Archbishop Boniface had incurred the bitterest
animosity, not only in his own diocese, but from the

[1] His collation of Constantine de Mildenhall to the living of
Hever is dated from Lyminge in 1264.
[2] Hasted's "Kent," tom. xii. p. 359.

citizens of London, by whom his very life is said to
have been endangered. All the chroniclers of the
age, however they may disagree in their views of
local events, are agreed in the intense animosity
towards the foreign pluralists, who, under the blight-
ing influence of the Papacy, had reduced the Church
in England to a state of poverty and dependence
which no other Church had ever endured, and which
few Churches could have survived. The case of
Petrus de Albi alone, which was by no means a
solitary one,—a foreigner spending in Italy the
fruits of his English sinecures, while the people of
his Kentish parishes were starving both in soul
and body—may well justify the resolute words of
King John, as Shakespeare has conceived them—
words so feebly carried out in the end—declaring
that

> " No Italian priest
> Shall tithe or toll in our dominion."

Boniface closed his long primacy at his castle in
Savoy, whither he had retreated in his last days, to
avoid the indignation which had been awakened
against him in England, and was succeeded by Robert
Kilwardby, a nominee of the pope, in 1272. Little,
indeed, is recorded of his primacy, and even that little
has a very slight bearing upon the history of the diocese ; though in his pastoral character and as visitor,
not only of his diocese but also of the province, he
appears to have fulfilled both his episcopal and primatial duties with a greater zeal and success than
most of his predecessors. He is said to have been
a regular preacher in his church, and to have been a

divine of no common order. He contributed also
not a little to the peace of the diocese by healing the
breach between the city of Canterbury and the monks,
which threatened the most serious results, and which
arose out of the refusal of the latter to contribute
towards an imposition set upon the city by the king
in aid of his intended expedition into Wales. It is
probable that the foresight of a renewal of this hostility led him to an act which must ever be regarded
as the most fatal blow which has ever been inflicted
upon its literary and historic possessions. He had
not presided over his church for more than five years
when Pope Nicholas III., by the offer of a cardinal's
hat, allured him to Rome, upon which he resigned
his archbishopric and hastened to Italy, bearing with
him a large sum of money, and also the whole of
the registers of the see of Canterbury, and several
of its most precious treasures of ecclesiastical plate
and ornament. In vain did his successor, Archbishop
Peckham, send a special commissioner to Rome in
order to recover these inestimable records—in vain
has every effort been made in a later day for the discovery of them. Among many others the writer may
make mention of two which he himself originated,
in one of which he was kindly aided by his lamented
friend, the late Cardinal Wiseman ; in the other by
Lord Talbot de Malahide. In the latter, Archbishop
Longley took the deepest interest, assisting in it
himself as far as was possible. Cardinal Wiseman,
through Dr. Theiner, then the sub-prefect of the
Vatican, and Lord Talbot, through Mgr. Talbot, used
every influence they possessed in regard to these lost

treasures of history, but in vain. Whether the examinations now being made at the Vatican under the direction of the Rolls Commission, which were so kindly assisted by the late pope, and have been equally favoured by his successor, will be able to throw any light upon the matter remains yet a problem. Cardinal Wiseman, though he informed the writer that in the vaults of the Vatican and under its vast library the correspondence of legates and the communications of the Holy See with its world-wide dependencies have been preserved from a comparatively early age, yet doubted whether documents so early as the lost registers of Canterbury could have survived the tumults and sackings of Rome during the succeeding centuries. When we consider that the missing records must have included those of Becket, of St. Edmund. and probably of even Lanfranc himself, the extent of our ruinous loss may be conjectured, though hardly estimated ; while the hope that it may yet be in some measure redeemed must be excited in the same degree. From our brief retrospect of the events of the period in which it has caused so fatal a blank we may proceed to make a few remarks on the development of the beneficiary system in the diocese upon which the register of Archbishop Peckham (beginning in 1279) throws back so instructive and suggestive a light. The many abuses which had grown up during the period over which this chapter extends, led on to many remedial laws, and these had so important a bearing on the state of the diocese at the present time that we cannot delay the mention of them to a later stage of our narrative.

M

The opening of the thirteenth century forms an important epoch in the history of the Church generally, and one which ought to be carefully noted in the history of the diocese.   In 1215 the Lateran Council under Innocent III., carrying out the provisions of several provincial Councils, decreed the establishment of perpetual vicarages in those churches which, from their connection with monastic and collegiate foundations, had hitherto been served by vicars or substitutes removable at the will or caprice of the body by whom they were appointed.   In the diocese of Canterbury, where the majority of the livings were appendant to the manors, and where the religious foundations held so large and increasing a proportion of the churches, the effects of a law like this must have been peculiarly felt.   It will not, therefore, be inopportune in this place to exhibit the state of the Church before this important change, in order that we may fully estimate its results upon the diocese. Between the year in which the law was made universal and the first year of Archbishop Peckham (1279) we have but little documentary evidence to fall back upon.   We find, however, incidental proofs that the Lateran decree was acted upon in the diocese within a few years of its promulgation, the vicarage of Bapchild having been made perpetual as early as 1229; while between that date and the close of the century the vicarages of Elham, Ash, Aldington, Herne, Newchurch, Eastry, Swalecliffe, Shepherdswell, and the churches dependent upon that of Minster in Thanet, viz., St. John's, St. Peter's, and St. Laurence's, were made perpetual, to which might probably be added those of Lyminge and Wrotham, which the non-residence of the rectors had so long deprived of spiritual oversight as to lead to the active intervention of Archbishop Peckham in 1280. But to give the reader a clear insight into this important change we will again have recourse to the words of Böhmer :—

"I proceed," he writes, "from canonical and capitular vicars to the parish clergy, who were the more bound to residence on the ground that the care of souls, which at no time could be suspended, devolved upon them. In these, however, non-residence was accidentally allowed after parishes, through an evasion of the law, had been by right of *union* attached to and consolidated with monasteries, abbacies, provostries, and cathedral or collegiate churches. For since these corporate bodies or representatives of the dignified clergy were unable to fulfil the office of parish-priest, and the union was made in favour rather of the prelates and monks than of the congregation of the faithful or the Church, the result was that the revenues of the parishes came to them, while it was tacitly permitted them to fulfil the office of parish-priest by means of a *vicar* to whom some portion of the parochial income was assigned." . . . " And the abuse from the first was the more serious in regard to these vicarages on account of the vicars being appointed *temporarily* and being removable at the caprice of the *rector* (*i.e.*, the *principal*) or of him to whose prelature the parish was joined by reason of the union in the same manner as a servant taken about with him might be dismissed at pleasure—an abuse which was reprobated and prohibited at last by various councils.

Thus, the Synod of Mayence in 1225 complains of the 'outrageous custom which is marked in some parts of Germany of putting itinerant priests (*conductitii sacerdotes*) as temporary vicars,' and severely prohibits the abuse, enjoining that the prelates to whose prebend a parish church is annexed shall appoint for such parish church a sufficient and perpetual vicar who shall have a fit portion (*portio congrua*) out of the income of the church. Hence it comes that these vicars (as they are now called) are ordinary parish priests, and to that end are duly ordained, and possess the certain income assigned to this vicarial office as an *ecclesiastical benefice*."[1]

The settlement of the question what ought to be the *congrua portio* of the vicar was made at that time in England (as it is now in countries where still the tithes are appropriate to religious foundations) by a suit in the Court of the Ordinary to whom properly the adjudication belonged. And hence we must regard the final decrees of the archbishops establishing perpetual vicarages in different churches as judicial determinations, and date from these several periods the fixed succession of the parish-priests in such churches. The fatal effects of non-residence and the frequent collation by the archbishops of aliens to some of the richest rectories in the diocese, gave occasion to the extension of this system of perpetual vicarages, even to churches not specially attached to the religious foundations. It is to this grave abuse of patronage, remarkably illustrated in the case of

[1] Böhmer; "Jus. Eccl." l. iii. tit. iv. s. xxxviii.

Archbishop Boniface, the Savoyard, that may be attributed the foundation of vicarages in the churches of Lyminge, Wrotham, Aldington, Newchurch, and many others. The establishment of perpetual vicarages was so much evaded by the monastic and capitular bodies that even in the time of the Council of Trent the Ordinaries are charged, in visiting churches thus united to religious foundations, to inquire diligently whether perpetual vicarages have been founded in them in every case, and to assign to such vicars their *portio congrua*. As late as 1686 the abuse continued in France, and was prohibited by a Royal edict in that year.[1] The monks and chapters whose object it was to retain these movable and temporary vicars were brought into constant conflict at this point with the bishops, whose interest as well as duty it was to create a perpetual benefice. This added another element to that conflict between the regular and secular clergy, which lasted up to the dissolution of the monasteries in England, and up to our own times in those countries where the religious orders have preserved their ancient endowments.

The description of the value of the livings in the " King's Book " gives in every case the *portio congrua* assigned to the vicarages, which, in the case of those in which no decree and date of foundation is named, must be held to represent a fixed composition between the patron and the vicar, not liable to change unless made the subject of a

[1] See van Espen, p. ii. tit. 34, c. i., where the whole subject is admirably explained.

special suit. In a deed of 1349, in the possession of the writer, the vicarage of Lyminge is described as " *non litigiosa* nec portionaria nec pensionaria," the first words apparently expressing the fact that the *portio congrua* was not in litigation, but had been settled by established custom.

To this great change in the beneficiary system, which provided a permanent resident priest in every parish, and removed those hirelings who had so long discredited the work of the ministry in the eyes of the people, must be attributed, far more than to any other cause, the great outburst of church-building zeal which distinguishes the thirteenth century, and made it the culminating period of Gothic art, both in England and in Continental Europe. The beautiful style improperly termed by us " Early English," but by our Continental brethren called with greater propriety the " first ogival," or Pointed style, was the fruit of this renaissance of Christian art, which perhaps has fewer examples in Kent (except in its plainer and more ordinary form) than in any other part of England. The chief reason appears to have been the extreme difficulty of moulding the native Kentish stone— generally of extreme hardness, and abounding with fossils—into the slender and refined forms of this highest development of Gothic art. Hence this style, except in few instances, presents in our churches rather the massive octagonal columns suggested by the Transition period, than the clustered shafts so rich with foliage and elaborate mouldings which adorn the structures of other counties where a more practicable stone is to be found. Yet this was, in Kent as well as elsewhere, eminently the age of church-building.

The chancel of Hythe presents an exquisite specimen of the finest work of this kind which the diocese possesses, but here the introduction of Caen stone and Bethersden marble indicates more ample means than an ordinary parish church could have adopted. The chancels of Cheriton, Folkestone, Alkham, and many others, are approaches to this higher stage ; while that of Stone in the adjoining diocese of Rochester, recently restored in a true conservative spirit, is perhaps the finest specimen, on the whole, to be found in the county. The magnificent choir of the Cathedral of Canterbury presents to us perhaps the most perfect instance in England of the transition between the Norman style and that which succeeded it, exhibiting to us in beautiful combination the circular and pointed arches which form the most distinctive features of the two systems. The octagonal columns which support the arcades of so many of the churches of Kent have here their earliest and most beautiful type, and evidently suggested to the local builders the imitation, as far as was possible, of the great metropolitical church.

The perfect calm which succeeded the death of John, and extended over the last years of the primacy of Langton, uninterrupted by the voluntary exile of St. Edmund, gave an opportunity to the Church of recovering the influence she had lost ; while the shrine of Becket was a mine of wealth for the church-building labours of the monastery which can hardly now be fully estimated. The great Monastery of St. Augustine,

whose revenues had never been disturbed like those
of the rival foundation, appears to have restored
many of its dependent churches at the same period.
That of Minster presents a beautiful specimen, both
of Norman and first-pointed work ; while the chapels
of St. Lawrence and St. John (Margate), built probably between the close of the twelfth and the early
years of the thirteenth centuries, and made parochial
(with that of St. Peter's) in 1299, were among the
fruits of this architectural revival.

A few remarks may here be made on the state
of preaching and doctrine in the diocese, for
although the scope of our present work precludes
any observations of a controversial nature, an
account of the diocese would be necessarily imperfect were not the general tendency of the teaching
of its ministry to be noted from time to time. We
have observed how closely the pastoral and practical doctrine of Lanfranc preserved the simplicity
of the first teaching of the Saxon missionaries, and
how perfectly the features of his exegetical teaching
resemble those which are still preached within the
walls of his cathedral. The same remark may be
made on the general teaching of the archbishops
during the period to which this chapter refers. The
impartial reader of the religious writings of the age
will at once observe, that not only the separate
features of this teaching, but their relations to one
another—not only the doctrines, but the proportions
of faith it delineates, are identical with those which
our Church has so happily preserved. A singular
proof of this is given us in the beautiful treatise of

St. Edmund of Canterbury, called the *Speculum Ecclesiæ*, which puts together the elements of Christianity in their proper form and order, and might be used in the present day as a safe and faithful manual of Christian doctrine. This was written during his exile at Pontigny, and very shortly before his death, at the time in which he was preaching from church to church as a mere monk, taking his turn with his brethren, and therefore fairly represents the method and course of his religious teaching. The comparison of such a manual as this with the elaborate scholastic system developed in the Catechism of the Council of Trent illustrates forcibly the too much-neglected truth that the Reformation was rather the assertion of the ancient proportions of faith, and their relations to the entire body and to one another, than a mere negation of mediæval doctrines or settlement of technical controversies. Short as was St. Edmund's primacy, the reign of his teaching has been a very long one : for no intelligent and unbiassed reader of the *Speculum Ecclesiæ* will fail to acknowledge that the scope of its teaching and the proportions of doctrine which it exhibits are the same as those which our Church still represents : the only points of difference being in the number of the sacraments, the supposition of a substantial change in the Eucharist, a single allusion to the intercession and merits of the saints, and a very faint reference to the doctrine of Purgatory. The constant repetition of the *Pater Noster* and the neglect of it for other and human compositions are both reprobated by St. Edmund. " Do not," he writes, " be careful in multiplying

Pater Nosters, for it is better to say once the Lord's
Prayer with a good understanding and attention than
a thousand times over without understanding or devotion . . . In the same spirit you ought to take
part in the service of the Church." The "internal
manifestation of God" he defines to be "by revela-
tion and reason;" His "external manifestation by the
Scriptures and by works of the creation." He admits
of no separation of worship when he writes, "Every
man is bound to *serve* God only, and faithfully to
adore Him." There is, therefore, no address to the
saints, or even the shadow of Mariolatry. It is necessary to observe this close resemblance of the teaching
of St. Edmund to that of our Church in the proportions and relations of Christian doctrine, as the
permanence of this kind of teaching to the days
of the Reformation throughout the diocese was
among the causes which occasioned that remarkable
unanimity with which, as we shall observe hereafter,
the doctrines of the Reformation were received in a
Church which might otherwise be reasonably expected
to have been the last to entertain them, as it was the
very first and most devoted of any in England to the
obedience of the See of Rome.

CHAPTER V.

FROM PECKHAM TO WARHAM.

OUR Diocesan history has been hitherto traced rather in the biographies of the archbishops than in the annals of the diocese itself. From loss of the registers of the see during the Norman period and up to the age of Peckham we are enabled to gain but few and distant glimpses of the diocese itself, which we see rather as an appendage to the primacy than as a distinct existence. Occasionally the various scenes in Kent which are connected with the lives of the archbishops become visible, and even clear to the eye, as the monasteries and churches with which they were connected, and the towns over which they held a peculiar jurisdiction, become prominent objects in our long retrospect. When we read of Lanfranc's almost mortal illness at Aldington and the vision of the white horses, on one of which was the sainted Dunstan, whose appearance was the omen of his victory over the rapacious Bishop of Bayeux, we seem to realize for an instant the picture of the diocesan life of the primates; while in the brief periods of Becket's visits and progresses in Kent, we trace the current of popular religious sentiment in that age of uninquiring obedience which represents the feudal period of faith. The miracles of the sainted archbishops, which are mentioned in connection with many of the lesser as well as of the greater towns of the diocese, are suggestive indications of the same state of simple devotion in the rural population of the diocese; and the lives of Dunstan and Lanfranc, the great re-establishers as well as reformers of Monachism in England, enable us in some degree to fill up the lines of the picture, and to measure the relative influence of the parochial and the monastic systems, and their bearings upon the religious and social life of the age. Yet our view, even with all these helps, is but transient and fragmentary. The diocese has no distinct individuality. Its towns and villages, not excepting even the important city from which it derives its name, appear only in the connection in which they stand with the chequered fortunes of the primates. Of those which lie along the route of their progresses, whether of triumph or to exile, we have occasional notices; but of their visitations of the diocese itself and the state of its parishes we have no record; and scarcely the faintest lines of the picture of the diocese as it presented itself in the days of Becket, of Langton, or of St. Edmund, remain. The seasons of exile of the archbishops, so frequent in the early period, are also blanks in the diocesan life; and the vacancy of the primacy even makes a corresponding vacancy in the history of the see. The accession, however, of Archbishop Peckham in 1279 opens a new page in our annals, and for the first time the history of the diocese separates itself from that of the primates and the primacy. The register of Peckham, at once the earliest and the most interesting of those which remain in the vast collections at Lambeth, was first brought into notice by Dr. Ducarel's proposal for its publication, and by his admirable reproduction of it, which is still among the " Additional MSS." of the British Museum, as well as in the Library at Lambeth.[1]

It was carefully transcribed, with a view to its publication, by Mr. Edward Rowe Mores, and is preserved in this very readable form in the same collection in the British Museum.[2]   It opens with a description of the progress of the archbishop from one to another of his great manorial residences, which took place immediately after his return from Paris to take possession of the temporalities of the see.   When we remember that these manors extended from one extremity of the diocese to the other—from Croydon and Otford in the west, to Canterbury, Wingham, and Ford, in the east—from Northfleet and Reculver on the north, to Romney, Aldington, Lyminge and Saltwood on the south, we cannot but see that such a progress was equivalent to a continuous visitation of his diocese, and that almost every part of it was under the ceaseless inspection of its chief.   The first place which is mentioned in the archbishop's itinerary is Lyminge, at which manor he arrived in the beginning of June, 1279.   It was here that the great Earl

---

[1] Among the additional MSS. the collection fills fifty folio volumes, numbered from 6062 downwards.   Up to Archbishop Arundel the work is carefully executed.   After this it seems to consist of Dr. Ducarel's rough notes preparatory to the completion of the Lambeth copy.

[2] Additional MSS. No. 6111.

of Gloucester, Gilbert de Clare, did homage for the
castle and lowy[1] of Tonbridge, and for the other
possessions he held of the see of Canterbury. In
right of this feud, the Earls of Gloucester were
hereditary seneschals of the archbishops, and presented
to them the cup at the banquet succeeding their
enthronization. By a special composition with the
primates (which is minutely described in the register
of Archbishop Meopham) the seneschal was to be
entertained at any one of their manors they might
choose in the four divisions of Kent, but were limited
to a retinue of fifty horsemen, and to a stay of two
nights ; receiving for their official perquisites " seven
robes of scarlet, twenty quarts of wine, fifty pounds
of wax, hay and corn for sixty horses for two nights,
and the cup with which the archbishop is served."
The office of seneschal devolved afterwards to the
Earls of Stafford as succeeding to the feudal holding.
The site of the palace of the archbishop at Lyminge
which covers the fields adjoining the church, and
was also that of the Saxon monastery, can now
only be traced by the mounds and depressions which
mark the position of its ancient walls. A portion of
the foundation, which appeared to be that of the
archbishop's chapel, was disclosed some years since,
but it shortly after perished from the effects of a
severe frost. The "chamber" or "hall" of the
palace, having been built upon the Roman foundation of the "Villa of Lyminge," has still left
a few traces of its existence ; and the vast collection of fragments of stone-work and of encaustic

[1] Lowy (*leucata*) is a kind of liberty extending for about
a league round a town or fortress.

tiles, which were found in the process of excavation,
indicated the place in which the earl took the oath
of feudal allegiance to the archbishop, which the
record before us thus describes :—" On the fifth day
of June the Earl of Gloucester did homage and swore
fealty to the archbishop in his chamber of Lymyngs
standing beside his bed on the east side (juxta lectum
suum in parte orientali) in the presence of the Dean
of St. Paul's " and other dignitaries and great officials.
" And the said earl declared and professed that he
held the honour of Tunbridge with all belonging to it
and all the land and whatever he possessed in the
Lowy of Tunbridge from the archbishop and none
other." The words of the oath are as follows : " Jeo
deveng (defend ?) vostre hon're Sir encontre tuz ceus
ki present vivre et murir de la terre que jeo tieng de
nul sauve la foy le roy et l'arcevesk se recente, sauve
son droit e lautri (?) la fealté en ceste jeo porterai
bone foy al Arcevesk de Cantor-Johan par la grace de
Deu, de vie et de membre et de tril (?) hon^r et leal-
ment contraire les services feray et les custumes que
la tre (terre ?) dong jeo claim de vous tenir, se Deu
m'aid et les soinz." On the same day Bertram de
Criol, the great Norman knight of Westenhanger, did
homage for a military feud held of the archbishop,
as did Bartholomew de Valoigns, whose name is as
illustrious in the history of the country as of the
county itself. At the same time and place appeared
William de Montecamero, to swear the same fealty,
but he is described as standing at the foot of the bed
(" ad pedes lecti ") a less honourable place it would
appear than that occupied by the great Norman earl.
A series of homages and great receptions is carried

on at Lyminge, till in the middle of July the archbishop passes on to Wingham, where in his chapel
he carried on the same tedious process, and doubtless
exercised the same feudal hospitality.   From Wingham he visited Charing, where among other tenants
appearing to do homage was Alexander de Balliol, of
that great house which gave a pretender to the crown
of Scotland as well as the founder of one of the
greatest of the Kentish houses, the Scotts of Scott's
Hall, whose stately monuments fill the church, and
even usurp the place of the altar at Brabourne.   From
Charing the archbishop proceeded to Cranbrook :
from thence into Sussex, to his manor of Mayfield, so
celebrated in a later day for its beautiful palace and
hall, which made it one of the favourite residences of
the primate.   From Mayfield he travelled towards
London, taking up his residence for a short space at
Mortlake ; then visiting Otford, famous in more recent
times for the costly restoration of its palace by Archbishop Warham, but chiefly memorable in that earlier
day as the frequent and favourite residence of Becket.
From Otford his progress was extended to Maidstone,
whence he proceeded to Tarring (in Sussex), Chartham, Teynham, afterwards reappearing successively at
Lambeth and Mortlake.   From this sketch of the
archbishop's first journeys we may be led to infer that
his knowledge of the diocese was personal and intimate,
and that he fulfilled the part of a diocesan as zealously
as he carried on the more conspicuous duties of a
primate.   We are also reminded that the state of the
rural districts in which most of these manors were
situated was one of primitive simplicity, the rents of

the tenants being rather given in kind than in money, the support of the archbishop and his retinue during his stay in his different manors standing in lieu of a money payment, at least in the case of the cultivators of his demesnes, among which all his principal manors were included. His visits to these manors were not, however, merely for the purposes we have already described. They enabled him to inquire into the state of the clergy and laity, and to redress any evils which might be occasioned by the negligence of the one or the necessities of the other. Thus, his visit to his manors of Lyminge and Wrotham was made the occasion of a remarkable letter of complaint and remonstrance to the pluralist rector, Petrus de Albi (or Blaune), a Savoyard, who had been promoted to the most lucrative offices by his countryman, Archbishop Boniface. This letter is a characteristic monument of his zeal both for the temporal and spiritual welfare of his diocese. "Lately," he writes, "making a progress through our said churches we found therein that the cure of souls was altogether neglected as far as belongs to our office; and the poor parishioners, from the want of a good steward, afflicted with hunger and (to sum up in few words) defrauded of all temporal and spiritual consolation. Wherefore we have enjoined our proctor, Master Poncius, for the need of the parishioners, whom you are bound to relieve both temporally and spiritually, to distribute among the poor parishioners of Lyminge a hundred (solidos?) sterling and to assign the same sum at Wrotham. For so great a famine has prevailed at this time, that none of them had anything of his own to live upon;

N

nor, as far as we have heard has there been any one, during the whole period of your incumbency of these churches to relieve the wants of the parishioners in our name, for which cause without doubt you have offended the Most High, Whom we believe that we also have displeased by allowing such conduct to pass by for so long a time under the shadow of dissimulation. It becomes therefore your own honour and will, we believe, be fruitful for the salvation of souls for you to take an early opportunity of coming to visit for some days the cures committed to your government, and to have an interview with us on several matters." The importance of this letter in its bearing upon the history of the diocese must be apparent to every reader of it. We observe the evil of non-residence developed in a very early period, and are led to see how irregularly and perfunctorily the services of some of the principal churches were fulfilled ; those in episcopal patronage being often habitually neglected, while those held by the monasteries as appropriate to them were for the most part served by regulars belonging to the house,—an abuse which prevailed largely as late as the period of the Reformation. This led, as has been already observed, to the foundation of perpetual vicarages, most of the earliest in Kent dating from the period of which we are writing. Albi, who seems to have been almost the evil genius of the archbishop, was not only chaplain to the queen who was the niece of Boniface, but also the executor of his will. Peckham in vain appeals to him to fulfil the duties of his executorship, by reimbursing him the vast expenses he had suffered through the dilapidations of his manor-houses and churches. "You well know," he adds, in the letter already referred to, " in what a state we received the manors belonging to the see, which in the time of my lord Boniface our predecessor, of good memory, were in a strange state of dilapidation (in parte notabili sunt confusa) by reason of whose neglect you know that we have already spent more than 2,000 marks." Every remonstrance, however, was vain in the case of an ecclesiastic who was at once an alien and a client of the queen, and could exercise, as executor of her uncle, the archbishop, so injurious an influence over the affairs of the see. The determined non-resident defied the power of the primate whose only remedy was first the sequestration of his benefices and then his deprivation. Equally fruitless in their results were the efforts of the archbishop to recover the treasures and registers of the see which had been taken away with him by Archbishop Kilwardby when he went to Rome to receive the Cardinal's hat. These are described as the "movable vessels and church ornaments, the books and judicial processes and the registers of the see." A proctor was sent to Rome with the special object of recovering these invaluable documents, but every endeavour of that earlier day was as unsuccessful as the many recent efforts which have been made in our own age, and the records of the see still commence with the primacy of Peckham himself. And indeed if the failure was complete at a time when Kilwardby was still living, it could hardly be successful after the lapse of so many centuries. Notwith-

standing, however, all these losses, and the expenses
he had incurred through the negligence of Boniface
and the dishonesty of his executor, the archbishop
planned the erection of a "decent chapel of stone"
at Otford, " since it was unbecoming that to so stately
a hall (tam solempni aulæ) as now exists there, a
mean wooden building should be attached." Ordinations to all degrees, both of the greater and lesser
orders, fill a large space in the register of the archbishop. These were solemnised at various of his
own chapels or churches in the diocese, the archbishop occasionally delegating the office to some
other bishop but generally fulfilling it in person. In
1281–1283 we find the primate engaged in another
progress through his manors, Aldington, Saltwood,
Charing, Teynham, Maidstone, and Lyminge being
visited in succession. The variety of the duties connected with the diocese which devolved on the archbishops is indicated from time to time in the pages
of his register. At one time he is called upon to
defend the clergy or his retainers from imprisonment
and other evils incident to feudal despotism. These
were assertions of what are called the "liberties of
the church of Canterbury," and gave protection not
only to the unfortunate cleric, as "William Wyldegos,
a priest of Canterbury," but even to the barber of
the archbishop. The value of a copy of the Scriptures at this time is indicated by a letter of Peckham
requiring the restitution of a certain Bible which had
been written out for his predecessor, and for which
113 marks had been paid out of the property of the
Church. The ancient discords which reigned peri-

odically in the priory of Christ Church were also an
object of the archbishop's solicitude—as were also
the needs of those churches in which the bishops
through age or infirmity were unequal to the labours
of their sees,—to whom he assigned "coadjutors,"
or, as we might term them, suffragan bishops.

But in the midst of his diocesan and primatial
work the archbishop was called upon to defray the
enormous charges which had been exacted or rather
demanded by the Court of Rome, and was even
threatened with excommunication and deprivation if
he should fail to satisfy its extortionate claims. Well
might he appeal to the Pope in almost despairing
words, complaining of the letter of the "curia" as
"horrible in its aspect and terrible in its sound," a
grievous addition to the trials which his efforts to
reform the state and manners both of the clergy and
laity had brought upon him. But the mercy which
he sought for at the hands of the pope was cruelly
denied to the unfortunate Jews, whom after the un-
christian fashion of the age, he ceaselessly, but
happily unsuccessfully, persecuted. He "hears with
horror that they are building a new synagogue in
London," and writes to the Bishop of London urging
him to unite with him in the severest measures of
excommunication against all who assist in the work.

In the appointment of the clergy to benefices he
exercised so wise a judgment as even to resist the importunities of the Pope in favour of one Bartholomew
de Ferentino, who is reported to be "not only ignorant
of the English language, but scarcely able to speak
grammatically (*satis literaliter loqui nescit*). His

numerous and important letters to the king and the
great officers of state upon European and political
subjects do not fall within our present scope, but
they indicate Peckham to have been fully equal to
the office he held in the secular, as he undoubtedly
was to that which he so ably fulfilled in the ecclesiastical world. His zeal and energy as a diocesan
bishop appears to have specially subjected him to the
taunts and depreciatory remarks of the chroniclers,
whose devotion to the monastic orders ever makes
them the severest judges of all who have maintained
the interests and improved the position of the secular
clergy. Seen, however, through his register, which
reflects also the progress of the diocese under his
government, Archbishop Peckham must ever be
regarded by the impartial historian as one of the
wisest and best of those who have united the larger
functions of the primacy with the more limited but
not less important labours of a diocesan bishop.
Probably his severity on pluralists and non-residents,
and the stern morality which he exacted from clergy
and laity alike, may have inspired a popular feeling
against him, of which the chroniclers became naturally
the ready exponents. Among the instances of his
severity against the moral delinquencies of the highest
classes was the penance he inflicted on Sir Osbert
Giffard for stealing two nuns out of the convent of
Wilton, which at least proved the impartiality and
independence with which he exercised the great
powers of his office. His foundation for a provost
and six secular canons in the church of Wingham
indicated a munificence which, but for the great dis-

advantages with which he entered upon the primacy, might have had still more conspicuous proof. Archbishop Peckham died at Mortlake in 1292, and was buried in his own cathedral, where his tomb (in the Martyrdom), with its singular recumbent figure carved in bog-oak, which has survived the stonework of many more recent monuments, is well known to every visitor. Few archbishops have conferred greater benefits on the diocese; by few, indeed, has the diocese been more fully known than by the good archbishop, who was almost better known by his cotemporaries under the name of " Brother John " than under any of his higher titles.

His successor was Robert de Winchelsey, elected in 1292. His register is described in the note of an early scribe, prefixed to it, as " mytch out of order, and the first years of his transacyion about the mydest of ye book." Probably the chief cause of this confusion was the conflict in which he was so early engaged with King Edward I. in regard to the subsidy of the fifth of the clergy revenues, in order to carry on the war with Scotland. The archbishop resisted this impost, and the king, appealing to Rome, banished him from the kingdom, his restitution not taking place until 1307. Winchelsey, like his predecessor, passed his time during his residence in the diocese in progresses from one manor-house to another, closing his days at his manor of Otford on May 11th, 1313. In 1302 he held an homage at Lyminge and at other of his manors ; but very little light is thrown upon the history of the diocese from his register. We find the ancient warfare between the monks of St. Augustine's and those of Christ-

church coming again into prominence, and the
"excesses" of the great exempt foundation are
brought by the archbishop under the eye of the
pope; but the influence exercised by the proctors
of St. Augustine's protracts the suit, and apparently
leaves it undecided—one of the numerous proofs of
the evils arising out of a distant appellate jurisdiction
like that of Rome.

The liberties of the church of Canterbury, and its
temporal rights, were as assiduously protected by
Winchelsey as by his predecessor, and the institution to
the office of janitor of the monastery has as prominent
a place in his register as that to the archdeaconry, or to
the highest dignities of the Church. Notwithstanding
the zeal of the primate for the foundation of which he
was the supreme head, the numbers of its monks were
at this time rather diminishing than increasing, the
rival monastery evidently presenting greater induce-
ments to those entering the conventual life; for the
archbishop has to admonish the prior " to increase and
fill up the number" of the monks of his foundation,
and also to complain to him of their wanderings
from the cloister (*super deragatione monachorum*).
The same complaint is made against the monks of
Ely and the Knights Templars, whose impending
fate " casts its shadow before " in the commission
issued by the archbishop to examine into their
" heresies." The old subject of the exemption of
delinquent priests from the secular authority—the
great bone of contention in the days of Becket—re-
appears during this as in many subsequent primacies,
the clergy of Canterbury receiving a large measure of

this mischievous kind of protection. Non-residence for special and not inconsiderable periods, some extending to three years, was frequent at this time, and must have greatly tended towards the more absolute forms of non-residence which at last roused even the reforming zeal of the Council of Trent, and evoked the really admirable bull of Pius IV. against non-resident bishops and priests.[1] The abuse of pluralities, the natural fruit of that of non-residence was now assuming, under the shadow of the dispensing power of the pope, very serious dimensions. It was usual at this time for dispensations to be given to those who could afford to pay for them, allowing them to hold benefices in plurality not exceeding in value a certain sum fixed by the papal chancery, and probably sufficiently elastic to adapt itself to the tariff of fees which the Roman court was able to exact without any fear of revision or taxation. One John de Sandale is accordingly instituted to the following charges :—The chancellorship of the churches of Dublin, St. Andrew's, and Dunbar ; the livings of Wymbish and Simonsburn in Yorkshire, and Mimms in Hertfordshire, with a canonry in Wells, to which the archbishop adds the benefice of Wimbledon, in Surrey, in his own gift.

Among the grants and concessions relating to the diocese there is one which to many will have peculiar interest. It is the grant to William de Brockhull permitting him "to celebrate divine service in his chapel at Saltwood," dated in 1310. A fragment of

[1] See the bull, "In supremâ militantis Ecclesiæ speculâ," A.D. 1564.

this ancient oratory now forms part of a cottage, which represents the last remains of the ancient house of Brockhull, a property which has descended in unbroken succession from the Norman period through the Criols, the Brockhulls, the Sellinges, and the Tournays to the present possessor, Mr. Allen Tournay, of Brockhull. An entry of general interest appears in connection with the chapel of St. John the Baptist at Sevenoke. It is an inventory of the furniture of the chapel and residence of the chaplain taken in 1313. Among the objects mentioned is a small chalice, a missal *not according to the Use of Sarum* (which would indicate that such a missal was in somewhat general use in Kent, the presence of a missal of different use here being alluded to as exceptional), a gradual, a psalter with hymns, a volume containing the office of St. John the Baptist, and other things,[1] an ordinal, a surplice with a poor rochet, a thurible, &c. The effects in the house and grange include a horse, worth ten shillings, and two oxen worth twenty. The visitation work of the archbishop seems to have been carried on less in a general form than at intervals, and separately in the different deaneries, and chiefly by officials acting under his commission. Hence our view of the diocese during his primacy, and, indeed, until the time of Courtenay, is very imperfect and fragmentary.

His successor was Walter Reynolds, promoted by the king in opposition to the choice of the monastery, which had fallen upon a member of the great

---

[1] The register is here somewhat obscure, there being a gap between the words " baptista " and "alia," but I conceive this to be the meaning.

historic family of Cobham. The pope eagerly confirmed the royal candidate in the possession of the
see, and in return for many gifts and pensions to the
Court of Rome, conferred upon him in eight successive bulls very extraordinary privileges, which largely
extended the power of the primacy. Unlimited
powers of visitation, absolution, dispensation for all
causes, reservations, pardons, and other concessions
were included in the papal grants, and the spiritual
interests of the diocese were fatally sacrificed in these
unprecedented efforts to increase the powers of the
primacy. The prospect of the diocese during this
period, as far as we can discern it from this register,
discloses constant changes in the places of the
clergy, and an accumulation of benefices on the
favoured few, among whom the chronicler Adam de
Murimuth, is conspicuous. Perhaps a yet more
flagrant instance, which even Murimuth ventured to
chronicle as the climax of Italian rapacity, was that
of the Cardinal Gaucelinus de Ossa, the nephew of
Pope John XXII., who on his coming to England to
negotiate a peace between the king of England and
Robert Bruce in 1315, acquired that year benefices
worth more than a thousand pounds a year, including
the rectories of Lyminge, Hollingbourne, and Pagham,
in the gift of the archbishop, the church of Hackney
in Middlesex, and the prebend of Driffield in York.
Not content with this accession to his non-residentiary
titles, he applied for the church of Stepney, then just
vacant. This large income he drained out of England
until the year 1349, when he died at Avignon, where
his uncle was carrying on the exile of the Papacy.

An account of the taxation of the archbishop's manors, which is given us in his register, presents a tolerably clear view of the possessions of the see in Kent while they were under the careful stewardship of Winchelsey. They are thus given :—

	£.	s.	d.		£.	s.	d.
Westgate	57	13	0	Bocton (Bough-			
Reculver.	61	6	8	ton)	52	14	4
Westhalimote	40	14	6½	Teynham	85	12	5
Wingham	249	3	7	Northfleet	107	2	5
Bishopsbourne	42	13	10	Aldington	133	11	10
Petham and				Charing	53	4	3
Waltham	22	0	9½	Maidstone	83	16	11
Dale	16	13	4	Otford	198	5	0
Lyminge	56	18	6	Bexley	40	0	0
Saltwood	22	0	4	Wrotham	80	15	0
				Gillingham	95	11	10
					1,499	18	7

To the total sum there is added from the manors in the diocese of London £128. 19s. 8½d., in Winchester diocese, £65. 0s. 0d., in Chichester, £354. 0s. 9¼d. The whole sum upon which the archbishop was taxed amounted therefore to £2,047. 19s. 0¾d., the property of the Priory of Christ Church being rated at £1,321. 18s. 1d. It is curious to observe that the greatest of the modern estates of the see was then one of the least; Lambeth being only taxed at £15. A comparison of this list with that given in Doomsday enables us to see how greatly the value of the estates in West Kent was beginning to predominate over those in the less fruitful districts of East Kent. Perhaps the most difficult problem is presented in the value of Wingham, while the enhanced value of

Otford, Northfleet, Gillingham, and Maidstone point
to the influence of London, and the water-communi-
cation which gave so easy an access to the metropolis.

During the primacy of Reynolds, the terrible blow
so long impending over the ill-fated order of the
Knights Templars fell with all its force of cruelty,
and even barbarism, but its effects in the diocese
were but little felt. The villages of Ewell, near
Dover, and Waltham, near Canterbury, still bear the
prefix which marks their connection with the order,
but its possessions in Kent were few and unimportant.
The primacy of Simon de Meopham, the successor of
Archbishop Reynolds, began in 1327, but only a
fragment of his register has survived. It is not,
however, without interest in its bearing on the history
of the diocese, as we find in it the entire form of
electing the prior and other officers of the Monastery
of Christ Church. The election of Richard de
Oxenden gave occasion to this full account of a
ceremonial which those acquainted with the cathedral will easily realise. When the archbishop had
taken his place in the choir a schedule containing the
votes of the monks was placed in his hands, upon
which he retired with his retinue to Chartham, a
village and then residence of the primates near the
city, where he conferred upon the matter with his
clergy, and, when he had fixed upon the most fitting
candidate, returned to Canterbury and proclaimed
the name of the prior elect. After this he placed
the golden ring of investiture upon his finger and
made him sit on his right hand in the chapter.
The "Te Deum" was then sung, and a procession

formed to the altar, at which an "oration was pronounced by the archbishop over the said prior;" and
the primate retired again to Chartham. A curious
and considerable portion of Meopham's register consists of a minute detail of the fees required by the
archbishop for consecrating in the cathedral the
suffragans of his province, by which it would appear
that the precedent of the Court of Rome was but too
faithfully carried out at Canterbury,[1] and the most
sacred offices of the Church discredited by a very
mercantile kind of taxation. The fees paid to the
Earls of Gloucester, and their successor the Earl of
Stafford, which have been already described, find
here their appropriate place. The archbishop is said
to have rebuilt the parish church of his native place,
Meopham, in North Kent, but his connection with
the diocese was rendered more painful and harassing
than that of any of his predecessors by reason of the
severe controversy carried on between him and the
monks of St. Augustine's. The monks prevailed as
ever against the unfortunate primate, being supported
by the Court of Rome against the ordinary, and the
archbishop was condemned to pay £1,210 to the
monastery for costs of the suit. Refusing to submit
to this judgment, he was pronounced contumacious,
and retired in great distress of mind to Mortlake,

[1] It was computed in the Parliament held in the 23rd year of
Henry VIII. that the Papacy had received out of England
for the investitures of bishops only, since the second year of
Henry VII., not much above forty years, £160,000 sterling, an
enormous sum for that day, but only an item in the long and
ruinous list of exactions which had impoverished the country
since its fatal connection with the see of Rome.

where he died under sentence of excommunication, and could not be buried until the Abbot of St. Augustine's had absolved him. A reversal of the unjust judgment was obtained by his successor, but the case remains as a monument of the degradation of the Church of England under the Roman yoke which has but too many parallels in its history.

The successor of Meopham was John de Stratford, whose register, while equally imperfect, is even less interesting. He was permitted by the king to form a park at Otford, a place which from the time of Becket to that of Warham seems to have been the favourite residence of the archbishops. He was rather a primate than a diocesan, and more a courtier and civil servant of the crown than either, attending on the king as his chancellor, and following him in his varied fortunes with singular fidelity. The fifteen years of his primacy give us scarcely a glimpse of the history of the diocese, and his chief work was the foundation of a college at his place of birth—afterwards far more celebrated as the birthplace of Shakespeare. His character is described to us as one of great gentleness and beauty, and his fidelity to Edward II., at the time of the fall of the Spensers, instead of involving him in their penalty, appears to have been the very cause of his safety.

Upon the death of Stratford the prior and convent elected Thomas Bradwardine, whose great work in defence of the Augustinian doctrines of grace has given him a name and a place in the history of the Church, and an influence over its teaching more than that which the longest enjoyment of the primatial dignity could have obtained for him. His possession of the see, however, lasted but for a few months, as he fell a victim to the plague which was then raging in all its intensity in London, dying miserably of that dreadful disease which the fatigue of his journey to Rome had brought upon him within five weeks and four days of his consecration, and before he could enter upon the temporalities of the see.[1] The vacancy was filled by the election of Simon de Islep, whose register has reached our day in a perfect form. It is, however, as deficient in interest as it is copious in details connected with the ordinary government of the diocese. We see less of pluralities than in former periods, but the licences for non-residence fill no less than thirty pages of Dr. Ducarel's index. Mention occurs of the castle of Saltwood and its park, the keepership of which is bestowed upon the archbishop's valet (valetto suo), Simon de Dinghurst. A visitation of the diocese was held in 1350, and a commission for another appears in 1357. We find a licence given in the case of a person too infirm to attend church to have a portable altar, while there are indications of an occasional resort to other churches than that of the parish, which seems to have been then as later a prevailing temptation. Burials in chapels, in derogation of the rights of the parish church, are severely dealt with, and a curious judgment of this kind was pronounced by the official of the archbishop at Maidstone, ordering the disinterment of one Sarah

[1] The short primacy of Archbishop Ufford, who was intruded by the pope, and died before his consecration, has here been omitted as having no bearing on the history of the diocese.

Cole, who had been buried in the chapel of Paddlesworth in derogation of the rights of the parish church
of Lyminge, whither the offending churchwardens are
charged to remove the body at their own cost.

Islep died in 1366, and was succeeded by Simon
Langham, bishop of Ely.   In 1368 he was created a
cardinal, and resigned the archbishopric.   But, during
his short tenure of office, he seriously disturbed the
good work of his predecessor, who had founded a
college at Canterbury[1] for secular scholars, by forcing
upon it monks instead of seculars.   Among those
whom he thus displaced was one whose name from
this period becomes conspicuous both in Church and
State—John Wycliff.   Among the many problems
which the life of this remarkable man presents, not the
least interesting in its historical bearing is suggested
by this, his first experience of the conflict between
monachism and secular learning.   Again an appeal
was lodged at Rome, and again the monastic influence
overcame both law and right.   A bull of Urban V.
against pluralities revealed, in the pages of Langham's
register, the vast proportions which this abuse had
reached, both in the diocese and in the country at
large. The bulk of his register consists of the returns
from the dioceses of the province of the livings held
by pluralists and *in commendam*.   As these were
always held under papal dispensations, the court of
Rome may be regarded in this instance as giving at
least a show of penitence for an error which, however
it may have left its infallibility untouched, gave fatal

---

[1] Other writers describe this as "Canterbury College" at
Oxford, which probably is the more correct account.

disproof of its moral integrity. Non-residence, however, which alone made pluralities possible, remained
still as a blot upon the ecclesiastical system of the
age, and licences of this kind are still among the
prominent documents of the archiepiscopal registers.

On the resignation of Langham, the primacy was
conferred upon William Whittlesey, bishop of Worcester, a nephew of Archbishop Islep. The first feature
which strikes us in his register in connection with
the diocese is the increasing frequency of exchanges
of livings, and the generally unsettled state of the
clergy, which must have seriously affected their influence with a laity with whom they could never have
been able to form ties of friendly intimacy or of
lasting interest. The power of the regular clergy
could not but have been increased in proportion as
that of the secular and parochial clergy became
diminished, in all the churches which lay within their
reach ; and the Church was virtually losing the
benefit of that institution of perpetual vicarages,
which was the greatest diocesan work of the thirteenth
and fourteenth centuries. It is not easy to believe
that this wide-spread system of exchanges was free
from suspicion of simony, and the eagerness with
which the beneficed clergy of the day bartered their
livings suggests a natural doubt of the purity of these
contracts, to which the archbishops seem to have
given too ready a sanction. Prominent among the
documents contained in this register is the "Royal
Prohibition against Papal Bulls," whose publication
in the kingdom is forbidden under the severest
penalties. The archbishop himself gives a token of

his independence by relaxing the rigour of the papal law in regard to the benediction of second marriages.

Whittlesey died in 1375, and was succeeded by Simon de Sudbury, who had been previously bishop of London. He was enthroned at Canterbury on Palm Sunday in the following year by the prior of Christ Church, assisted by the Bishop of Rochester, the priors of St. Augustine's, Battle, St. Radegund's, Langdon, and Rochester, with many other eminent persons, both lay and cleric, the Earl of Stafford officiating as seneschal. The accumulation of benefices in England upon foreigners had now become one of the scandals of the age, and a letter of inquiry in regard to this abuse is a feature of interest in Sudbury's register. The diocese of Canterbury suffered probably more than any other from this draining away of its revenues by aliens; the sinecure rectories, as well as the dignities of the cathedral, having been frequently bestowed on the favoured candidates of the court of Rome, the representatives and emissaries of the pope, who, on the pretext of some political mission, set forth to gather the richest fruits of a country of which Pope Innocent IV. said, "vere hortus noster deliciarum est Anglia et puteus inexhaustus ; et ubi multa abundant de multis multa sumere licet."[1]

The register of Sudbury throws but little light upon the diocese, and it would appear that the political troubles in which he was involved and which closed his life so tragically disabled him from entering as fully into his episcopal duties as many of his prede-

[1] Matth. Paris.

cessors. The frequent appointment of the parochial
clergy as advocates in the Court of Arches is indicated
at this period, and must have tended to disturb them
in those duties which more properly belonged to
their office. The extension of the diocese of Canterbury over Calais and the adjacent districts, effected by
a bull of Urban VI., reminds us of the English occupation of that part of Picardy, and denotes its ecclesiastical results. The presentation of one William
Grene to the parish church of St. Mary in Calais, and
of a Yorkshire priest to the Church of St. Nicholas in
the same town, shows that the king, in whom the
patronage vested, however intolerant in regard to an
alien clergy in England, was by no means scrupulous
in regard to the same grievance, when inflicted by
himself upon another country. Andomarus de la
Roche, or as he is commonly called the Lord Andomar
de Rupy, was at this time Archdeacon of Canterbury
and one of the great pluralists of the age. Mixing
himself up with the dangerous political movements of
the period he brought upon him the censures of the
pope and of the archbishop, and was finally deprived
of all his benefices and dignities. These included,
with the archdeaconry, the rectories of Lyminge,
Teynham, the vicarages of Hackington, St. Clement
in Sandwich, St. Mary in Sandwich; and their proceeds were given by the king to Sudbury to carry on
the great work which he was engaged in on the nave
of the cathedral, whose date may, therefore, be fixed
at this period. The kindred zeal of the archbishop
for the memory of his predecessor, St. Augustine,
was indicated by his making his feast a "double"

one.[1] In the year 1378 the archbishop appealed for a voluntary subscription (charitativa subventio) for the fabric of the nave of the cathedral, probably the earliest instance of an appeal of this kind for church-building purposes, which the wealth and the zeal of the monks had in former ages been sufficient to effect without external aid. Non-residence seems still to have prevailed, as we find a monition on the subject put forth as early as 1377, while the licences for non-residence are fewer than in previous records.

A papal subsidy was demanded by Gregory XI. from all the dioceses of the province, and as we gather from one of the numerous documents relating to this ruinous impost, was ruthlessly exacted, extreme measures being taken against all defaulters. Our restricted space has hitherto prevented any reference to the numerous and very interesting wills which are interspersed throughout these registers, though they illustrate in many of their directions and bequests the state of the religious feeling of the age, and might well give the materials of a work of great historical and doctrinal interest. But the will of Edward the Black Prince, indicating his burial-place in the cathedral, has too direct a bearing upon our history not to find mention here. The words of his last testament run thus :—" Nostre corps d'estre enseveli en l'Eglise Cathedrale de la Trinité de Canterbrygg, ou le corps du vray Martir Mons. Seint Thomas repose, en ma lieu de la chapelle de notre Dame Undercrofte,

---

[1] Mandatum Archiep. de tenendo festum St. Augustini sub duplici festo (A.D. 1396, f. 18, b).

droitement devant l'autier, si que le bout de nostre tombe dont les pees soit dix pees loing de l'autier, et que mesme la tombe soit de marbre de bone masonerie faite." [1]

The opening of the great Schism of the west discloses itself in the year 1378, the first symptom of it being a bull of Urban VI., announcing his election, which was presently followed up by a monition of the cardinals declaring the invalidity of the election, and charging the faithful everywhere · to withhold their obedience. This latter document was not admitted by the English clergy, who adhered to Urban. In close and significant connection with this breach in the "centre of unity" we find the first proceedings taken against Wycliff, which assume considerable proportions in Sudbury's register. We have already seen the early but brief relation in which the great reformer stood to the diocese, and we now find him putting forth those famous "conclusions" on religion and philosophy which called for the intervention of popes and bishops, but were not finally condemned until the assembly of the Council of Constance, in 1415. We may here observe that the "heresies" of Wycliff ought not to be confounded with the doctrines of Lollardism, whose unfortunate professors find such frequent mention in the succeeding registers of the see. The Lollards were rather a sect of pietists than of philosophers, and though many of the more educated among them held also the philosophical conclusions of Wycliff, the majority of them belonged

---

[1] F. 90, b. 91, a, b.

to a class whose education was far too limited to enable them to follow his teaching. Thomas de Elmham, writing in 1414, clearly separates the two, and as clearly indicates the point of union between them which made the clergy and monastic orders of the day so envenomed in their hatred of both. This was the hostility of both alike to the wealth and territorial position of the Church. Both these and other heretics, as Elmham writes, endeavour to root up "the flowers of ecclesiastical property."[1] He naturally deduces their pedigree from the mythical Thunor, whose attempt to frustrate the good design of the king at Minster in Thanet the reader will doubtless remember. Gregory XI. addressed a mandate to Sudbury and the Bishop of London to proceed against Wycliff without delay, which was followed up by a citation of him to Rome. His "conclusions" are put into a regular form and a new citation issues. Those relating to the eucharist seem chiefly to have terrified the clergy of the day, for we find a special attempt to refute these on the part of William de Brecon, chancellor of the University of Oxford. The violent death of Sudbury during the rebellion of Wat Tyler, which was closely connected with the opening persecution against the Lollards (the archbishop having imprisoned one, John Balle, a popular preacher in Maidstone jail, for maintaining heterodox doctrines), more properly belongs to the history of the country than of the diocese. To the latter as to the church and city of Canterbury, he was

---

[1] "Hist. Monast. S. Augustin." p. 214: ed. Hardwick, 1858.

a munificent benefactor, as his work at the cathedral
and his rebuilding of the Westgate, besides other
monuments, very fully testify.

He was succeeded by the lordly Courtenay, who
had filled successively the sees of Hereford and
London, and was, soon after the death of Sudbury, translated to the primatial see. No less
than seven separate bulls were needed for this
translation, a process whose enormous profits to the
Court of Rome were only equalled by its tedious-
ness and ruinous loss to the church and to the country.
The archbishop, who, in the baronial castle of his
ancestors, had rather realised the military than the
civil side of feudalism, found on his entrance on the
see that the expense of keeping up so large a number
of manor-houses was as great as the danger of living
in such defenceless abodes in an age of civil and religious commotions, as well as perils from foreign
invasion. He obtained, therefore, the licence of the
king and of the monastery to pull down all his less
necessary residences and to build and embattle the
castle of Saltwood, so as to render it at once a palace
and a fortress, a union of beauty and strength, of
pleasure and of defence, which should make it in every
sense a fitting abode for himself and his successors. A
castle of some importance appears to have existed
here from very early times, and the learned members
of the Archæological Institute during a recent visit
held that the mounds and earthworks around it
might well have belonged to the very earliest period.
The castle itself, which is entirely the work of Courtenay—for the most ordinary observer would con-

clude that the whole is of one structure, and that no inferior or earlier building could have been incorporated with a plan so grand and symmetrical— exhibits that transition between the mere military stronghold and the feudal residence which begins in the early part of the fifteenth century, and is so beautifully developed towards its close. De Cammont, in his admirable treatise on early military architecture, points out that from the year 1450, after the re-taking of Normandy, the change of the fortress residence into the castellated abode of a palatial character began in France. In England, however, the change appears to have been somewhat earlier.

The introduction of fire-arms, and especially cannons, in the fifteenth century, "diminished the importance of the ancient castles, whose strength depended on the height of their walls. It was foreseen that this system of defence would soon be greatly changed, and that less importance would be attached to all which formerly constituted the main strength of feudal mansions. Nevertheless, a number of the castles, even of the latter half of the fifteenth century, preserved outwardly a certain appearance of strength —the entrance was defended by towers, portcullis, and drawbridge—the walls adorned with towers and machicolations."[1] This description gives a perfect picture of the castle erected by Courtenay, whose magnificent ruins, grievously as they have suffered from age and neglect, prove that the execution of his work was not unworthy of the grandeur of its design.

[1] "Cours d'Antiquités Monumentales," p. v. p. 844.

Everyone who surveys the stately towers and gate-
way and the mutilated wall of the castle of Saltwood,
may easily fill up in imagination the picture of
princely magnificence which the primacy displayed at
this culminating point of its splendour. A commission was issued in 1382 to pull down the houses on
several of the archbishop's manors, and to sell the
stones and other materials in order to carry on the
great work in which he was engaged, reserving a
portion of them for the reparation of the neighbouring
churches or chapels.

The numerous parks and chases, so expensive
and useless to the see, were now gradually disused
or consolidated. The ancient park of Lyminge was
added to that of Saltwood and placed under the
management of the same keeper, by another commission dated in 1387. It does not clearly appear which
of the manor-houses were actually taken down, and
which merely disused and suffered to fall into ruin.
From an inquisition taken on the attainder of Archbishop Arundel in 1398 being held at Lyminge, we
may conclude that this ancient residence was yet
undestroyed though disused. Otford, which had
been the principal and favourite residence of so many
of the primates, was doubtless spared, awaiting the
magnificent restoration of Archbishop Warham. The
influence of this change upon the diocese was marked
in the less intimate relations which it involved between
the primate and his diocese, relations which, during
the period from Lanfranc to Courtenay, were so close
and personal. The registers, as a natural consequence, throw less and less light upon the diocese

and more upon the primacy, and the great estates of the see were managed by stewards and bailiffs or seneschals, whose accounts of the different manors have been only recently disentombed from the numerous bags in which they were gradually wasting away. These are now being carefully catalogued and arranged by a skilled hand, and may at a future time furnish materials for the social and statistical history of the county of the greatest value and interest. Though Courtenay's primacy extends from 1381 to 1396, the events which it comprises are comparatively few and unimportant. Wycliff comes but once on the scene in a letter addressed to the Bishop of Lincoln. In his visitation of the Priory of Dorchester three Lollards, William Smith, Roger Dexter, and Alicia, his wife, are brought before him to abjure their heresies and seek absolution from the excommunication they had incurred, which, after the performance of a due penance, is accorded to them. We do not find that Lollardism has much hold on the diocese at this period, and there are no traces of the cruel persecutions with which Archbishop Arundel followed it up in Kent. A "Lollard chaplain" is not remitted to the stake, but "restored to the unity of the church," while others are described as "reconciled." How far these persons held the condemned opinions or "conclusions" of Wycliff does not appear. Archbishop Courtenay held a general visitation of the diocese in 1393, beginning his visitation at Lenham. As we shall have occasion to give a picture of the visitation of Archbishop Warham rather more than a century later, it will be unnecessary to dwell upon this earlier and less important survey of the diocese.

Archbishop Courtenay died on the last day of July, 1396, and was succeeded by Thomas Arundel, son of Robert, brother of Richard Fitzalan, earl of Arundel by his wife Eleanor, daughter of Henry Plantagenet, earl of Lancaster. His enthronisation took place at Canterbury with great magnificence in the presence of the king himself. But the royal favour soon forsook him, and his very nearness to the throne involved him in the dangers which invariably attended it in that day of rivalry and intrigue. Under a charge of high treason, he was attainted and the whole of his possessions sequestrated and kept in the king's hands. The death of Richard II., however, freed him from danger and restored him to his former offices and estates, and the favour of the new king rendered his subsequent career one of almost unexampled prosperity. He is chiefly known to us as the bitter and cruel persecutor of the Lollards, whom he followed up with unrelenting severity in his own diocese, as well as throughout the province. Except in his gifts to the cathedral, whose completion he greatly assisted, building the spire on the north-west steeple, —since destroyed with the tower on which it rested, to give place to a tower exactly modelled after the corresponding one on the south-west,[1]—we read of nothing great or good done by this primate. In 1401 we find him consecrating the " chapel of

---

[1] This attempt to make the west front uniform at the expense of historical association and picturesque variety was disapproved of by many at the time, including the late Archdeacon Croft.

St. Mary and St. Thomas à Becket," in the castle of
Saltwood, upon the exact position of which recent
antiquaries have been divided. It appears from one
or two obvious indications to lie to the right of the
great hall, which some have erroneously identified
with it. In one of the grisly *oubliettes* of this stately
ruin several unfortunate Lollards expiated the guilt
of holding a simpler creed and observing a more
spiritual rule than those whom their example at once
rebuked and exasperated. These unhappy people
were evidently looked upon as worse than felons,
whose guilt received frequent absolution from the
archbishop. Campanologists might claim Arundel
as an early devotee to their art, for we find him
engaged in blessing bells for his chapel at Otford,
and also for that at Maidstone, while he left a peal of
five bells to the cathedral dedicated to the Trinity,
the Virgin Mary, the Angel Gabriel, St. Blaize, and
St. John the Evangelist. In 1401 a general collection
was made throughout the diocese towards the defence
of the Eastern Emperor, Manuel Palæologus, and the
city of Constantinople, then threatened by the
Saracens. There could have been little, however,
left out of the archbishop's treasury to give to this
urgent cause, when he had to provide such enormous
sums to meet the demands of the court of Rome on
his predecessor and himself. We find a receipt or
acquittance given for 350 golden florins, followed
up by another for 2,300 ; while the enormous sum
of 5,000 golden florins is presently claimed for
the insatiable curia. Not content with this plunder,
the court of Rome threatened to sequester the estate

of Archbishop Courtenay in order to satisfy a claim upon him for 1,575 golden florins. Well might a wit of these times write :

> " Roma capit marcas, Bursas exhaurit et arcas
> Ut tibi tu parcas, fuge Papas et Patriarchas."

The court of Rome was now, however, in the throes of the great schism of the west, and the popes and cardinals on either side are compelled to become rather suppliant than peremptory rulers, soliciting the king and the archbishop to recognise their conflicting claims. We find in Arundel's register a state of the side-light thrown upon the fragmentary records of Archbishop Sudbury's primacy. It appears that Sudbury's register was stolen from the chest of the see at Reigate, as was also that of Courtenay.[1] All that Arundel can do is to excommunicate the offenders, a process of law which could only strike an undiscovered thief in the conscience, a faculty of which he was probably destitute.

The fatal zeal of the archbishop against the Lollards culminated in the terrible part he took against Sir John Oldcastle, in right of his wife, Baron Cobham, and those who suffered with him or in the same cause. In some cases a revocation and reconciliation saved the life of the convicted person at the expense of his faith, and we read of the " revocation " of John Becket, a name hardly suggestive of Lollardism ; while one, by name John " dictus de Scyvonus " (Sevenoke ?), undergoes the gentler process of " conversion."

---

[1] This latter must have been recovered, unless it existed in duplicate, as the original seems to be that still to be found at Lambeth.

The churches and residence-houses of the diocese were at this time in such a state of disrepair as to need a general monition of the archbishop for their reparation throughout the whole of his jurisdiction. This might well be borne in mind by those who are interested in the architectural history of the churches of Kent, as much of the early Perpendicular work which abounds in them might with great probability be traced to this period. An interesting list of the benefices in the gift of the archbishop, given us in this register, enables us to see the extent of his patronage and the value in marks of every separate piece of preferment. Whether this return was in any way connected with the charge to repair the churches and residences already mentioned does not distinctly appear, though it may be reasonably conjectured. The park of Aldington was now added to those of Lyminge and Saltwood, for the purposes of the keepership and the economic policy of Courtenay is thus carried on in the case of these unnecessary appendages to the primacy. The same evils of non-residence and pluralities remained though in lesser degree, for the serious changes which impended over the Church compelled the clergy to begin the long-neglected work of setting their house in order. In some sense Arundel may be said to be the last (if we except Bourchier) of those princely archbishops whose alliances with royalty gave then an exceptional place in the long succession of the primacy, and who had a kind of posthumous representation in our own day in Archbishop Manners-Sutton, who found a seat in the House of Lords his natural place, being enabled to

recognise all the greater peers around him as his own
kinsmen. The closing years of Arundel carry us on
into the fifteenth century, extending to the year 1414,
when he was succeeded by the munificent Chicheley,
whose name has so far more lasting a memorial from
the great foundation at Oxford, which has made the
very greatest in the land anxious to prove their kindred to one whose origin was more obscure than that
of most of his predecessors in the primacy. His
connection with the diocese seems from his register
to have been but slender ; and though his gifts to the
city of Canterbury and the cathedral find an appropriate recognition in the mandate of the prior and
chapter directing the place and ceremonial of his
burial, he seems rather to have had an eye to the
splendour of the temporal reign than to the higher
duties of his spiritual office. A significant proof of
this is given us in the bull of Martin V., authorising
him " when he had begun his visitation, to turn his
attention to other things, and to continue his visitation by the agency of a commissary." It is singular
that the founder of so many imperishable educational
monuments should have been so anxious to build
himself a mausoleum, in his case so little needed.
Yet we cannot read without interest, however it
may be mixed with surprise, the document in
which the prior and chapter consent to the erection
of this splendid tomb, in which the taste of the renaissance seems struggling into life in the midst of so
many triumphs of mediæval art and skill. After a
preamble setting forth the special affection which
the archbishop "ever bore to his church, and which

led him in his lifetime to select a burial-place for himself in the cathedral, namely, on the north side of the choir, between the place of the relics and the entrance of the choir leading up to the high altar," and setting forth "that to the honour of God and the adornment of the church he hath built and completed a sumptuous monument or mausoleum, and arranged it for the reception and burial of his body," it proceeds : " Therefore, we, the prior and convent aforesaid, having regard to the intention of the most reverend father, and considering that he hath given certain goods and jewels for the use and ornament of our church, and hath spent large sums of money in the reparation of the said church and of the bell-tower thereof, and specially hath given money for the construction of a new library, and furnished it with divers precious books relating to all the faculties, have given and granted as follows—that whenever the body or bones of the same father shall be brought to our church for burial, we, or our successors, shall receive the same body and remains and cause them to be borne, processionally, as is the custom in the burials of the archbishops, and placed solemnly in the said tomb or mausoleum." The archbishop carried out with a care which indicates the fear which the popular preaching of the day inspired, the constitution of his predecessor to prohibit preaching without a licence. The growing fear of Lollardism is thus again indicated, and is farther illustrated by a letter of the archbishop for the purgation of one John Barton, a physician of London, " long-time charged in London and elsewhere with heresy and Lollardism." Another

P

absolution for the same charge (on March 31, 1420), and processes taken against various heretics, remind us that the impending danger was only averted for a season. We find in this and several earlier registers frequent entries relating to the removal of the feasts of the dedication of the churches of the diocese to more convenient days—a precedent which might well be followed by those who are reviving this long extinct observation. Archbishop Chicheley died in 1442, and was succeeded by John Stafford, translated from Bath and Wells. The light thrown upon the diocese at this point becomes faint indeed. The frequent ordinations made in various places in the diocese, to both the lesser and greater orders, fill a large portion of this register, and indicate the fact that, however the monastic system had become weakened by its contact with the increased learning and civilization of the age, the ranks of the secular clergy were still well filled.

The wills which are incorporated with the other records of the see become occasionally invested with a more general and public interest. We find the well-known author of the " Provinciale," John Lyndwode, official of the court of Canterbury, and keeper of the privy seal of the archbishop, after directing his interment in the chapel of St. Stephen, Westminster, where he received his " consecration," adding this provision : " Also I will that the book which I have compiled on the Provincial Constitutions shall have chains and iron clasps put upon it, that it may be kept safe and sound in the upper part of the chapel, or else in the vestry."

Whether this useful provision was carried out or the
book preserved to our day, the historians of the palace
of Westminster can best determine.   Very remarkable,
and illustrative of the growing luxury of the age, is the
will of the Duke of Exeter ; while in touching contrast
to its costly directions stands the will of the Duke of
Suffolk—" My wretched body to be beryed in my
charterhouse, where I wol myn ymage and stone to
be made, and the ymage of my best beloved wyf by
me, she to be there with me if she lust."

Stafford was succeeded in 1452 by John Kempe,
afterwards cardinal, whose primacy, lasting for less than
two years, is as sterile in its fruits for the diocese as it
was brief in its duration.   He was succeeded by Thomas
Bourchier, of the great house of the Earls of Ewe,
representing also the historic family of the Bohuns,
Earls of Hereford.   Whether the state of the diocese
was exceptionally bad at this period (which is but too
likely from the neglects of the primacy of Chicheley
and Stafford, and the brief reign of Kempe which
succeeded them, which left little opportunity for
diocesan inspection), or, on the other hand, the new
archbishop was merely fulfilling a formal and perfunctory office (for which, however, we do not observe
any direct precedent), we find among his first acts a
commission addressed to his principal official "to
reform the crimes and excesses of the clergy and laity
of the diocese of Canterbury."   Reversing at this
point the policy of his predecessor, Courtenay, he
added to the palaces belonging to the see the magnificent house of Knole, in Sevenoke, which, as it lies
within a few miles of the palace of Otford, upon

whose extension and reparation so much had been already spent, and so vast a sum was afterwards expended by Warham, was a most unnecessary and burdensome addition to the heavy charges on the primacy. He had the honour of crowning King Edward IV., and afterwards of marrying him to Elizabeth Woodville, the year after which he entertained the king and queen at Canterbury for several days together with great magnificence. His long primacy of thirty·two years appears to have left the diocese much as he found it; and although an increase of church-building and restoration was the natural fruit of so long an episcopate, as the wills in the registry at Canterbury indicate, the spiritual condition of the people remained apparently unadvanced or at least gave no proofs of increased activity. He was succeeded in 1486 by John Morton, also afterwards cardinal, who is more celebrated for his singular fidelity to King Henry VI. in all his troubles than for his devotion to the higher duties of his spiritual office. He had contributed largely to the buildings of the see by repairing and increasing his houses of Knole, Maidstone, Aldington, Charing, Ford, Lambeth, and Canterbury, and the central tower of the cathedral was chiefly his work. He died at the first-mentioned of these manors in 1500, and was succeeded by Henry Dene or Denny, who, dying in the beginning of 1502, before his enthronisation, left only the record of his name in the history of the diocese. To him succeeded the justly eminent Archbishop Warham, the precursor of the Reformation, whose primacy is the link which connects the close of the feudal system with the comparative freedom of modern times. With him the learning and life of the primacy may be said to revive ; and the friend and patron of Erasmus was also the first to break off the yoke of that foreign allegiance against which England had so long vigorously, but vainly, contended. He was enthroned at Canterbury with even unusual splendour, the last glories of ecclesiastical feudalism shedding their lustre upon its final scene. In 1509, he entertained the king with the wonted magnificence of archiepiscopal hospitality, and two years after entered upon that important visitation of his diocese which from the peculiar bearing it has upon our history will be described in a separate chapter. At the present time, and in order to prepare the reader for the later history of the see, it will be well to examine, as far as our space permits, the civil and social changes which during the fifteenth century passed over the face of the diocese, and which will best prepare us for the great reconstruction it experienced in the days of the Reformation. We have already seen how large was the proportion of the estates of the Church in Kent at the period of the Domesday Survey to those of the other great feudatories of the Crown. They not only extended throughout the country in every direction, but were by far larger in their territorial extent than any of the manors held by lay owners. The very few tenants under the Crown mentioned under Kent, in Domesday, were increased considerably by the breaking-up of the great estate of the Bishop of Bayeux, whose 184 lordships were confiscated on his disgrace, and granted to new favourites. Fifty-seven manors, however (as Mr. Furley observes), alone remained in lay hands even after this great change, forty-nine of which fell to the lot of Hugo de Montfort. The sub-infeudations (or holdings under the first grantee) as far as we find them recorded in the Survey, were less numerous under the ecclesiastical than under the civil lords, and a vast extent of the property of the archbishops was held in Demesne, managed doubtless as it was in the thirteenth and later centuries by bailiffs and seneschals, while the principal manors of the monasteries, being assigned to different objects connected with the monastic life, were managed much in the same manner. The result was that a vast portion of Kent was peopled by a very impoverished class of inhabitants, a result which the destitution described at Wrotham and Lyminge in the letter of Peckham vividly illustrates. During this earlier period we can discern no intermediate class between the great feudal nobility and the tenants who held under them, either immediately or as sub-feudatories. When, however, these great houses, the Montforts, the Clares, the Sayes, the Leybournes, the Badlesmeres, and others were represented by co-heiresses, which was generally the case in two or three generations, their properties became divided ; and a change took place in the county which tended to enlarge the number of the resident nobility, and to bring a general accession of prosperity to those parts of it in which the lay holders of land predominated. It was not, however, thus with the great estates of the Church, which, though divided by sub-infeudations almost as largely as the lay-feuds, could not be so easily relieved of the pressure of a lord-paramount, or convey to a tenant so secure and permanent a position as was given by the actual division of the estate, or by an hereditary connection between the tenant and the feudal lord. Under the shadow of the Church and the greater earls and barons a second rank of nobility had gradually sprung up, whose origin can be traced to the Domesday period, and which formed the nucleus of those great knightly families which dominated in the county when the massive estates which were centred in the few names mentioned in the Survey were broken up. The number of holders under the few churches or families between whom the whole of Kent is parcelled out in Domesday, appear very clearly in that Survey, but their names have in most instances no distinct mention. We find, however, in these the ancestors of that second dynasty of mighty families who were celebrated in the county during the thirteenth and fourteenth centuries, and who became, with very few exceptions, absolutely extinct in the middle of the fifteenth century. A very important cause was added in this century to the natural process of extinction through failure of the male line, which had operated in the case of the earliest nobility. The power of transferring land which previously was incapable of alienation, together with the great increase of personal property by means of mercantile adventure or agricultural success, produced a revolution in the state of the county and of the diocese which it is difficult fully to estimate. We may instance the progress of this transition in the history of the now extinct family of Hardres, deriving its name from the ancient village of Upper Hardres, near Canterbury, which held a feud under the arch-bishop, in his manor of Lyminge, at the time of the Conquest.[1] Their principal lands were held under the great family of the Clares, whose chevron is borne over the lion rampant of their own arms, to denote this feudal relation.   As the greater house failed they naturally held a place in the foremost rank of the newer nobility, and carried on their male line until the close of the last century, when their ancient inheritance passed away into the hands of strangers. But they were among the last representatives of this second dynasty, the Pluckleys, Surrendens, and Hautes, having failed in the male line three cen-turies before, while the Peyforers, the Sandwiches, the Northwodes, the Septvans, the Leybournes, and a number of knightly houses had passed away at even an earlier period.   Upon the ruins of these greater houses came in the ancient families which have since gained so great a celebrity in the political history of the county—the Derings succeeding to three of these families by a fortunate marriage in the middle of the fifteenth century,[2] the Knatchbulls purchasing their estate at the same period; the Brockmans acquiring first Shuttlefield, and then

---

[1] Robertus de Hardres is described in a register of the manor of Christchurch cotemporary with the Domesday-book.

[2] The authentic pedigree of the Derings in the male line begins at this period. See the full pedigree in the "Arch. Cant." (vol. x. p. 327).

Beachborough ; while many other ancient houses, both in East and West Kent, became prominent at the same period. But the mention of these names recalls to the mind so forcibly the eloquent words of the late lamented antiquary and genealogist, whose loss to the county and diocese can never be repaired, the Rev. Lambert Larking, in his Inaugural Address on the formation of the Kent Archæological Society, that we cannot but fall back upon them here ; "Hence," he writes, "in earlier days sprang the Nevills, the Maminots, the Says, the De Crescies, the Clares, the Crevecœurs, the De Chilhams, De Thurnhams, De Leybournes, the Averenches, the De Burghs, the Criols, the Rokesles, the Cobhams, the Malmaynes, the Beauchamps, the Greys, the Poynings, the Valorigns, the Strabolgies, the Badles-meres, the Northwoods, the Peches, the Freming-hams, and Hauts. Hence, in after ages, sprang the Wyats, the St. Legers, the Cheynes, the Bulleyns, the Sydneys, the Guldefords, the Ropers, the Isleys, the Woottons, the Moyles, the Hales, the Cromers, the Harts, the Bretts, the Levesons, the Scotts, the Roberts, the Kempes, the Monins, the Twysdens, the Derings, the Knatchbulls, the Tokes, the Darells, the Colepepers, the Walsinghams, and Fanes. Hence, too, the Astleys, the Richmond Stuarts, the Sack-villes, the Finches, the Vanes, the Filmers, the Maneys, the Brockmans, the Tuftons, the Botelers, the Clerks, the Selbys—the men who at all periods stood up for the freedom of England at home, and her aggrandizement abroad. With such examples as these to look back upon, we may be forgiven our attachment to the past; our reverence for the homes which gave birth to such men, and that home-loving and homely feeling which characterized their lives in its most chivalrous aspect."[1] The reader will observe the kind of stratification in the ancient nobility and gentry of the county which Mr. Larking, with almost the discriminating eye of a geologist, here so distinctly marks, and how gradually that ancient landed aristocracy which unhappily is so rapidly passing away in Kent, was formed. The rapid disintegration of the Domesday Settlement is sometimes attributed to the system of the equal division of land, known under the name of gavelkind, but this is an insufficient cause, as most of the larger estates were early "disgavelled," and entailed in the ordinary way. We may safely conclude that that third stage of our social history which exhibits the first ground-plan of its present structure, and which was laid down in the middle and at the close of the fifteenth century, was mainly the result of the causes we have previously suggested, and tended very greatly to prepare the diocese for that great religious change by which the feudal power of the Church was as entirely broken up as that of the lay feudatories of an earlier day. From the many indications given us in the parochial history of the diocese, and which the reader of Hasted and of the local papers in the "Kent Archæologia" will readily recall, the state of the church-manors and parishes was far below that of those under lay influence at this period. On the former there were scarcely any residents who could

[1] "Arch. Cant." tom. i., introd. p. 17.

be called opulent, or even independent, and though
the interest taken in the churches was remarkably
displayed in the constant bequests left to them in
the wills, even of the poorest holders of land, from
1390 to 1500, whether in the lay or ecclesiastical
parishes, the comparative opulence of the former is
everywhere visible, and the churches and manors
farmed for the archbishops and sinecure rectors fared
far worse than those held by or under a lay-proprie-
tor. A resident gentry had, in fact, sprung up in
the middle of the fifteenth century having an interest
in the diocese as well as in the county, which could
not have well been awakened either in the distant
and non-resident primates, or in their often needy
and always unprogressive tenantry. The amount of
park and woodland which still covered a large portion
of East Kent, rendered large districts unproductive
except for fuel and game, while the gradual severance
of the dennes in West Kent from the East Kent
manors impoverished the inhabitants of the latter
district, and offered another obstacle to their progress. The great pilgrimages to the shrine of Becket
had reached their culminating point in the previous
century, and the tide which had once set in, not only
from the different parts of England but of the Continent, and which had once flowed so freely, was now
on the ebb.[1] The visits of the archbishops to the

---

[1] A great number of Nuremberg tokens, and similar inferior
money, found in many parishes in East Kent, and most probably
dropped by pilgrims, indicates a poorer class of visitors to the
favoured shrine than that which bestowed such priceless gifts
upon it in an earlier day.

cathedral city had become fewer and shorter, and
the office of diocesan was becoming rather an appendage to the primacy than a co-ordinate dignity,
as it was in earlier days. At the same time, it
cannot fail to be observed that the absorption of
nearly all the churches of the see into the patronage
of the archbishop, or of the religious houses, prevented that strong tie being formed between the
higher laity and the clergy which is so valuable a
result of private patronage, and tends so much to
awaken the interest and promote the liberality of the
laity.[1] Even late in the fifteenth century the bequests for church purposes were generally given in
kind, as we shall see presently illustrated in the
complaints of their non-payment in Warham's visitation. On the whole, a survey of the period comprised in this chapter leads us to regard the later
portion of it as in all respects as much a transition
period in its social and ecclesiastical history as it was
in its architectural development. In regard to the
outward fabric of the church which this comparison
suggests, we may observe that the style which is
termed (from the tendency of the lines of its window
tracery, and the comparatively debased forms of its

[1] The proportion of private to public patronage in the
present day in the original parishes of the diocese is about 109
to 270, but many of the livings originally belonging to the
archbishops were surrendered by Cranmer, and at a later period,
rendering the disproportion more apparent. With very few
exceptions, all the largest are in the gift of the archbishop, not
even those connected with the most ancient residences in the
county (as Pluckley, Mersham, Great and Little Chart, Leeds,
Godmersham, and others) being in lay hands.

mouldings and characteristic ornaments) the "Perpendicular" style, became universally prevalent from the time of Bourchier and Morton, and almost all the churches in Kent present some features of reparation, and often of extensive reconstruction, peculiar to this style. The extreme difficulty of moulding the native stone into the more graceful curvilinear features of the previous period probably made this style earlier in Kent than in most other counties. We observe in one or two places, and notably in the beautiful gate of Christ Church which leads into the precincts, an attempted imitation of the "flamboyant" style, which was coeval with the so-called "Perpendicular" on the Continent. But this, unless the softer Caen stone was within reach, could never become acclimatized in Kent, where the intractable nature of the material compelled the masons, even of the "Decorated" period, to confine themselves to the massive and plain octagonal columns which are to be found so commonly dividing the nave from the aisles in the churches of East Kent. The flood of light which was thrown upon the Norman and "Early English" churches by the insertion of the large Decorated and Perpendicular windows of the fourteenth and fifteenth centuries, not only illustrates the increased security of the worshippers from the fear of assailants, but fitly symbolizes that approach to a more enlightened and intelligent worship which appeals to the ear and to the understanding rather than to the eye—a change heralding the approach of the age of reading and printing which the primacy of Archbishop Morton was the earliest to witness, and that of his successor saw so fully developed in the presses of Frobenius and the literary labours of Erasmus, which they recorded for all time. Yet the fatal estrangement between the clergy and the laity in the diocese and in the country was rather increased than removed by the reviving learning of the age. The cruel persecutions with which the Lollards had been in a manner hunted down by Arundel, and even by his more enlightened successors, had led·the people to regard prelacy much in the light in which their Puritan descendants regarded episcopacy in the days of Laud. The vast wealth and pomp of the prelates and of the regular clergy, who were under the obligation of poverty, draws forth the severest censure from the popular religious writers of the age. ·In the treatise of the Carmelite Henry Parker, in the reign of Edward IV.,[1] after the description of the earlier bishops of the Church, we find them thus contrasted with the prelates of the time : " But now God may say, Prelates have reygned in holy churche but not of me, ne by my plesance. I made them not, I chose them not. . . . . For prelates for the most parte seke more their owne profite thanne the profite of man's soule. Such prelates and curates be not faders of the people, but wolves of raven that devoure Goddes people *sicut escam panis*" (p. 147). Of their negligence in their spiritual duties he complains elsewhere. " There is neither bishoppe, ne prelate, ne curate, ne preacher that will speke ayenste the vices and errors that been so highe ayenst Goddis wor-

---

[1] London, Berthelet, 1536.

shyppe. And so by misuse and sleuth (sloth) of men of holy churche, vice is taken for vertue, and error for treuthe, the fende is worshypped, and God is despised " (p. 69).

Such is the picture drawn by a not unfriendly hand of that Church of which the archbishops of Canterbury were the recognised head, and of which their diocese might be expected to present the most perfect type. It may well prepare us for the apparent indifference with which the men of Kent beheld the crushing blows which fell upon the religious houses which had so ill fulfilled their trust, and on the vast estates of the primacy, which had rather tended to promote the temporal and spiritual poverty of its tenants than to advance their interests in soul and body. Such was the state of the age which preceded the Reformation, and the picture of the diocese as it comes before the eye in the visitation of Archbishop Warham tends to confirm the impression which the words of the English Carmelite cannot fail to convey to the unprejudiced mind.

CHAPTER VI.

THE DAWN OF THE REFORMATION.

At no period of the history of the diocese can we obtain so perfect a view of its religious and social state as in the year 1511, during which Archbishop Warham, in the eighth year of his primacy, made a general visitation of it, the record of which, carefully condensed by the late Mr. Maitland, discloses the exact condition both of the conventual houses and of the parish churches and foundations throughout the county. The editor of it, by whom it was communicated (unfortunately in irregular fragments) to the " British Magazine,"[1] observes that not only is its ecclesiastical interest very remarkable, but that it supplies materials of great value to the philological, the antiquarian, the topographical, and genealogical student. It begins with the visitation of the monasteries and conventual foundations of the diocese, including also the hospitals and other charitable establishments, and this is given throughout in Latin. It then proceeds with the visitation of the parishes grouped together under their respective deaneries, and these, as the inquiries and returns are given in English, have an obvious interest

---

[1] Vols. xxix. xxx. xxxi. xxxii.

to the philological student.   The visitation of the
monasteries begins with that of Christ Church, whose
members are given by name under the certificate of
the prior, and include one or two of historical interest, memorably those of Richard Deryng and
Edward Bokyng, who were executed as the principal
instigators of the imposture of the famous Elizabeth
Barton, the "Holy Maid of Kent," in 1533—a fate
which was shared by Richard Master, the successor
of Erasmus in the rectory of Aldington, and one in
which even the archbishop himself was all but entangled on account of the encouragement he was supposed to have given to the prophecies of the unfortunate victim of the political intrigues of those in a
much higher station.

The celebrated Cuthbert Tonstal, chancellor of
the archbishop, accompanied him throughout his visitation, which began on the 9th of September, in the
chapter-house of the cathedral, after mass of the Holy
Ghost, and a Latin sermon on the appropriate text,
"Behold and visit this vine" (Ps. lxxx. 14).   On the
next day the archbishop sat judicially in the same
place, and after enjoining the prior and other officers
to reform some general defects which had been found
in the house before the following 1st of April, he sat
in the chapel of the palace to visit the chaplains of the
several chantries, who exhibited their letters of orders
and letters of institution of their chantries.   The
Priory of St. Gregory was next visited (Sept. 11th).
A sermon was preached by John Thorneton, afterwards prior of St. Martin's *Novi Operis* at Dover, on
the text, "Wherefore standest thou without? for I

have prepared the house " (Gen. xxiv. 31). This
visitation revealed some of those internal dissensions
which exhibit the weak side of the conventual life of
that period, in which the zeal and devotion which
gave the first impulse to the religious orders had so
completely died out. William Tailor, the " pre-
ceptor," is accused of sowing strife and discord
among the brethren, and is accordingly admonished
by the archbishop. The Priory of St. Sepulchre, a
foundation of nuns, was next visited, after a sermon
on the text, " Hearken, O daughter, and consider,
and incline thine ear " (Ps. xlv. 10). The prioress
confesses that they do not rise to matins in the middle
of the night, but at daybreak, because the enclosures
of the convent are under repair, and great tumults
were heard around the church. The House of the
Sisters of St. James was visited on the same day by
the chancellor. The prioress, who was eighty-four
years old, was charged by the sisters—two of whom
were past eighty—with defaming their character, to
the great scandal of the house. The visitor admonished her accordingly against using contumelious
words, requiring the sisters to be obedient to her rule,
as required by their profession. The collegiate
church of Wingham was next visited, after a sermon
from a text which seems rather singularly chosen for
the occasion, " Though ye have lien among the pots,
&c. ;" although as several of the houses of the canons
were in a ruinous condition, and called for injunctions to repair them from the archbishop, there would
seem to be some grounds for the selection of such a
theme. At this visitation one or two suggestive cir-

cumstances are to be noted. None of the canons resided at his own house and kept his own table, which was contrary to their statutes ; almost all the houses were in a state of disrepair ; several canons exhibited letters of orders and dispensations, which " were nothing to the purpose," and so were peremptorily ordered to cease from performing service ; others appear as pluralists ; others complain that the benefices which they ought to have had are given to strangers. This visitation called for many admonitions of the archbishop. The Convent of St. Martin at Dover was visited on Sept. 18th, after a sermon from the very doubtful text, " Nosce tempus," probably an excerpt from the words " Non est vestrum *nosse tempora*." The inquiry disclosed the fact that the monastery was in many places ruinous ; that the constant access of the brethren to the town produced great irregularity and many scandals. Complaints are made of the mayor and townsmen, who seem to have been on ill terms with the monks ; the third prior is accused of punishing the novices for small and trifling offences, and even inventing charges against them. Complaint is made that they have linen instead of woollen sheets, as the rule of St. Benedict requires, also that there is no teacher to instruct them in grammar. On all these points the archbishop gives precise and strict injunctions. The house called the Maison Dieu, at Dover, was then visited, but the complaints in this case are comparatively trifling. The Priory of Folkestone was visited on the 22nd of the same month. Here also nothing worthy of note is mentioned. Then followed the visitation of the

College of Wye, where also nothing noteworthy occurs. The Nunnery of Davington passes a good examination, while the Domus Dei at Ospringe is found to have dwindled down into a mere sinecure, the master or *custos* being its sole representative. He wisely submits himself and his hospital to the reformation and ordinance of the archbishop, who adjourns his visitation to Feversham. This convent appears to have presented a very degenerate state. Eatables and drinkables are withdrawn from the poor and given by the monks to their friends; women have ingress and egress into the cloister; the food is not duly served in the refectory; the abbot is charged with extreme severity to a monk, who had been reduced in consequence to great necessity. Another complains that the butler and all the monks are hostile to him; while the sacrist is charged with being so contumelious and quarrelsome that he creates discord among the monks. Another complains that sufficient clothes are not provided him; while the butler is again accused of ill-behaviour, and of conducting himself more like a master than a servant. The cellarer is accused of spoiling the food for the refectory, it being scarcely half-boiled or roasted. Altogether, the picture of this important house is not an inviting one, and it may well point a moral to those who too anxiously desire to see the revival of monastic life in England. The view of the Priory of Leeds has features which are still less attractive. The prior is accused of acts of violence and outrage, one of the brethren charging him with laying violent hands on him and treading him under foot. He therefore naturally prays that the prior may

not in future lay hands and feet on his brethren (non
mittat manus et pedes in confratres suos).   The archbishop gives the necessary admonitions and injunctions in this as in the previous cases, which indicates
the fact that they had been sufficiently proved.   The
Nunnery of Minster in Sheppey next underwent examination.   The chief complaint here was the want of
a female servant ("a convente servante") to serve
them with food, and as a nurse in sickness.   The
prioress is enjoined to find one, and also to bring up
the number of her nuns to fourteen.   The fact that
the nunneries of England were failing in numbers
shows that the taste for a conventual life was gradually dying out, and prepares us (among many
other causes) for the general apathy with which
the dissolution, already impending, was received by
the people.   The visitation of the College of Maidstone contains nothing of special interest.   That of
the Priory of Cumbwell indicates the same decadence of monastic life and observance which was instanced at Feversham.   There are the same complaints of violence, of neglect in the matter of food
and raiment, of inattention to the care of the sick,
of educational destitution, of disrepair of the buildings, which we have found elsewhere, and the same
injunctions to amend all these particulars by a fixed
time.   We now pass from the conventual to the parochial portion of the visitation, which to us is far more
interesting, not only from the light which it throws
upon the present state of the diocese, but also from
the fact that it is written in English, and gives a vivid
retrospect of social and parochial life in Kent at this

period. We need not here follow the archbishop in his progress through the various deaneries into which the diocese was then, as now, divided. We shall better fulfil our purpose by regarding the visitation in its three principal features : those of the **fabric of the Church, with the** incidents connected with it ; **the ministry of the Church, and** the disclosures relating to it ; **and the religious and social** state of the parishes as it reveals itself to us in the course of the visitation. In regard to the first of these subjects, we are led to the conclusion that the portion of the Church which depended upon the parishioners for its support and reparation was generally in a very satisfactory state. With a few exceptions the complaints are here confined to the state of the windows and their glazing, or of the roof, but we rarely find the dilapidation to be of a serious kind. Ivychurch is a striking exception, where the churchwardens complain that "the parish church is sorely decayed, and likely to fall down ; " while Eastry Church is said to "need great reparations." The duty of the rectors and impropriators of the great tithe appears to have been far less carefully fulfilled. The ruin and dilapidation of the chancels are a constant subject of complaint. The neglect is most conspicuous in the case of those churches which belonged to the monasteries and religious foundations, whose representatives are admonished to repair them without fail within a certain time. Equally negligent are the executors of the wills of those benevolent parishioners who left money or cattle or grain towards the reparation of churches, or in order to found in them obits either temporary or perpetual. From the earliest period to which the wills in the Registry of Canterbury extend, we find innumerable bequests left for the reparation of churches or roads, or public works of other kinds, and for the celebration of religious services, or the provision for lamps and candles at the various altars with which every church more or less abounded.   These gifts appear to have been continually delayed or appropriated, and the executors of the wills under which they were given were accordingly summoned to give account of them and to promise their immediate restitution.   On some occasions the existence of them is denied and the counterclaim admitted, but in most cases the churchwardens are described as being in treaty with the parties interested. A curious feature in these returns is the farming-out of cows and kine for the benefit of the church, a provision which is necessarily precarious, and offers a great temptation to the farmers of them to turn them to their own profit.   Thus the Church of St. Dunstan in Canterbury purchases a cow "to be put to farm for the behoof of the church, the money for the purchase of it having been withdrawn, and the cow also." Two kine and another cow are put out to farm for the same church, but those who had to procure them died in such poverty as to make the churchwardens return the cases as "desperate."   This is a very frequent case in these returns.   But if the beneficial keeping of cattle is thus "withdrawn" from the church, the injurious results of cattle of another kind are no less pathetically detailed.   The churchyards seem very generally to be unfenced and "haunted with hogs," or, as it is elsewhere expressed, "embruid and foul with beasts that goeth to pasture there." A curious complaint occurs from Barham, " That the trees in the churchyard are an impediment to them that bear the cross in procession, insomuch that it cannot be borne upright for the boughs." Many other nuisances are reported and removed, but the most important result of the visitation in regard to the temporal interests of the Church was the restitution of a large amount of real property which had been abstracted and appropriated, and which, under the terrible threat of excommunication, was restored to it on this occasion.

The state of the ministers of the Church is no less diligently inquired into and reported upon. First, we have the charge of non-residence, which under various circumstances continually recurs. Notwithstanding the ordination of perpetual vicarages in almost all the churches in Kent, where a resident rector was not established, a number of cures appear still to have been served by itinerants from the monasteries, and canons of the several foundations, by which abuse the people were deprived of all spiritual comfort in regard to parochial visitation and relief. Thus the Church of Holy Cross, Westgate, returns that " there is no secular priest that serveth the cure these three years, but the Prior of St. Gregory's of Canterbury causeth one of his own canons to serve it, the which goeth to the priory every night, and when we should have him, oftentimes it is required in the night season, we cannot have him." The same charge is made against the same prior in regard to the Church of Thanington. In the Church of Sibertswould, of

which the Prior of St. Radegund was impropriator, a
singular conflict between the regular and secular
priest is recorded. The archbishop had augmented
the vicarage which sorely displeased the canons—one
of whom " came unto me," complains the vicar, "and
spake many opprobrious and contumelious words
openly, and said, 'Thou priest, what doest thou here
in our church? get thee hence or we shall pluck thee
out by the head ; howbeit thou beareth thee bold, and
was instituted by my lord of Canterbury, he hath
nought to do here, for we are exempt from him, and
so tell him '—with many more words long to re-
hearse." The abbot and convent intended an appeal
to Rome, in this instance, certainly, hardly a " centre
of unity." At Monk's Horton "the parson had
not been among the people for five years," and
having been called to residence by the archbishop,
did not appear, and was therefore deprived. The
complaints of non-residence were numerous in the
more distant and rural parishes, and appear to have
been always proved. In the case of Ivychurch the
" parson " is described as " an outlandish man, who
has never come among us sith his induction." Neglect of duty is another charge of frequent recurrence,
and one which naturally arose from non-residence ;
while pluralities are another just cause of complaint.
Exactions in matters of tithe and offerings occur
not unfrequently, while in some cases the moral
character of the clergy is very severely animadverted
upon. In not a few, their social asperities are matter
of curious complaint. Thus the Vicar of Stodmarsh
is complained of as " sometimes malicious and looking

on his neighbours with a grym and sower countenance
where they think him, God knoweth, no hurt." The
Vicar of Bridge is accused of "giving no rights
(?rites) to them that will not content his mind,
and when they do not agree with him after his
pleasure." Almost all these subjects are entered into
judicially, and the result is generally a solemn admoni-
tion to amend, accompanied by the threat of excommunication in case of a continued delinquency. The
state of the people was naturally affected both socially
and religiously by the decadence which this visitation
reveals in that of the clergy. The neglect of the
services of the Church is one of its more immediate results. Some (as St. Dunstan's, Canterbury), "keep the
tavern and alehouses" in the times of service—others
resort to the monastic churches instead of their proper
parishes; one is accused of "letting the people of
their devotions;" another of neglecting to furnish a
" pair of silver shoes for the Roode of Chislet "—left
charged upon a certain house. The failure to render
an account of legacies left to the various churches,
and the complaints that they are never satisfied, fill
a very large portion of these returns. The reader
unacquainted with the vast collection of early wills
in the Registry of Canterbury, would be surprised at
the number and sometimes the amount of bequests
for every imaginable purpose connected with the
Church. The visitation of Warham shows how very
seldom these were carefully accounted for and secured
to the several churches at this time. Masses and
obits appear to have been neglected very commonly—
and those who have seen the almost fabulous account

of the masses which were thus neglected even in Italy in the last century— which in the single Church of St. John and St. Paul at Venice amounted, in 1743, to 16,400—and in that of the Madonna dell 'Orto to 14,300,[1] will hardly wonder at the more moderate defalcations of the fifteenth century in England. Some are charged with not assisting to pay the salary of the parish clerk, and several of the returns refer to that official now so generally dispensed with. A man who is charged with "laying violent hands upon his ghostly father for asking his tithes" (Seasalter) is remitted to the common law, at which, instead of in the ecclesiastical court, the vicar is prosecuting him. An interesting instance is here presented of the manner in which the canon law had been superseded, even in a matter which a century or two before would have exclusively dealt with crimes against the clergy. One Valentine Cole is charged with "troubling the Church by reason of his evil disposition," who is accordingly enjoined, "ut sit in Ecclesiâ orans sedendo non fabulando aut garrulando" — (Herne). The Church of Knowlton is remarkable for having only a single parishioner from time immemorial. He is, however, required to procure a chalice for the church, which hitherto had only borrowed one. At Elham, Thomas Rigdon is accused of "letting the people from their devotions because drinking in the church is put down." At Willesborough a similar complaint is made—indicating that the practice of drinking in

---

[1] See the "Scrittura del Segretario Pietri Franceschi sopra le messe testamentarie," addressed to the Councillor of State, Marc Antonio Grimani, in 1763.

the church at obits and other celebrations had been
recently prohibited in the diocese. In the will of
Thomas Duffyn, vicar of Lyminge (1508), a sum of
money is left to build a place for the regaling of the
parishioners at the anniversaries—doubtless with a
view to supply the need occasioned by this prohibition.
Among the complaints against laymen for withholding
the goods of the Church, we not unfrequently find
cases in which chalices were thus held in lay keeping.
In all these a promise is given to restore the articles
thus held in pawn, but a suspicion naturally arises
that they were held as pledges for money lent either
to the parish or the minister.   Dr. Maitland amusingly
notes that while Sir John Russell is charged with thus
withholding a chalice, Sir Robert Pele, vicar of Chilham, is accused of withholding a legacy.   At Wye
we have the case of a man impeding the celebration
of matrimony between a certain couple, and menacing
the priest, saying, "If thou ax them any more here,
I will styk thee."   A terrible series of charges is made
against one Richard Ricards, of Kennington, who
has threatened to slay the vicar, has slain a man, with
many other serious accusations—all which he denied,
and is required to "clear himself with six honest men
of his neighbours."   In many cases the charges
appear to have little or no foundation, while in others
the parties are remitted to the archbishop, or the
cause is adjourned.   Numberless charges of scandal
are brought both against clergymen and laymen, and
many again are charged with being slanderers and
propagators of slander.   A number of curious illustrations of the religious life of the diocese appear in

this visitation. We find days mentioned which are evidently rather of local than general celebration, as " hopp monday " (Little Mongeham), " Relic Sunday," under Rolvenden. The latter was the day appointed for pilgrimage to the relics—probably to Becket's shrine. The vicar is reported to have declared that for " every foot that a man or a woman set to the relics-ward he should have great pardon." Whereupon John Baylis replied to his wife who told him this, " He said so because he will have folk's money ; " a very sensible speech for days of greater enlightenment, but born at this time out of due season. He accordingly had to purge himself *quartâ manu*, as the phrase was—in other words, by four witnesses lay and cleric. The failure to provide books and ornaments for the church is another frequent accusation, the graduals and antiphoners being chiefly in request. Books containing masses for new festivals are wanting in some churches, viz. the Feast of the Visitation, of the Transfiguration, and of the Name of Jesus (Great Chart, &c.) Surplices are wanting in many churches, and rochets in others. The "farmers of the rectories" who have constantly to appear to answer to charges of neglect, appear to have left the churches under their care in a very dilapidated state. The poverty into which the diocese had fallen at this time is perhaps one of the most remarkable of the circumstances which this visitation disclosed. The support of a Church whose ritual observances and ceremonial were so expensive, fell heavily on the poorer parishes of the diocese, and the bequests of very many in this behalf fail on account of the poverty, and even

destitution, of those who left them in the vain hope
that their limited means were equal to such a burden.
The fact that pews and regular sittings in churches
belonged to this period, and even to a much earlier
one, is indicated not only by numerous wills in the
Registry of Canterbury during the fifteenth century,
but by a petition of the inhabitants of Minster in
Sheppey that they might remove the effigies of a
knight and his wife, "and lay in the place a plain
stone with an epitaphy, that the people may make
setts and pewys where they may more quietly serve
God." The Church of Middleton (or Milton) had a
simple rood "that lacketh Mary and John." This
important defect has of course to be restored. A
certain widow holds the erroneous opinion (which,
however, she denies) that "whensoever she shall curse
by these words, I curse thee by St. Germayne's curse,
they shall never prosper in bodily health nor in goods."
She escapes on her denial; but James Morris, in the
parish of Sutton Valence, has to undergo a severe
penance, being enjoined "to go before the processions
made in the Church of Sutton, on the three following
Sundays, bareheaded and barefooted, wearing only a
shirt, and holding in his hand a taper, value 2d.; and
that on the third Sunday, after the Gospel should
have been read at high mass, at the time when
Christians offer, he should humbly and devoutly offer
the said taper into the hands of the officiating minister."

Our space will not admit of the examination of all
the details of this remarkable visitation, which exhibits
the state of the diocese in the period immediately
preceding the Reformation. Those who look back

upon the pre-Reformation Church with too lively a regret, might learn from it that the former days were not so far better than those in which they live. They were days of transition, which we are too apt to neglect when estimating the work of the Reformation and the changes it brought about, apparently with so much suddenness, but truly by many and gradual stages of development. Already in the age of Warham the ties between England and Rome, so often severely strained, and at several periods almost entirely broken, were giving way almost imperceptibly in the scene of Rome's earliest conquest. In the constantly recurring complaints during this visitation of the refusal or neglect to pay " Peter's pence," and in the rash threat of the Canon of St. Radegund's to carry his appeal to Rome, we see the symptoms of a change of feeling, which present a striking contrast to the devotion with which the Anglo-Saxon converts in Kent regarded the Roman Church. We are apt, perhaps, to forget in this contrast the fact that a new power had sprung up in what we term the " Court of Rome " which might have led even the docile Saxons, had it developed itself in their day, to an open rupture with the see which was under so terrible and galling a yoke. We cannot wonder in any case that if Warham so soon after shook off his allegiance to the Roman primacy, his diocese even at an earlier moment should have found their obedience to it giving way ; and that when the power of the regular clergy was broken down by the dissolution of the monasteries, the secular clergy should have sided with the primate, in opposition to the Papacy which had made the yoke of monasticism

so oppressive to them. The character of the gentle
and courtly Warham, whose portrait has been drawn
for us by the hand of Erasmus, was singularly fitted
for this period of transition, and resembles in many
of its features the contemporary life of the great Leo
X., who as the patron of learning became uninten-
tionally the promoter of the Reformation. In the
dedication of his edition of St. Jerome to the primate
who had been his constant friend, Erasmus affirms
that the memory of that great Father could have no
higher honour than its connection with the name of
one who " virtutum omnium episcopalium circulum et
harmoniam mirè temperavit." Of the progress of
England (and we must naturally include the diocese
in this compliment) " in religion, righteousness, and
moral culture," he gives his testimony in this dedication ; which written originally in 1516 he renews in
1533 as a kind of epitaph to the primate that " incomparabilis heros "—" vir ex omni virtutum et orna-
mentorum genere concinnatus." One portion of his
eulogy, though brief, is very significant, and to those
who estimate the labour involved in this visitation in
a day when travelling was comparatively difficult will
be readily appreciable. " Nemo vidit illum nihil agen-
tem." Erasmus, to whom he had given the valuable
rectory of Aldington, must have had ample opportunity
of estimating his conduct in his diocese ; and we may
remember with pleasure the often neglected fact that
Warham was the President of that convocation which
abrogated the Papal authority in England, and was
in a certain sense the first Primate of the Reformation.
The gradual removal of the Papal legislation was

easy after the great principle of the independence of
the English Church was established, for as the rule
of the canon law affirms, " Non firmatur tractu tem-
poris quod de jure ab initio non subsistit ; "—and "quæ
contra jus fiunt, debent utique pro infectis haberi."
The Court of Arches, from which the Canon of St.
Radigund threatened to carry up his appeal to Rome,
had now recovered its natural rights, and the freedom
of the archbishops and of the Church of England
began before the primacy of the " incomparabilis
heros " of Erasmus had closed.

CHAPTER VII.

FROM WARHAM TO PARKER.

THE visitation of the entire diocese by Archbishop
Warham in 1511 may be said to present the last
complete view of its state in the pre-Reformation
period. The church-building zeal which had been
carried on from the close of the twelfth to the beginning of the sixteenth century was now exhausted. If
we may believe the historians and writers of the age,
this zeal had taken a worldly and secular form, and
had become rather a rivalry of towns and villages
and a mark of the increasing luxury of the age than
an indication of that deep religious sentiment which
had first inspired it. The towers of the churches of
the southern districts of Kent, with their beacon-
turrets and manifest contrivances for defence and
security against invasion from the Continent, were
naturally the work of this period or of that immediately preceding it ; and these beacon-turrets formed
a system of coast-guard defence similar to that of the
Martello towers of a later age.[1] In the rare and
remarkable Dialogue, written in the time of King
Edward IV., by Henry Parker, a Carmelite monk of
Doncaster, which we have already cited, we find a
passage which probably expresses too well this deca-

---

[1] The beacons are hence carefully marked in maps of the
time of Elizabeth.

dence, both in the outward work of the Church and
in the spirit which had once animated it :—" If the
makyng of churches and the ornamentes and the
service in this londe were done principally for devocion and for the worshippe of God, I trow this londe
passed all other londes in worshyppinge of God and
holy Churche. But I drede me, that men do it more
for pompe and pride of this worlde to have a name
and worshyppe thereby in the countreye, and for envy
that one towne hathe ayenst another, not for devotion, but for the worshyppe and the name that they
see them have by araye and ournamentes in holy
Churche, or elles by slygh covetyse of men of holy
Churche . . . for the people nowe adays is full
undevout to God and to holy Churche, and they love
but a lytell men of holy Churche, and they ben lothe
for to come in holy Churche when they be bounde to
come thyther, and fulle lothe to here Goddis service.
Late they come, and sone they go awaye. If they
ben there a lytel while, them thinketh full longe.
They have leaver to go to the taverne than to holy
Churche. Leaver to here a songe of Robynhoode or
of some ribaudry than for to here masse or matynes,
or any other of Goddis service or any word of God.
And sythen that the people hath so lyttell devocion
to God and to holy Churche, I canne not see that
they do suche coste in holy Churche for devotion ne
for the love of God. For they despise God day and
nyght with their evylle and wycked lyvynge and their
wycked thewes."[1] When we add to this picture that

---

[1] "Dives and Pauper." London : Berthelet, 1536, p. 69.

of the convents and religious houses, as given by the same impartial witness,[1] we shall easily come to the conclusion that the Reformation was less a violent revolution in the spiritual world than a revival of religious life taking the direction of the Augustinian theology as opposed to the petrified divinity of the schools. The fourteenth and fifteenth centuries had witnessed in the inextinguishable flame of Lollardism, and the extraordinary vitality of the theses and doctrine of Wycliff, the first inspiration of this great movement. In the work we have referred to this popular teaching appears in all its force, very thinly veiled under the scholastic distinctions which abound in the text. The diocese of Canterbury was one of the earliest of those in which, in spite of the almost crushing influence of the archbishops, the new doctrines proved their vitality. Archbishop Arundel had vainly attempted to extinguish it in the terrible dungeons, or rather *oubliettes* of Salt-wood. In the venerable ruins of that castle may be seen to this day the vaults where the persecuted Lollards expiated the then fatal guilt of professing a more spiritual faith than agreed with the worldliness of the age. The succeeding archbishops down to Warham had generally (and in his case most reluctantly) to lend their names and their influence to the reign of persecution, which seemed to the authorities of that day to be the only means left them for resisting the gathering tide of spiritual life and power. As the political divisions of the kingdom and the

---

[1] "Dives and Pauper," pp. 139-142.

power of the collateral branches of the Royal family
had assisted in so great a degree the progress of the
doctrines of Wycliff, so it was ordained that the excesses and even sins of the autocratic Henry should,
by freeing the Church of England from the papal
yoke, bring in the reign of a reformed church and
faith. The inauguration of this great work belonged
not, as is too popularly believed, to Cranmer, but to
Warham himself, who presided over that convocation
in which the papal authority in England was reduced
to that of an ordinary bishopric, and the freedom of
our Church placed upon the same basis as that upon
which the Council of Ephesus established the independence of the island of Cyprus. It is very remarkable that in no diocese of England was this
change effected with such ease as in that of Canterbury—and that the scene in which the papacy was
most absolutely worshipped in the day of the conversion of England, was the first to throw off that
allegiance in the period of the Reformation. But
there are many reasons to account for what must at
first appear to be so difficult to explain satisfactorily.
The first is the immense power of the archbishopric
while its estates were still entire, a power which was
absolutely transferred to the Crown and its most devoted adherents when the vast estates of the Church
were surrendered under the specious pretext of exchanges with the king. To this may be added the
influence which the continental reformers exercised
so specially in Kent, in which their exiles had a
residence, and a freedom of worship assigned them
in Canterbury, Sandwich, Maidstone, and other

places, which could not but be most favourable to the progress of the reformed doctrine. Yet another cause presents itself in the danger which every popish recusant incurred by residing in a county which was so immediately under the eye of the Government, and which on account of its being the place of transit to the Continent was watched by means of a regular *espionage* whose head-quarters were at Dover Castle.[1] But whatever may have been the causes of the early and paramount reign of the principles of the Reformation in Kent, the results are conspicuous and undeniable, for scarcely a recusant of note could be found in the county at periods when they abounded elsewhere. And almost the last of the ancient county families professing the faith of Rome in our day are those of the Darells of Calehill, and of the Hales of Hales-place, near Canterbury.[2] These preliminary observations will tend to prepare us for the great changes which the Reformation effected, both in regard to the spiritual state and to the outward constitution of the diocese. The tokens of this spiritual

[1] There was till recently in the Dering Collection at Surrenden a MS. book containing the correspondence with the Government of the celebrated Sir Edward Dering, of the Long Parliament, when he was Deputy-governor of Dover Castle. From this it appears that every one passing to and from the Continent suspected of Roman tendencies was most carefully watched, and a chaplain to convert recusants was specially appointed for that important place of transit.

[2] The writer made this observation many years since to the late Cardinal Wiseman, who agreed with him that on no other grounds could the sudden and entire alienation of the diocese from the Papacy be accounted for.

revolution became very marked as the primacy of
Warham drew on towards its close. His letters to
Wolsey, with whom his relations were very far from
cordial, and who in everything endeavoured to in-
terrupt his course as primate, were (as a recent
writer[1] has termed them) "grimly civil," and contrast strangely with the jocose letters he addressed to
his friend Erasmus. They discover, however, fears
which were common to both alike of the great movement which was so rapidly extending from Germany
to England. One of them recounts the committal
of a priest (by name Sir Adam Bradshawe) for pulling
down the writings and seals of the papal condemnation of the theses of Luther from the too-famous
Abbey of Boxley. This was in 1522. In the same
year the archbishop mentions his receipt from Dr.
Sampson of the "Lutheriana damnatissima opera," and
certain MSS. of Wycliff, "non minoris malitiæ ac
hæresis." He congratulates the cardinal on their possessing so "pious, holy, and catholic a king;" and yet
a sad presentiment appears to lurk in the words which
follow. "But if his majesty (which heaven forefend !)
shall fall from the Catholic faith, not a little loss would
accrue to the Christian commonwealth."

Disaffection to the king in the matter of subsidies, especially on the part of the religious
houses, gives another indication of the coming
change. The miserable state of poverty into which
the diocese had fallen at this time is pathetically
urged by Warham as a ground of its relief from the
subsidy, which originally claiming a third of the

---

[1] "Arch. Cant.," vol. i. p. 10. Letters of Abp. Warham.

revenues of the clergy, was afterwards reduced to a
sixth, even this being an intolerable burden. A far
more interesting feature in the history of the diocese
is the attempt which was now being made to convert
several of the conventual foundations into public
schools, a plan which in another form was so successfully carried out by Edward VI. and Elizabeth.
The archbishop, in a very interesting letter, inquires
into the views of the people of Tunbridge, offering
them a free school for forty scholars, with exhibitions
at Oxford, in lieu of their ancient priory. The
majority of the inhabitants, however, prefer the
monastic institution to the scholastic, and the project falls to the ground. This is in 1525. Another
matter in this correspondence of peculiar interest to
the diocese, and one which placed the primate in
very imminent danger, was his patronage of Elizabeth Barton, the Holy Maid of Kent, whom he
introduces to the cardinal in order that she may
have a private interview with him. He describes
her as a " very well-disposyd and vertuouse woman
whiche hadd all the visions of our Lady of Courtup-
street." These letters are almost all dated from
Otford, where the archbishop, having quarrelled with
the citizens of Canterbury in the matter of his palace
there, had laid out the then enormous sum of
£33,000, in order to make what he still continues to
call his " poor house of Otford" a palace worthy of
the primacy. It is strange to read his pleas of exemption from the subsidy, in connection with this princely
expenditure. One of the most suggestive of these
letters is that addressed to Wolsey, in 1522, in which

the archbishop excuses himself from meeting the legate at Canterbury on the occasion of the visit of the Emperor Charles V. and King Henry VIII. to that city. This was almost the last gleam of royal splendour that shone on the scene of the "martyrdom" which had witnessed in earlier days so many pilgrimages of almost equal grandeur, but with a spiritual object of so far deeper a significance. Warham excuses himself on economical grounds, having already so lately entertained the king's grace at his "power (poor) house at Otford." His real purpose was doubtless to avoid meeting the hated legate, and the fear that he could scarcely dissemble his joy at the narrow escape he had had from greeting Wolsey as pope. In an equally interesting letter of Longolius, the friend of Sadolet, Bembo, Pole, Erasmus, and our own Linacre, we find how near the chance of Wolsey's election had become. "While I was writing this," are his words, "news was brought to our friend Pole that Thomas Wolsey, of York, that Briton, I mean, has been made a pope. If that has happened nothing has happened more wonderful in the memory of our fathers and our grandfathers." Further on he writes, "When I had finished my letter I received yours, from which I learned that not Wolsey, but our own Hadrian, has been declared pope." [1] Perhaps Wolsey was as anxious to dissemble his indignation at Canterbury as Warham to conceal his joy.

But there is a dark side to the brightest character, and we cannot but regret that the cruel persecutions which followed the earlier converts to the reformed

---

[1] Christ. Longolii Epp., l. iii. Ep. 10, ed. Basil, 1558, p. 185.

doctrine were carried on by Warham with a severity
which stands in singular contrast to the gentler
features of his life. We must, however, remember
that not even the highest persons or the most enlightened minds of the age, whatever may have been their
influence, could have resisted the tide of barbarism
which rendered the laws of England under the Tudor
dynasty a code of the most refined and vindictive
tyranny, whose traces survived in English criminal
jurisprudence up to our own day. Warham, in the
dreadful part he took against the earlier martyrs of
the Reformation, was a mere instrument under the
law to which he himself nearly fell a victim. He and
his still more eminent commissary, Cuthbert Tonstal,
were associated together as colleagues in the execution
of a law which they were unable to abrogate, or even
to mitigate. The charge of heresy, less pardonable
in that darker day than murder itself—inasmuch as
it was supposed to involve the ruin of the soul as well
as the body—had been one of life or death, even
from the enlightened age of the great Justinian, whose
code is as deeply stained with the capital law against
the Manichæans, as that of Elizabeth is with the judicial
murder of the unfortunate Baptists. The blot which
rests upon the name of Warham rests also upon that
of Cranmer, and in a far higher degree upon that of
Calvin ; and when we think of the horrible punish-
ments inflicted upon the alleged traitors of a later
day, and remember that almost every offence against
property was punished by death in our own, we shall
look with less severity upon those who were the
instruments of a sanguinary law in an age of twilight

like that in which Warham lived. An immense and
uncontrollable power had been introduced into the
world by the invention of printing; and almost the
earliest use which was made in England of this great
discovery was the multiplication and propagation of
the works of Wycliffe and others, by whom many of
the received doctrines of the Church and its entire
hierarchy were held up to the animadversion and
often ridicule of the multitude. The early settlement
of French, Flemings, and other foreigners in West
Kent, Sandwich, Canterbury, and other places, rendered the propagation of such doctrines too easy,
and the danger (as it appeared) to the clergy very
imminent. The very year of the visitation, which
the archbishop conducted with so much gentleness
and moderation was marked by a process against a
number of alleged heretics in the diocese of Canterbury, whose names being chiefly of a foreign origin
lead to the belief that they were among those immigrants who established so many industries in the
Weald of Kent, and in the principal centres of its
commerce. We have William Carder, of Tenterden,
weaver—a name doubtless derived rather from his
craft than from his forefathers. Then there is Agnes
Grebil—an evidently foreign name—who was accused
(among others) by Stephen Castelin, also of Tenterden, William Olbert, of Godmersham, and by
many of her own nearest relatives, including her son
and husband, and brought on their evidence to the
stake—a hideous proof of that utter extinction of the
most sacred ties of kindred which is effected by the
doctrine of heresy as it is laid down in the Roman

Church. William Carder, though he professed his
repentance if he had held an heretical doctrine on
the sacraments, and his willingness to conform to the
Church's teaching, was yet condemned by the archbishop, though (as Fox alleges) there is no appearance
whatever in the register that he had relapsed, and
was delivered as an excommunicated person to the
secular power.

The unfortunate Agnes Grebil, against whom the
archbishop acted with even less pardonable zeal, was
condemned on the evidence of her own husband and
of her two sons, who were compelled to bear witness
against their sexagenarian mother, and in a manner to
deliver her to death ; as though the terrible prophecy
of our Lord were now a second time fulfilled, with
circumstances of even augmented horror. Numbers
who escaped the last penalty, but were supposed in
some degree to be compromised by the conversations
they had had with the unhappy victims, were compelled nevertheless to abjure, and among these were
Christopher Grebil and John Grebil—both of Benenden ; William Rich, of Benenden, William Olbert, of
Godmersham, Agnes Ive, of Canterbury, Joan Colin,
Stephen Castelin, William Olbert the younger, John
Frank, of Tenterden, and others. These names, as
we observed before, lead to the supposition that the
new doctrines had been propagated in West Kent by
the immigrants from France and Flanders, who had
so early settled there. The spectacle of these terrible
and revolting cruelties which even in that day must
have shocked the public mind, contributed not a
little to prevent the spread of the reformed doctrines

in Kent. In any case it is clear that during Warham's primacy, and especially in its intermediate portion, there was a great lull of religious activity in Kent, ominous, perhaps, of the violent convulsion which was so soon to change the face of the diocese and of the country.

The wills of this period, which give so clear an impress of the prevalent religious sentiment, offer no indication of the coming revolution. The offerings to particular shrines, the devotion to patron saints, the foundation of masses and obits, are as general as they were in an earlier day, and even the political events which were so rapidly developing themselves in the closing years of Warham's primacy seemed little likely to open so new a scene in the religious life of the country. Nevertheless the results of the discovery of printing and the manner in which the public mind was being almost imperceptibly educated for the reception of the doctrines of the Reformation were now gradually appearing, and the influence of the clergy in the diocese, from the primate downwards, was perceptibly reduced, while that of the religious orders had altogether passed away. Only the terrors of the law remained, a significant token of which appears as late as 1535, in the municipal records of Canterbury ; where we find 14s. 8d. paid for "the expenses of bringing a heretic from London, and for one and a half load of wood to burn him, 2s., for gunpowder, 1d., a stake and staple, 8d." As a set-off to this great expense, and as a proof of the levity with which its object is regarded, we find immediately after, "Receive 11s. 8d. from sale of John Barley's harness."

But while the penalties of heresy, from which Warham was sufficiently safe, were so easily incurred, the political danger which involved like results was not escaped so lightly. The case of the unfortunate nun of Court-at-Street, in Lymne, was a startling indication of the difficulties through which the highest in the land, both in Church and State, had to thread their way between the temporal and spiritual perils which bristled along their path on either side. The chapel of Court-at-Street, situate at a small hamlet, called in Domesday Billerica, in the parish of Lymne, had been built in early times for the inhabitants of that village, and had fallen into a state of such neglect and disrepair at the time of Henry VIII. that it seems to have been mostly occupied by a hermit. To hinder, it would appear, its total ruin, Richard Master, the rector of the neighbouring parish of Aldington, encouraged the unfortunate Elizabeth Barton, whose name has been already mentioned, to begin a course of prophecies, and to pretend that she held miraculous conferences with the Virgin Mary, to whom the chapel was dedicated. These began in the year 1525, and were continued for some months, till the celebrity they were acquiring among the common people induced the archbishop to appoint a commission to report on them, at the head of which was Dr. Bocking, one of his chief officials. The members of this body rather countenanced the imposture than inquired into it, for they attended a service held at the chapel, in company with many of the gentry of the neighbourhood, as well as near 3,000 of the common people.

Soon after this the archbishop became compromised in the matter by his appointing the "Nun of Kent," as she was afterwards called, to a vacant place in the convent of St. Sepulchre, in Canterbury, where she continued to see visions and to work miracles in a more extended sphere and from a more conspicuous position. As long as her prophecies were of a purely spiritual nature, and consisted of earnest appeals in behalf of the pilgrimages and vows, which were now beginning to be held in such light esteem and even openly denounced, the archbishop and his clergy could only have regarded her teaching as a providential antidote to that of the poor martyr, Agnes Grebil, whose seventh heresy lay in the assertion that "pilgrimages to holy places and holy relics be not necessary nor meritorious to soul's health," and in moving her to Canterbury may have had an eye to the transfer of her influence to Becket's shrine from the obscure and dreary scene of her first revelations. But scarcely had she entered on her new scene than the project of the king's divorce turned her prophecies into a new and more dangerous channel, and she ventured to predict that if the king carried on his suit he would not remain on the throne for one month longer. The attention of Henry being thus called to the "Holy Maid of Kent," as she was now termed, it was not long before all who were implicated in what might have turned out to be a very serious conspiracy were brought before the Star Chamber and compelled to confess that the whole affair was an imposture—a confession which brought the extreme penalty on all engaged in it, and would probably have involved Warham himself in the condemnation had he not passed away from the scene just before the gathering storm had burst. Elizabeth Barton herself, Edward Bocking, and Richard Dering, monks of Christ Church, Richard Master, rector of Aldington, Henry Golde, rector of Aldermanbury, and Richard Risby, gent., were executed at Tyburn in 1534; while the great and good Bishop Fisher, afterwards cardinal, with others were found guilty of misprision of treason, and adjudged to forfeit their estates and to be imprisoned during the king's pleasure. The severity of this sentence must strike us very forcibly, and though it forms no contrast to the ordinary cruelties of the age, we cannot but remark that while the intercession of Queen Anne Boleyn was put forth for the unhappy followers of the poor visionary, neither Cromwell nor Cranmer lifted a finger in their behalf. The suggestive entry we have referred to, from the records of Canterbury, was made during the primacy of the latter, and the Act of Conviction must have been signed by his hand. A long letter of Cromwell's is extant in the Cotton MSS., upbraiding Fisher for the mildness with which he had acted in regard to the deluded or deluding nun, but we see no effort to mitigate the very disproportionate punishment with which her error was visited, and seem to read throughout this long reign of crime and lust and suffering the fulfilment of the divine declaration, that "they who take the sword shall perish with the sword." Burnet ascribes the severity of the sentence to some fresh intrigues which were discovered between the nun and her accomplices. But of these he gives no sufficient evidence.

We now approach the history of a period, which, as our adversaries affirm, has made such a change in the history and the teaching of the diocese, and such a break in the continuity of its succession, both of teacher and doctrine, as in a manner to have created a new primacy and a schismatic body, and to have left the Church of England as a severed member of the great and once united Church of the West. It must be admitted that the strangely extended ignorance of the history of the Reformation in England, and the principles upon which it was conducted, have too much contributed to justify such specious misrepresentations to the public mind. In taking up, therefore, the thread of our history at the time of the nomination of Cranmer to the archbishopric, it will be necessary to point out as briefly as possible the regularity of those stages of progress, both in point of law and doctrine, through which the diocese has reached its present state, and the unbroken continuity, both of orders and teaching, which we claim in behalf of our Church. Our Reformation rests upon the great principle which our Church, even during the Roman usurpation, claimed and exercised, that every national Church, as it has a right to call a provincial synod (from which the African Church admitted no appeal)[1] and to lay down therein definitions of doctrine and rules of discipline and reformation (as the same African Church did at Milevis and Carthage),

---

[1] See the notes of Justellus on the African canons—(Cod. Cann. Eccl. African. not. p. 35).

has no necessity to apply to any external and foreign authority either to authorize the convocation of such an assembly or to confirm its decrees when established. In virtue of this right, inherent in every national Church, and necessary to its very existence, the Church of Poland, notwithstanding the reclamations of Pope Paul IV.,[1] and the fact that the Council of Trent had then been already summoned, convoked under the presidency of its primate, Nicholas Dziergowski, archbishop of Gniezno, a national synod, in which it put forth a body of doctrine and discipline as large as the Tridentine decrees themselves, and even fuller in its definitions and statements. This is called the Confession of Catholic Faith, " made by the Fathers in the Provincial Council of Piotrkov, in May, 1551," and was published at Posen in 1557 (while the Council of Trent was yet sitting) under the Royal authority. Exactly the same course was taken by Warham in England, though the results of the deliberations of the one council were so different from those of the other. Dziergowski and his colleagues elaborated a system of doctrine resembling, though by no means identical with, that afterwards manipulated at Trent, while the English synod, first under Warham (whose only act was to relieve it of its Papal restraints) and then under Cranmer, who had resumed under the Royal sanction the title of Metropolitan, promulgated those articles and canons which form the basis of the teaching and discipline of the Anglican

[1] See his dissuasive letter addressed to the Archbishop of Gniezno, given by Le Plat, " Monumenta Concil. Trident." tom. iv. p. 567.

Church. The words of the Archbishop of Gniezno might well have been those of Cranmer himself:—— "Since many sought our offices as bishops in this matter, and held that we were not free from blame in not having prescribed a certain form of teaching to the clergy in which they might rest, . . lest we should seem to any to be unwilling to provide for the salvation of our flock, we have called together a synod hereupon, in which, when we had deliberated on laying down our religious views (" de constituendâ religione ") every one agreed that certain articles should be drawn up on which all the bishops should severally give their opinion, the obligation of an oath being added that no one should be permitted to teach otherwise."[1] These words are in his opening address to Sigismund, the then king, in which, strangely enough, there is not even an allusion to the pope. The idea of the Papacy, which is conveyed in this confession, is of a very limited character. The pope is described to be of the same honour and dignity as the humblest bishop, though he has the *plenitudo potestatis*, while they have only the *pars sollicitudinis*. His appellate jurisdiction is only defended on the ground that he has assessors from among the most learned men everywhere, by whose advice he determines the more weighty causes. Therefore, " no one ought to think that it is only Paul or Julius that gives judgment in such cases." The infallibility would seem therefore to rest rather in the counsellors than in the counselled, or simply to be re-

[1] I quote from the rare folio edition published at Posen (Joanne Patruo Bibliopola Posnaniensi imprimi curante) A.D. 1557.

solved into the notion of irreformability, on the ground
of the Court of Rome being an ultimate tribunal. To
this, Bossuet, in his " Defence of the Declaration of
the Gallican Clergy," does in fact reduce it.

But to return to our immediate subject, we may
observe that while *our* synod, at least in regard to
doctrine, was free, and fairly represented the English
Church, the Council of Trent was a body so entirely
influenced by the pope as to be unable even to
initiate a subject, the legates insisting on this as their
exclusive right—while it was packed with Italian
bishops, and bishops *in partibus*, who outnumbered
by an overwhelming majority the bishops of every
other country in Europe. Many of them, moreover,
were so poor that the pope had to find their daily
bread, while none of the representatives of the Protestant states were even allowed to speak or to appear,
except to retract their alleged heresies. But there
was even a more serious obstacle than these,
great as they were, to the reception of the decrees of
Trent in England. Every one of the ancient doctrines of the English Church was repudiated, through
the fatal influence of the Jesuit Lainez and his followers in that assembly. The doctrine of Justification by Faith, maintained by all the great Roman
divines, including Cardinals Cajetan, Contarini, and
Pole, and that eminent bishop, Pflug, with the divines
of Cologne, was absolutely condemned at Trent, and
this unexpected result led to the departure of Pole
from the council, to which he never returned. The
doctrines of grace, which from the time of Archbishop
Bradwardine's great treatise had been one of the

distinctive features of the teaching of the Church of
England, were reduced at Trent to a semi-Pelagianism,
in which it is hard to recognise a single relic of the
Augustinian teaching. If, therefore, the Church of
England arrived at different conclusions from the
Italian bishops on these subjects, it must be remembered that her teaching from the days of Lanfranc had
been essentially different from theirs, and that she had
never learned that Jesuit casuistry which is represented in the conflicting teachings of the chapters and
canons of Trent. We may here observe, in vindication of our own position, that the discrepancies of
teaching in the decrees of the Council of Trent arise
not only from the studied endeavour to avoid giving
offence to the conflicting orders of the Roman Church
and to the chief leaders of the council, but also from
the fact, too generally overlooked, that there were
properly two distinct councils of Trent, and that very
few of those who took part in the former one lived to
take their place in the latter. The protest of the
orators of the King of France to the council in 1563
affirms that their sovereign sent orators "to the *First
Council of Trent* and then to this *second one*," and
constantly we find the first and second council contrasted (Le Plat, tom. vi. p. 233). The development
of doctrine by the Jesuits between the two councils
produced what was virtually a new religion, and
hardened into a dogmatic form the floating opinions
of the innovating divines of the age. The almost
entire ignorance of Greek which pervaded the council,
and the absolute ignorance of Hebrew which prevailed in it, must disqualify it in the eyes of all who

do not actually believe in its inspiration for the great
work of doctrinal definition on which it entered.
Cardinal Pole, almost the only representative in it of
the English Church, left in disgust, after a doctrine
of Justification so opposed to that of the ancient
Church of his country, was propounded ; and even had
he remained, the representatives of all the other
Churches in the world might have said of the Italian
bishops, " What are we among so many ?"—the latter
numbering 187 against the 81 which represented the
rest of Europe, only one Englishman taking part in
this truly Italian council.   At all events the English
Church *was* represented in the Convocation of 1562,
and by her own lawfully-consecrated bishops, having
both order and jurisdiction.

It would lead us far indeed from our subject were
we to enter upon the mazes of the controversy on
what is called "Apostolic succession," which by an
imprudent afterthought the Roman Church has so
pertinaciously denied to our episcopate. This has
been exhaustively treated by abler hands, and we
may be contented to say of it what the Polish
orator said at Trent,—"It does not become our
dignity in these calamitous times to waste our
time in interminable genealogies."[1]   The progress of the great work of the Reformation was
much slower and more gradual than is generally
supposed. The office of the mass remained almost
unchanged in the earlier directions of Edward, the
communion of the people being merely substituted
for the reception by the clergy alone.   The small and

[1] Le Plat, tom. v. p. 577.

slender chalices which gave so much scope to the
skill of mediæval artificers then gave place to the
large and rude cups of a more debased workmanship.[1]
The vestments and other goods of the churches in
Kent were, until 1552, carefully preserved, and probably many of them were still used on festival days.
They are minutely described in the return of the
commissioners who were appointed to take account
of them ; and their report has been reproduced in
several of the later volumes of the Kent Archæological
Society.   It is difficult to believe that some at least
of these costly vestments were not included in the
much-disputed rubric which falls back on the practice
of the second year of Edward VI.   The course of
the Reformation in Kent cannot perhaps be better
traced than by taking up as a clue to it the history of
its progress in a single parish in which its record has
been preserved.   We are fortunate in possessing the
churchwardens' accounts of many parishes both in
East and West Kent, some taking us beyond the Reformation period, while others begin about the time
when the great change was approaching.   The records
of the Church of Hawkhurst belong to the latter class,
and give us so clear a view of the transition from the

[1] In the work by Mr. Wilfrid Cripps, recently published, on
Silver Plate, the most learned manual on the subject in the
language, this change is fully illustrated.   The rude and ancient
cups at Lyminge and St. Laurence Jewry, in London, were
among the earliest chalices of the reformed rite which came
under his observation.   From the visitation book of Archbishop
Parker, in 1562, it appears that the Lyminge chalice was
bought in that year, and it is, therefore, one of the earliest
instances of a cup for the communion of the laity.

usages of the primacy of Warham and those of
Cranmer that we cannot but accept them as a kind
of typical example from which the change in the
diocese itself may be fairly estimated. In 1548-49,
the sale of various articles of church furniture, rendered useless under the new doctrines which had now
spread so generally, takes place, including a holy-
water stoup, an old sepulchre frame, a "Mary Mau-
delen tabernacle," St. Laurence's tabernacle (the
patron of the church), the high altar frame and altar
stones, two altar tables, and (which is in some sense
more to be deplored) a quantity of glass—painted
glass without doubt—besides a vast number of other
items connected with the earlier form of worship.

The late lamented secretary of our Archæological
Society observes hereupon :[1]—"These entries of
1548 are interesting as showing the activity with
which the work of the Reformation proceeded immediately on the accession of Edward VI. Cranmer
had commenced it in November, 1547, by his great
speech in convocation, exhorting the clergy to 'throw
out all the popish trash which was not yet cast out.'
In February came the letter of the council to Cranmer, ordering that all images should be taken down,
and commanding him to look to it in his own diocese, and to give injunctions to the bishops for theirs.
Accordingly, in his visitation of that summer, he inquires whether his clergy have 'removed and destroyed all images, shrines, and monuments of feigned
miracles, idolatry, and superstition,' and in these

[1] Mr. T. Godfrey-Faussett, "Hawkhurst Notes," by W. J.
Lightfoot—"Arch. Cant." vol. v. p. 55, n.

accounts we find the result. The items of sale of church goods begin immediately after an entry dated May 20. The holy-water stoup is first disposed of, tabernacles of saints—even of the patron, St. Laurence—albs, altars, and sanctus-bells, carved wood, brass and iron-work, stained glass, wax-candles, and other not less suggestive property follow in quick succession. From the third item in the expenses of this year we may suppose an auction of some of the 'implements' to have taken place. The visitation itself is mentioned, and immediately follows the destruction of St. Laurence's tabernacle, as if the vicar had returned, smarting from the archbishop's rebuke, and had lost no time in obedience. Then follows a large expense in whitewashing, to hide the paintings with which we may suppose the interior walls to have been covered, and in glass, doubtless a very poor substitute for the departed glories of mediæval art."

The articles of visitation of Cranmer for the diocese of Canterbury, which are here referred to, are of the most searching and inquisitorial character, but are too well and generally known to need any full description of them here.[1] The completeness of the spiritual change, or rather revolution, which they indicate must excite wonder in every mind, that it was accomplished with so little displacement of persons or violent disturbance of the feelings and habits of the rural population. Such a convulsion, at a time when the dogmatic systems on either side of this great controversy had been fully developed, and in a

---

[1] They are given in Bishop Sparrow's collection and in all other similar republications of the articles and canons of the Church.

manner stereotyped, would have been impossible.
But at this period the rural, and in great measure the
urban population, knew nothing of doctrine but the
Apostles' Creed ; of Christian practice, but the Ten
Commandments ; and of the Christian liturgy, but the
Lord's Prayer, and the short courses of devotion then
in use. Preaching, except on very rare occasions,
was unknown, and when practised was limited to
moral duties, and even in Cranmer's visitation was
only obligatory four times in the year. And as by
the same articles the pope's supremacy and the king's
were to be handled, the one negatively and the other
positively, the same number of times yearly, there
could have been little opportunity to enter upon doctrinal subjects in the vast majority of the parishes of
the diocese. It was quite a different question in the
conflict of the Church with Puritanism in later days.
In this case, doctrine was the great and only test,
and the change of parties produced an entire displacement of the principal advocates on either side.
The great difficulty of the earlier period arose out of
the destruction of the furniture and ornaments of the
churches, so historical in their character, and so naturally endeared to the people by the associations with
which they were bound up. This was a reckless act of
spoliation, which has no parallel in Christian history.

Every subsequent age has mourned over this whole-
sale destruction of all the treasures of art and works
of mediæval piety, which the iconoclastic zeal of the
period assumed to be incompatible with the revived doctrines of the primitive Fathers, and the severer school
of teaching which was now imposed upon the Church.

The words of the psalm come upon us with all
their force, "He that hewed timber afore out of the
thick trees was known to bring it to an excellent
work ; but now they break down all the carved work
thereof with axes and hammers." Yet, if we could
realize the spiritual dangers and necessities of the
rural population of that darker day, as well as we can
measure the Vandalism and immoderate zeal of their
guides, we might discover some "extenuating circumstances" in this process of ruinous destruction,
which has left us only the outer shell of the ancient
worship, and (until the recent revival of ecclesiastical
taste) has fitted up our parish churches with the
modest furniture of a cottage. The completeness of
the destruction of the vestments and instruments of
the Roman service on the accession of Mary is illustrated by the directions of Cardinal Pole, in his "Reformation of the English Church," in which, among
his visitation questions, is this suggestive inquiry,
"Whether there is, in every parish church at least,
one clergyman serving at the mass in a clean and
decent surplice?" When we read how vast a number of the ancient vestments were still in existence in
1552, this visitation question, only four years after,
seems suggestive of a sad destruction.[1]

As a necessary preliminary to these important
changes in the forms and requisites of public worship,
the monasteries and convents, out of which so much
of the ritual magnificence of the Roman Church and
its multiplied festivals arose, were dissolved and de-

[1] Le Plat, "Mon. C. T." tom. iv. p. 597.

stroyed, a work of demolition which was far more
disastrous to the archæology of the county than any
which has ever fallen upon it in its long history.   In
this place, therefore, we may well give a passing view
of the monasteries, greater or lesser, which fell under
this summary process, not only of " disestablishment
and disendowment," but of ruinous and final destruction.   The first step in this act of confiscation was
the suppression of all religious houses which were
under the clear annual value of two hundred pounds.
By this first act fell the Abbey of West Langdon, the
Priories of Folkestone, Dover, Bilsington, St. Gregory's in Canterbury, St. Radigund's, Cumbwell, Horton, Hedcorne, Mottenden, Aylesford, Newenden,
and Sandwich, with several lesser foundations in Canterbury, and the Nunnery of Minster in Sheppey. Soon
after the greater foundations falling under the displeasure of the king, for the part they were supposed
to have taken in fomenting the disturbances which so
naturally followed an act which combined sacrilege
with robbery, were successively surrendered to the
Crown, under that irresistible pressure which was
afterwards applied to the archbishop himself in a
more disguised form.   In this list were the great
foundations of Christ Church and St. Augustine's, the
Priory of Faversham, the Abbey of Boxley, and the
Nunneries of Malling and St. Sepulchre's in Canterbury.   Then followed Dartford Nunnery and Leeds
Priory, the commanderies of St. John of Jerusalem
(or Knights Hospitallers), at West Peckham and
Swingfield, and after these all colleges, chantries, free
chapels, hospitals, and guilds which had not been

hitherto surrendered. These included Eastbridge, Maynard's, and Northgate Hospitals in Canterbury, Harbledown, Hythe, St. Bartholomew's Sandwich, St. Laurence, and St. Margaret's in Canterbury, founded for poor priests, St. Bartholomew's and the Maison Dieu in Dover, the Hospitals of Thanington, Sevenoke, Bredgar, Maidstone, Wingham, Cobham, and Wye. The suppressed chantries and free chapels were as follows :—

Ash (by Sandwich).	Penshurst.
Bapchild.	Pepenbury.
Chidingstone.	Petham (Deepdene
Cranbrook.	Chantry).
Herne.	Reculver.
Horton Kirby.	Sandwich (St. Peter's).
Maidstone.	Sevenoke.
East Malling.	Sittingbourne.
Orpington.	Teynham.

The sites of these venerable buildings, and the lands attached to them, were for the most part granted to the numerous favourites of the Crown, but they passed more rapidly into other hands in the case of the Kentish monasteries than those of the great foundations in other counties. The monastery of Christ Church was, however, dealt with in a manner worthy of its early history, being transformed from a conventual building into the cathedral of the metropolitical see, which thus became one of those cathedrals designated of the "new foundation." Of this great centre of the religious life of England, and scene of some of the most re-markable events of her history, nothing remains but

the fabric of the cathedral itself and a few suggestive
and picturesque ruins of the surrounding monastic
buildings.   Out of these scarcely-connected frag
ments, by the aid of documentary evidences, Pro
fessor Willis has constructed a description of the
entire monastery, with scarcely less skill than that o
Professor Owen, who, out of a few bones, was able
to construct in theory a perfect skeleton of the Moa
which was verified at last by the recovery of every
missing link in the marvellous structure.   It is im
possible in this place, without transgressing our ap
pointed limits, to give even a sketch of this remark
able restoration on paper of the venerable monastery
of Christ Church, which is given in the "Archæologia
Cantiana," with those illustrations so necessary to it
full apprehension.[1]   We will pass on, therefore, to
what might be termed the second act of this great
confiscation, the transfer of the most ancient and
valuable of the estates of the archbishopric, under
the specious pretext of an exchange with the king, in
order to add yet more of the plunder of the Church to
that new and most unconstitutional treasury, "the cour
for the augmentation of the revenues of the Crown.'
In the thirty-first year of Henry VIII. (1539–40), Arch
bishop Cranmer, by a single act of surrender, and in
one most comprehensive deed, transferred to the
king, under the specious pretence of an exchange for
other of the confiscated lands of the Church, four o

[1] "The Architectural History of the Conventual Buildings
of the Monastery of Christ Church, in Canterbury," "Arch
Cant." vol. vii. pp. 1–206.

his oldest and largest manors and lordships, **viz.,**
Aldington, Lyminge, Saltwood, and Croydon, with
all their dependencies in the Marsh and in the Weald
of Kent. Never was a more flagrant robbery con-
cealed with a more transparent misrepresentation.
The agents of the king produced a comparative valu-
ation of the properties to be "exchanged," without
giving the archbishop the benefit of a valuer on the
part of the Church, and thus these great estates
passed away for ever from the possession of the see of
Canterbury. Aldington was kept in the king's hands
for a considerable period, and it is said that he designed to retain it as a royal park ; a plan, however,
which was never carried out. Lyminge, after having
been held for some years, was granted to the Master
of the Jewels, Sir Anthony Aucher, for a fixed sum
and an annual payment. Saltwood was granted to
Cromwell, earl of Essex, reverting to the Crown on
his attainder ; and other surrendered possessions of
the see passed into the hands of other equally favoured
courtiers, a transfer which tended greatly to establish
the influence of the Reformation in East Kent, as the
new proprietors of these great estates were even more
devoted to the Crown than the archbishop himself,
and were more zealous advocates of its supremacy.
It is to be regretted, however, that by this severance
of the most ancient ties of property which had connected the primates with the diocese, the evils of
episcopal non-residence were fatally increased ; and
when even the palace of Canterbury itself was surrendered, almost the last link which connected the archbishop with his diocese was broken, and that *soli-*

tudo ecclesiarum which Cardinal Pole and his colleagues deplored in their report on the state of the Church to Pope Paul III., as existing in Italy, through the non-residence of the bishops, was witnessed for the first time in the Church of England.

The life of Cranmer was too constantly entangled in the complicated political events of the age to enable him to fulfil his duties as a diocesan in the manner of his predecessors in the see. He lived for the most part in a comparatively distant scene, Lambeth and Croydon having been his chief residences, and his visits to Canterbury itself seem to have been few and far between. The close connection between the archbishops, as abbots, and Christ Church had now ceased, and the tie between the primate and the new prebendaries, who had superseded rather than succeeded the prior and his monks, was slender and feeble. Christ Church was now a kind of Crown foundation, having very little connection with the life or duties of the primates. The independence of the new dean and chapter of the archbishops contrasted strangely with the relations which had subsisted between the monastery and its ancient heads, and the surrender of the palace in Canterbury and its entire secularization was an ominous token of the spiritual severance of the cathedral and the primacy. The public life of Cranmer as it affected the diocese rather indirectly and generally, than immediately and in connection with its local history, cannot well be dwelt upon in a work of such limited scope as the present. His sentence, however, against the unfortunate Joane

Boucher (or Bocher), commonly known as the Maid
of Kent, who had advanced erroneous doctrines in
regard to the humanity of our Lord, and its cruel
execution, has left a stain upon his memory which is
all the deeper from its having been carried out in the
reign of the young and gentle Edward VI., who
pleaded so touchingly against it, and while Cranmer
was in a position of power all but supreme. This
mournful process and the documents which embody
it exist yet in the register of the archbishop, and
must have led both the clergy and laity of the diocese
to look upon the similar fate which afterwards fell
upon himself with but little sympathy. It seemed,
indeed, a kind of Nemesis that the pardon he received
on the ground of his treason made the very charge
he had brought against the unfortunate Joane
Boucher to fall back upon his own head. He had
rekindled the fires of persecution in a day when a
single breath might have extinguished them, and
could hardly wonder that they blazed with new fury
under the reign of a reactionary queen. The connection of the primate with the diocese was somewhat
strengthened by the appointment of his brother to the
Archdeaconry of Canterbury, whom he loaded with
preferments with a lavishness not unworthy of those
of his predecessors most noted for their nepotism.
Edmund Cranmer in 1534, was collated to the archdeaconry and the provostship of Wingham, and had
several other rich benefices conferred upon him by
his brother soon after. In 1549 he was made a prebendary of Christ Church, and promoted to the
rectories of Cliffe and Ickham in the diocese—all

T

which offices he held until the year 1554, in which, on the accession of Mary, he was deprived of all his preferments as being a married priest, and compelled to fly to Germany in order to save his life. The process against him, which is fully recorded in the registers of the see, gives an interesting view of the course adopted against the married clergy. He had plainly confessed his marriage, and maintained its lawfulness, alleging that he could never forsake his wife with a clear conscience. Upon this confession sentence of deprivation and of separation from his wife was pronounced upon him. Against such a sentence there was, of course, no appeal at such a time as this.

Scarcely were the death of Edward VI. and the accession of Mary known in Rome than Julius III. hastened to declare Pole his legate. The letter of the pope, after recounting the religious and political changes which this early loss of the youthful king had brought about, enumerates the motives which induced him to commit to Pole, and to none other, a legatine office of so great difficulty—the "love of his native soil and its citizens," the "knowledge of their language, manners, and feelings," the "royal blood from which he derived his descent, and the authority and favour he acquired thereby," his "singular prudence and eloquence," and, "what was chief of all, his burning love of God and of the Lord Jesus Christ, and love and devotion to His holy Catholic Church." The choice was indeed in all respects a wise one, and yet the jealousy of the court of Rome led it in the ensuing pontificate to attempt to supersede the man whom it had so lately declared to be unique and perfect, " Non sanè primus sed solus omnium."[1]

The terrible death of Cranmer, and the great reaction which took place in the country and in the diocese when the work of the Reformation, so far advanced during the reign of Edward, was so suddenly checked, must have been specially felt in Kent. Closely connected as the county was in all its parts with the leading nobility of the period of the Reformation, the trusted friends of Henry VIII. and Edward VI. who had succeeded to the vast estates of the primacy, we cannot wonder that it formed the centre of the rebellion of Sir Thomas Wyatt, and that many of its influential inhabitants took part in that abortive project.[2] The suppression of Wyatt's rebellion, which gave new firmness to the authority of Mary, was naturally succeeded by a strong reactionary movement in the direction of Roman rites and usages. We find accordingly in the Hawkhurst records already cited, the purchase of two albs, an amice, a cope, a stole, baldrics and corporalia, a mass-book, a processional, and two " portasses,"[3] a cross and altar, and a " holy-water stick." " We may date these items," observes Mr. Faussett,[4] " early in the spring of 1554,

---

[1] Julii III. Ep. ad Reg. Pol. in Ep. Sadsleti—Append., tom. v. p. 287.

[2] As Sir William Cromer, of Tunstall, Sir George Harper, of Sutton Valence, Sir Henry Isley, the Knyvets, the Culpepers, the Rudstons, and many others. (See " Arch. Cant." vol. iii. pp. 179-183.)

[3] Breviaries.

[4] " Arch. Cant." vol. v. p. 69, n.

when Wyatt's attempt being suppressed and Mary firm on the throne, the act repealing King Edward's laws was passed and the old service restored. In Kent at least, Wyatt's own Kent, we may well suppose that there would be no unnecessary alacrity for the change." The terrible cruelties that followed this fatal and ill-advised movement were more unfortunate to the queen than even to the sufferers, for they awakened a feeling of reaction towards the doctrines and the work of the Reformation that might have gradually languished had severity at least been tempered with mercy. " Executions took place daily. Never in its long and eventful history had London witnessed such a scene as now ensued. Fifteen gibbets with eighty men dangling from them filled its streets with horror. 'At all crossways and at all thoroughfares,' said Noailles, the French ambassador, 'the eye was met with the hideous spectacle of hanging men.' So did the queen pursue her vengeance until even the lords, poor though they were in number and spirit when compared with that proud body who had awed the Plantagenets, plucked up courage to remonstrate. For Elizabeth, on that day, and it was Palm Sunday, had been committed to the Tower, and gloomy apprehensions existed as to her probable fate. Lord Paget was their messenger. 'He found Mary in her oratory after vespers ; he told her that the season might remind a sovereign of other duties besides revenge, already too much blood had been shed ; the noble house of Suffolk was all but destroyed ; and he said distinctly that if she attempted any more executions he and his friends would interfere; the hideous scenes had lasted too long, and as an earnest of a return to mercy, he demanded the pardon of six gentlemen. Mary, as she lamented afterwards to Rénard, was unprepared. She was pressed in terms which showed that those who made the request did not intend to be refused, and she consented. In the course of the week the council extorted from her the pardon of Northampton, Cobham, and one of his sons, with five others. . . . It was at the close of the year 1555 that the reconciliation with Rome took place; and when Cardinal Pole made his progress through Kent on his way to London, Lord Cobham received him on November 23rd at his castle of Cowling."[1] The cardinal did not display the insignia of his legatine power till he reached Gravesend on the following day. If it were even possible (and it is devoutly to be hoped that under the present altered circumstances of the Papacy it never may be) to reconcile our Church with Rome, the precedent of Cardinal Pole's primacy and the spirit in which his work was conducted might well claim the attention and invite the imitation of the promoters of this often-attempted reunion. The early life of Pole had been spent among the greatest and noblest of those whose lives and writings would be an ornament to the purest ages of our faith, and would do no discredit to the more enlightened learning of a later day. Associated with Sadolet, Con-

---

[1] I am here indebted to the interesting paper in the "Arch. Cantiana," by Mr. J. G. Waller, on "the Lords of Cobham, their monuments and the church" (vol. xii. p. 123). The included quotation is from Froude's History.

tarini, Ægidius of Viterbo, and many of the best and greatest ecclesiastics of the day, he had joined in that celebrated report to Paul III. on the abuses of the Church, which had it been acted upon might have retained vast numbers in the communion of Rome. A zealous advocate of the doctrine of justification by faith in the Council of Trent, his influence with that of Contarini (whose writings alone represented him in the council) and of many others went far to carry the day against the Jesuits, who repudiated the teaching of St. Bernard, on the "Imputed Righteousness of Christ," and confounded justification with sanctification, founding upon the mistranslated verse of the Apocalypse, "He that is righteous, let him be righteous still," or, as the Vulgate has it, "Qui justificetur, justificetur *adhuc*," an inherent and increasing justification, unknown to the ancients from the days of Origen downwards. Against this doctrine both Pole and Contarini had contended, one in the council itself, the other in his famous "Letter on Justification" read in the council, but their reclamations were in vain. Even Cardinal Scripandi warned the bishops at Trent to beware, lest in condemning Luther, they did not condemn their own party, especially Contarini and Ægidius of Viterbo, both cardinals, with Pighius and a host of great divines. As soon as it was clear that the council intended to set aside the received views on the "imputed righteousness of Christ," the "certitude of grace," and the doctrine of justification by faith, this ominous announcement appears in the records of the council,—"On the 31st of October, Cardinal Pole, the third president of

the council, on account of ill-health, departed from
his legation with the consent of the pope."[1]   On all
these subjects the council was most bitterly divided.
Twenty-one to fourteen were for the doctrine of the
"certainty of grace," while on the doctrine of justification we are told by an eye-witness, Jacobus de
Jacomellis, bishop of Belcastro, that "in full congregation" (in pleno senatu) "there were found those
who contended for the absolute dependence upon
the righteousness of Christ as imputed to ourselves,
and an absolute renunciation of all claim to salvation
on the ground of the merit of works," as though they
were fighting "pro aris et focis."[2]   It is easy to see
how the 187 bribed Italian bishops turned the
scale against the most zealous and eminent representatives of other Churches.   It is not too much to say

[1] Le Plat. tom. iii. p. 475.

[2] The work of Giacomelli, "De Justitiâ Christi Imputatâ,"
has never been published. A MS. copy on vellum, written
in the council and dedicated to Cardinal Farnese, is in the
possession of the writer. Its introduction is suggestive and
important : "Superioribus diebus cum de impii justificatione
in Sanctâ hâc Tridentinâ synodo ageretur . . . fuêre quidam
. . . eruditi viri meo judicio et diserti, qui summâ nobis con-
tentione summâque eloquentiâ persuadere conati sunt, opera
nostra quamlibet in gratiâ patrata quamlibet a charitate eman-
antia longe abesse ab eo ut sufficiant et quæ satisfaciant legi
Dei et quæ gloriam mereantur, nisi ad justitiam Christi ad
misericordiam Patris novo quodam modo nescio unde eruto
confugiamus. Manca enim ipsa nostra opera esse et debilia
quamvis a divinâ gratiâ fulciantur. Ipsis propterea non
fidendum, a Christi meritis, a solâ justitiâ Christi opem et
auxilium implorandum. Appellabantque hanc justitiam, justitiam imputatam."

that the doctrinal views of Cardinal Pole on this vital point were in as close resemblance to those of our Article on Justification as they were in absolute dissimilarity to those of the Council of Trent, which he refused to ratify by his presence. His views regarding the general doctrines of the Church and the restoration of its ancient discipline are fully conveyed to us by his scheme for the " Reformation of the Church," which is well known to every student of ecclesiastical history.

Here, it is notable, he makes the Council of Florence, and not that of Trent, whose first portion was now promulged, the groundwork of his doctrinal system, and recognises the Florentine Council as the *eighth* General Council ; thus ignoring all the intermediate councils of the West which claim œcumenicity, including the Lateran Councils, and that of Lyons, which introduced so many innovations into the Church.

The establishment of cathedral schools and seminaries of learning is an important feature of his projected reformation, and the directions he gives in regard to this subject are as judicious as they are minute. It may, indeed, be said that this first work of the cardinal on his entrance upon the primacy is a monument of wisdom, which shows that he, if any ever could be, was the rightly-chosen man for bringing about what is termed the "reconciliation" of England —and his complete failure must render the problem for ever an increasingly difficult, if not an actually insoluble one. To all these qualifications for his arduous task must be added those of a simplicity of life and a sanctity of character but rarely seen in these days of laxity of manners and indifference to all but worldly gain and selfish aggrandizement. The picture of the private life and character of the cardinal, as seen in his writings and letters, and in those of his most intimate friends, is one of singular beauty. He had passed through strange vicissitudes and heartrending trials. A touching letter of Cardinal Sadolet describes the fortitude with which he bore up against the dreadful afflictions which had fallen upon his house, the murder of his venerable mother —for murder it truly was—the almost extinction of his family at the hands of one, who, as Sadolet writes, "can hardly be called a king, as the barbarity and magnitude of his cruelties have scarcely left him the name of a man." "To hear from Pole," continues his friend, "the bitter lot of his family, and know that his noble house had been almost extinguished by the cruelty of that barbarous tyrant, affected me so deeply with the sense of its misery and cruelty, that unless I had been soothed by the virtue and wisdom of him upon whom all this injury was inflicted, I could not have put any bounds to my grief. But he, who is of such singular constancy and moderation under anything that happens to him, ever submitting himself to God, and ever ready to obey His will, spoke of all his bitterest trials as though they had happened to a stranger, and bravely bore up against his domestic affliction, while he was most deeply moved at the public injury which had been done to the Christian name."[1]

[1] Sadoleti, Epp. Rom. 1764, p. iii. Ep. 318.

The connection of Pole with the diocese had been made slender indeed through the surrender of those great manors and estates to which Cranmer so fatally submitted, and which he appears rather to have encouraged than endeavoured to prevent. This second great act of the plunder of the Church was even more serious to its interest than the first, for the loss of the monasteries was a lesser evil than the crippling of those vast means which might have extended the episcopate according to the manifest design of the reformers, and prevented the strange anomaly of the Church of the nineteenth century possessing an episcopate fitted to it in the sixteenth, —the one ever growing, while the other remained unchanged and unchangeable. Pole had indeed too large a work in the reconciliation of the whole kingdom to what was now a new faith to enable him to reconstruct the episcopate. But one point he devoted himself to with an energy worthy of its importance, and this was the residence of the bishops in their sees, upon which he has an important chapter in his decrees of Church Reformation, and which he so greatly promoted, as one of the commission of cardinals under Paul III. ; in whose report the evils of episcopal non-residence are so eloquently denounced. How far the effects of his reformatory labours were felt in the diocese will be best shown by the results of his visitation of it, which we propose to examine hereafter. His efforts to restore the cathedrals to their proper place as seminaries of teaching and centres of theological and genera learning, were worthy of his close relations with those Royal founders of schools and colleges whose example he was so anxious to emulate. The few and touching words which his friend, the younger Sadolet, wrote to one who was almost his brother, Luigi Priuli, describe a life which every age may well regard with admiration, and a death which even his greatest opponents might well have envied.

"Your letter of the 17th of April . . . . together with the precious treasure of peace invoked for me by that blessed soul on its departure from the world, have so bound up my heart with sweet and bitter tears and thought, renewing the grief with which on the first news of his death we realized that great and unspeakable loss, that I am forced to pray your Holiness to excuse me if I write confusedly and interruptedly. I had heard last summer the death of this unequalled lord (quell' unico signore) at first with different and varying accounts, which aggravated my grief; although he was indeed ready for death, since he died in company with his good and beloved queen, before the new tumults of that kingdom, quietly and honourably, and not without an evident mystery of Divine Providence."[1]

After dwelling on "his persecutions, and the manner

---

[1] It is curious to see this observation, so commonly made by those of our own Church in regard to the deaths of the queen and the cardinal on the same day, employed here by one of the Roman obedience. In the eyes of the one party they were taken away from the evil to come, in those of the other to make way for good things to be again restored.

in which he had borne up against these earthly injuries, sustaining the weakness of others with his invincible constancy, regulated by true Christian piety and charity," he adds, "but both in life and death one sees clearly that that angelic spirit has confuted and confounded everyone who wished to be the adversary and calumniator of its irreprehensible virtue; that he has heaped upon the heads of his enemies the burning coals of his charity for their amendment, if they are indeed capable of it, and for our example, as evidently appears from this declaration of his last will and belief, so conformable to all the actions of his life. Pray to God in my behalf, not indeed for his salvation and heavenly glory (for in this he has no need of our feeble prayers), but that I may become worthy of that most honourable lot of being esteemed during his life, and numbered at his death, among the dear friends of that dear lord."[1]

Letters like these, springing from the heart, and written by the hand of one who had been among the chosen friends of Pole and whose life was like his, have a freshness and an eloquence which can never fade, even under the withering detractions of the most searching modern criticism. They tell us of an inner life, which only the most intimate friendship can know and estimate, and lead us to form a juster judgment of the public life of those to whose secret counsels they seem to introduce us. The death of the queen and her favourite cousin, whom she so

[1] Pauli Sadoleti, Epp. (App. Epp. Sadoleti, p. 290.)

little resembled, occurring on the same day, the stage on which the great reactionary drama was opened with so much solemnity and magnificence was cleared at once for new scenes and new actors. The corpse of the cardinal, who had re-entered his native land with all the triumphant accessories of a conqueror, was consigned to its tomb in his own cathedral, silently and almost secretly, and the brick vaulting with its broken stucco, the only token of his burial-place, stands in strange and suggestive contrast to those of his royal kinsmen and ancestors in the Trinity Chapel of the Cathedral.

The most magnificent tomb could hardly tell so grand a history as this strange memorial, whose only interpretation (now read no more) was the coat-armour of the illustrious man who reposed beneath, with its quarterings.

As this blazoning is now almost entirely obliterated, it may not be uninteresting to the heraldic reader to record it here :—

The coat of Pole was of eight quarterings—

1st. Quarterly, France (3 lys) and England ; over all a label of three points.
2nd. Per pale ; a saltire engrailed, for Pole.
3rd. A saltire and label of three points, for Neville.
4th. A fesse between six cross crosslets, for Beauchamp.
5th. Chequy, a chevron ermine, for the old Earls of Warwick.
6th. Three fusils in fesse, for Montacute.
7th. An eagle displayed, for Monthermer.

8th. Quarterly : 1st and 4th, three chevronels, for
        Clare ; 2nd and 3rd, a fret; over all, a
        bendlet, for Spencer,

representing the blood that had been shed during
centuries of civil wars and religious persecutions : a
moral teaching too deep for words, yet fatally un-
learned in the century which followed, and which
opened the ancient warfare on another field.

Falling back upon the history and state of the
diocese during this period of reaction, we are naturally directed to the only document which represents
it—the visitation of the diocese by the archbishop,
which he entered upon early in the year 1556. The
previous year had witnessed his solemn consecration
in the presence of the queen, on the day after the
dreadful death of his predecessor, and in the deep
gloom of horror which succeeded that revolting
spectacle. It is difficult to picture a volume more
singularly suggestive than that which contains the
visitation of his diocese by the cardinal, with a view
to the reconciliation of it to its ancient state of reunion with the Roman see. Though carefully written,
and evidently the original copy, it has a bald and
fragmentary appearance, containing many blanks
which have never been filled up, and many inquiries
which seem to have been never satisfied. When we
compare it with the perfect pages of Warham's visitation, where every one of the *Comperta et detecta* are
most clearly exhibited, and the judicial investigations
arising out of them are fully developed, we see at
once that the ancient power of the primacy had
passed away, that the excommunications which gave

so terrible a sanction to Warham's injunctions, had ceased to be effective ; for here the power of the keys finds no mention whatever. Everything is feeble and tentative, timid and faltering. The magic influence of the undivided Church was at an end ; and the apparent haste, and even slovenliness, of all the proceedings remind us of the strange and touching features of the death of their author—of the burial by night and in haste, of the hurried service— of the mean and unfinished grave. And yet like that grave which was only known by the grand historic quarterings which filled the coat-armour painted on the wall above it, the volume now before us bears this proud title :—

"Acta habita et facta in visitatione ordinariâ reverendissimi in x͞p͞o p͞ris et dni, dni Reginaldi miseratione d͞ia tituli Sancte Marie in Cosmedin, Sancte Romane ecclesie p͞bri Cardinalis, Poli nuncupati, Cantuar̄. Archiep͞i. totius Angliæ Primatis et Ap͞lice sedis legati nati[1] necnon ad illustrissimos in x͞p͞o principes Philippum et Mariam sanctissimi d͞ni n͞ri Papae et ejusdem ap͞lice sedis etiam de latere legati, exercitum in et per civitatem et diocesiam Cantuarien̄."

---

[1] The title of "legatus natus " was little more than honorary, as was proved when Archbishop Chichely contended in vain for precedence against Cardinal Beaufort. The letter of Pope Eugenius IV. written from the Council of Florence to Chichely tells him that a legate *de latere* denotes his belonging to the very body of the Pope, and presents the most curious specimen of the snubbing of Lambeth by the Vatican which is to be found anywhere. (See Tamagna, " Origini e prerogative dei Cardinali della S.R.E.")

The ruin and desolation which the churches of Kent presented at this period discloses itself in every page of the Visitation. Altars, fonts, vestments, books, not to speak of images and ornaments less necessary even from a Roman point of view, had been desecrated and destroyed everywhere. In St. Mary Bredman three altars, with all their necessary furniture, including books, the lamp for the Sacrament, and the image of the crucifix, with Mary and John and that of the patron of the church, are all wanting. The two last works of art are found wanting everywhere, and the destruction of crucifixes here indicated was sometimes attended with acts of blasphemous irreverence. For in the Church of Buckland, near Dover, one Thomas Hide " destroyed and burnt the crucifix, maliciously uttering these words on the said crucifix, ' If it be God, let it rise and come out of the fire.' " In many places, both in town and country, charges are made against parishioners for " refusing to come to the Sacrament, or to be sprinkled with holy water, to receive the sanctified bread, and to join in the processions." A not unfrequent charge is that of looking down on the ground at the elevation of the host to avoid worshipping it ;[1] one of these delinquents is accused of hiding himself behind a column of the church with the same object.[2] " Contempt of the Sacraments and ceremonies of the Church " is a constant ground of accusation ; and still more common is the refusal and neglect to receive the Communion

---

[1] As at St. John's, Thanet (Margate), and at Wingham.
[2] At Wingham.

on the greater festivals. A priest in Thanet is charged
with not "using a decent and becoming vestment
suited to the clerical order." At Birchington one
John Alchorne, besides his contempt for the ceremonies, is guilty of possessing "certain schismatical
books." A priest[1] is charged with "visiting a sick
man without a light and bell," and a layman (Wingham) with blaspheming the Sacrament, by saying "the
Masse is an Idoll[2] and the Sacrament of the Altar is
the Sacrament of the Halter"—a sad indication of
the irreverence which the extreme party in the Reformation had occasioned among the common people in
regard to the most sacred and touching ordinance of
Christianity. A certain William Jackson is reported to
the cardinal as "suspected of heretical pravity;" while
many of the married clergy (whose wives are treated
with every name but that to which they were entitled)
are accused of not deserting them, and still keeping
company with them either openly or clandestinely.[3]
Strangely enough, in the same parish in which a
married priest is very hardly dealt with, a woman is
accused of not attending the church, alleging that "it

[1] At Stelling.   [2] The same charge is made at Buckland.

[3] In Bekesbourne, "Compertum est quod Marmaducus
Smyth fuit conjugatus et quod nonnunquam habet accessum ad
concubinam suam, et etiam accedit ad civitatem Cantuariensem
una cum dictâ suâ concubinâ, ubi palam et publice cum illâ
epulare et potare non erubescit in grave scandalum et offensam
aliorum Christi fidelium." He is charged also with serving
other churches "quia omnia quæ lucrari possit non sufficient
sustentationi concubinæ et liberorum suorum." From a later
entry (under Patrixbourne) we find that the poor wife is "expelled from the diocese."

is a diabolical thing to hear the divine service celebrated by a married priest, and that those are accursed
who hear it." It would seem from this that the mere
state of marriage did not disqualify a priest who was
living apart from his wife from fulfilling his duties at
this period. The remarkable moderation of Cardinal
Pole in enforcing the laws of the Roman Church has
been noted in a paper by the writer on a " Passage
in the History of the Twysden Family,"[1] illustrating
the dispensing power of the Papacy as asserted by
the Crown, and partially conferred on the primates.
Marriage places the priesthood in the fatal guilt of
" apostasy," and yet it would appear from this passage
of Pole's visitation that a married priest was not involved in this ruinous charge. There is no objection
made to the claim of the priest in question to either
orders or jurisdiction, though Cranmer most probably
conveyed both. And here it may be noted that the
Bishop of Aghadoe (Acadensis) in the Council of
Trent asserted and persuaded the fathers there that
the English Orders had every element of a perfect
ordination but one, viz., the papal confirmation—
whose absence, he alleged, invalidated the sacramental
authority.[2] So much for the fabulous histories and

---

[1] "Archæol. Cant." vol. viii.

[2] Acadensis Ibernus ostendit &c. . . . "In Angliâ Rex
vocat se caput ecclesiæ Anglicæ, et creat Episcopos, qui con-
secrantur a tribus Episcopis, aiuntque se veros episcopos qui
sunt a Deo, nos vero id negamus, quia non sunt a Pontifice
Romano adsciti, et recti dicimus, hâcque tantum ratione illos
convincimus non aliâ, nam et ipsi ostendunt se fuisse vocatos,
electos et consecratos, missos." (Le Plat. "Mon. Conc. Trid."

grotesque conclusions with which Sanders and his followers of a later day have endeavoured to obscure both fact and law in the cause of their idol of the Papal supremacy. In the same parish of Bekesbourne, which enjoyed the ministry of a married priest, we find one "Susanna Barret and her maidservant receiving the communion in both kinds, and according to the English form" (sermone Anglicâ). As an atonement for her sin she is required to attend mass on the Sunday after the 5th September, 1556, and to exhibit due reverence at the elevation of the host. At Littlebourne, the curate, John Woodye, is accused of preaching and affirming "that if any one bows down before an image in the church he commits idolatry;" also, "that in the sacrament of the Eucharist, when it is elevated by the priest in the mass, those who see it with carnal eyes see bread only." Perhaps this good man had remembered the older teaching of Aquinas's famous hymn—

> " Præstet fides supplementun
> Sensuum defectui,"

for an absolute presence like that assumed by his accusers needs no faith to realize it. At Elmsted, William Swaford and his wife are charged with uttering contumelious words against the cardinal's "inquisitors," viz., "that they were knaves and bludsuckers"—a charge which they afterwards denied. At Folkestone, a long list of persons refusing to give due

tom. v. p. 578). This was in 1562, on the 30th of November, nearly three years after Parker's consecration and the invention of the Nag's Head fable. This Irish bishop forgot that the Council of Florence recognised the Eastern Orders, notwithstanding this supposed defect.

worship to the Sacrament is given, but none of them seem to have made any appearance or to have cleared themselves of the charge. The pages exhibit a succession of names at long intervals, and with ominous blanks intervening. To account for this catalogue of recusants we find the notice that "meetings (conciliabula) and illicit and clandestine conventicles are held there." On the visitation of the ancient church of Northbourne an original petition of the churchwardens to the cardinal is bound up with the visitation. This describes the utter destruction of the church by fire,[1] and appeals to the archbishop for assistance in the work of restoration. To those who remember that the stone-work of this church is clearly of Norman structure, and that no such complete destruction could possibly have occurred, this address to Pole must be very inexplicable. Perhaps this evident exaggeration may give a clue to those earlier accounts of church conflagrations which have misled so many, and may suggest the belief that even the Danish devastations were not so ruinous as the monkish chroniclers, too eager to celebrate the church-restorers of their age, would lead us to conclude. We have reserved to this point of our review the account which is given us of the absolute plunder of the Church of Womenswould, or Wymlingswould, in East Kent, as it gives the fullest idea of the work of destruction which fell, in the earlier days of the Reformation, in more or less degree, upon all the

---

[1] "Not alone their parish churche with the chauncell and steeple be hooly consumed and destrowed, but also the mansion howse of the vicaradge," &c.

churches of the diocese. The church, it appears, was without a curate, and the following articles were robbed from it under the pretext that they were no longer necessary for public worship, viz., A surplice, a rochet for the clerk, a latten[1] pyx, five corporaces, with cases; two mass books, the one of parchment; one manual of parchment, one portis[2] of parchment, one chrismatory, a pax, a cross of copper, a cross with the image of St. Margaret, a streamer and four banner-cloths, a stained (painted) cloth of the Salutation before the altar, a pendant over the same of blue and red silk, fringed with silk, two curtains at the end of the altar, stained; seven altar-cloths, a houseling towel of diaper, a Lent cloth, stained; a cloth for the rood, a font cloth, a sepulchre cloth of red and green silke, a shippe chest in the rood-loft, two stalls in the quire and certain paving stones taken away; the vestry, the rood-loft, the partition between the church and chancel, the church porch (tiled), and the lead of the steeple all pulled down and taken away, and a dove-house thereof made. Item, the font-stone taken away, and it is used to serve swine in. Item, an altar-stone taken away also to make a grave-stone.

Some almost hieroglyphical letters, which might puzzle even an expert, follow this melancholy cata-logue, written in another hand.

Reparation in a case like this was hopeless. All that the cardinal could do was to restore, as far as pos-sible, the losses of his own cathedral, which were not

---

[1] A mixed metal much used in the vessels of the church at this time.

[2] A portis or portas is a breviary.

a few. In a precious fragment which the loving care of Mr. Sheppard has preserved among the relics of the cathedral documents, and carefully mounted in one of the scrap-books he has formed out of them, is an imperfect list of the vestments of the church, which is evidently merely the last portion of a paper of considerable length. After describing the costly "chesibles" and "tunicles" which closed the list, one embroidered with griffins, another with circles of gold and red roses; another with "orfrays" of gold; others with vines, burrs (tufts?), "hyndes and running orfrays," fleurs-de-lys, and birds, including a precious relic of the Prior Goldstone of blue damask with orfrays of tissue, we find a list of the "ornaments geven by the late L(ord) Cardynalle Poole," viz. :

A mytre of sylver and gylte sett with pearls and stone wayeing xx. li. xvii. oz. defaced.

A payre of gloves of knytt crymson silke embrodered with golde and tassells also.

Another payre of gloves of white knytt sylke embrodered with gold and crimson sylke.

A payre of Buskyns and a payre of shoes of cloth of golde and a payre of shoes and a payre of buskyns of white taffeta.

A payre of Tunycles of crymsen Taffeta with a crosse and borders of purple taffeta lyned with crymsen sarcenett. Another payre of Tunycles of white Taffeta layed with lace and fringe of golde.

A Cambricke clothe edged with golde to take the mytre off tharchbusshoppe's heade.

A vestment of clothe of golde braunched with whyte sylver and the crosse of purple clothe of tissue.[1]

These last relics of a parted faith and an obsolete ritual followed, without doubt, the fate of their pre-

[1] Archiv. Chr. Ch. Cantuar. MS. Scrap Book, C. 23.

decessors, and but for this mutilated record would have perished as completely from memory as they have done from sight.

The death of Pole and the queen on the same day left a clear field for Elizabeth, who now stood the only claimant of the vacant throne, and who hastened to appoint the chaplain of her mother, the unfortunate Anne Boleyn, to the primatial dignity. Matthew Parker, like very few of his predecessors, had ancient Kentish blood in his veins, his mother having been of the family of Monyns of Waldershare, descended from Sir Simon de Monyn of the Castle of Mayon, in Normandy, who attended the Conqueror in his expedition to England. His successor in the reign of Henry VI. acquired Waldershare through an heiress of the great Norman family of Malmaines, and their granddaughter, Alice Monyns, was the mother of Archbishop Parker.[1] Everything in the diocese and in the Church at large fell back, on this great change, upon the usages of the last days of Edward. The work of the Reformation, interrupted during the years of reaction of Philip and Mary, was resumed without delay. The laws repealing the acts of Edward were in their turn repealed, and the shadowy reconciliation of England with Rome passed away like a fitful dream. The fear of being called upon to restore the property of the Church had hung like a threatening storm over the courtiers and the higher nobility, and the return of a reformed government was hailed by them on grounds of self-interest as

[1] Burke's "Extinct Baronetage," p. 362.

gladly as it was welcomed by the masses of the population from the deliverance it gave them from the deeper fears which the cruelties of Mary had everywhere awakened. But the opening of the second Reformation period must be reserved for another chapter.

CHAPTER VIII.

FROM PARKER TO LAUD.

THE state of the diocese on the accession of Queen Elizabeth and the elevation of Parker to the archbishopric was naturally one of the greatest uncertainty and confusion. The temporalities of the Church had been fatally plundered. The brief reign of Cardinal Pole had rather raised the ghost of a departed faith than restored its substance and reality. The churches which were beginning their return to the usages of the past rather under the gentle guidance than the severe injunctions of the Legate, must have presented a melancholy and almost grotesque appearance, exhibiting the last struggle between the Roman and the reformed ritual. The ruin which is disclosed by the *Comperta* of Pole's Visitation would now become increased by the further destruction even of those modest restorations which were there rather suggested than enjoined. After the suppression of Wyatt's rebellion, and the security thus given to Mary's plans, we find that at least the more important and richer churches had been compelled to purchase again the implements and furniture of the old ritual. At Hawkhurst, where the churchwardens' books have been so fortunately preserved, we find a long succession of these purchases. Books, albs, mass-books, crosses, manuals, cruets, amices, girdles, vestments, a "holy-water styck," corporas cloths, stoles, candlesticks, porties (breviaries), a rood made and painted, and numerous other items connected with the revived faith, follow one another during the years of Mary's reign in rapid succession. But the scene presently changes, and we trace the steps of the returning Reformation as clearly as those of the Marian reaction. Here, however, we find a noteworthy fact, on which Mr. Godfrey-Faussett has remarked with his usual historical precision. The "making of a scaffold to paint the rood" is mentioned as succeeding the purchase of the book of "Artycholls" which is the first indication of the return to the reformed ritual. "Observe," writes Mr. Faussett, "that nevertheless the rood is newly painted after this purchase, Elizabeth being well known to be tender of images, and her injunction against them not being issued till the visitation of the summer of 1559. Later still, Edwin Sandys, afterwards archbishop of York, remonstrated with the queen on the crucifix still kept in her private chapel, and seems to have obtained its removal after some displeasure on her part."[1] What became of the remade or repurchased articles of the Marian period we know not, and can hardly safely conjecture.

The transition to the restored forms of worship appears to have been unattended by any resistance, and probably the return to an English service after the brief restoration of a ritual in an unknown tongue

---

[1] Hawkhurst Notes, "Arch. Cant." vol. v. page 71.

was even more welcome to the vast masses of the
rural population than it had been on its first introduction. The right of all Christian people to hear
in their own tongue the wonderful works of God,
a Pentecostal law which no human authority could
supersede, when once recovered could not be easily
parted with, and the more learned of the reformed
clergy must have remembered that the greatest divine
of the Roman Church within their own times had
written that " it would conduce better to the edifi-
cation of the Church if the public prayers which were
said in the hearing of the Church were said in a
tongue common to the priests and people rather than
in Latin."[1]   In the same place, on the words, " If I
pray in an unknown tongue, my spirit prayeth, but my
understanding is unfruitful," he observes, " Experience
shows that when anyone ignorant of the Latin tongue is
moved by the Holy Spirit to pray in Latin, his feeling,
that is, his feeling part, prays, but his mind, that is, his
understanding, does not reflect upon the sense of the
words he utters, does not contemplate their meaning,
nor is able to penetrate it, and thus his mind . . .
is without its proper fruit, which is to be nourished
by the meaning of the prayer, and the things signified
in it."   The return to an intelligible service had produced an intelligent body of worshippers, and we
can have little wonder that it was unattended by
those disturbances which a great change, when it
is also an unpopular one, never fails to occasion.
But while the new ritual was thus favourable to the

---

[1] Cardinal Cajetan on 1 Cor. xiv.

inner life of the spiritual body, it cannot be denied
that it was eminently the reverse to the external
form and comeliness of the Church, and to the
material results in which a less enlightened faith has
ever been so prolific. Church building and restoration ceased in the ever-present fear of still farther
works of sacrilege and destruction under the influence
of Puritanism, which so soon became prominent and
powerful. The means which the clergy possessed of
contributing to the repairs of the church, and to those
new works which we find from the wills of the fifteenth
and sixteenth centuries to have been almost uninterruptedly carried on in every church in the diocese,
and the motives by which they were enabled to
influence others in the same direction, were now cut
off altogether. The fifteenth century towers which
adorn almost every extended landscape, both in
East and West Kent, constitute the last of the glories
of the dispensation which was passing away. The
rude and massive tower at Lyminge, begun about
1480, and only finished, and then with the greatest
difficulty, in 1527—the actually unfinished tower of
Aldington, begun in 1507, the final stage of which
was not built till 1557, and represents the last failing
effort of the Roman revival, are among the countless
instances of this architectural decadence. " Sir
Thomas Duffyn" (as he is called), the vicar of
Lyminge in 1508, who had left more than £30 for
the tower of the church and a new bell, was represented in 1575 by John Grimston, who was only able
to leave £3. 5s. 8d. a-piece to his nine surviving
daughters, the tenth, whom he significantly named

"Sufficient," having died before him. The great
and important churches belonging to the monasteries
of Kent were now left to the precarious support of
the parishioners, who were burdened not only with
their churches, but with the poor who once received
what the Italians would call the "carità de' frati,"
at the convent-gates, a method of relief which would
hardly be approved of by the economists of a later
age. From the sudden drying-up of all these sources
of charity a poor law had become a necessity ; and
this greatest of all the burdens upon land has so
borne down the agricultural interest for the last three
centuries that we can little wonder that churches have
fallen into decay, livings become united, parsonage-
houses taken down or left in a state of perilous dilapidation until our own age, which has witnessed so great
a *renaissance* in the ecclesiastical state of the diocese.
The severance of the ties between the archbishops
and the diocese, which, beginning in an earlier day,
was completed by Cranmer's fatal surrender of all
his greater manors, was followed by the breaking-up
of those ties which had hitherto connected the foundation of Christ Church with its dependent churches.
The cathedral, as Henry VIII. originally designed
it, was to have included within itself not only a
grammar-school, such as was ever connected with
such an establishment, but also a perfect school of
divinity, which would have enabled it to become not
only the model but the motive power of the spiritual
life of the diocese. Readerships of divinity in Greek,
Hebrew, and Latin; readers in civil law and medicine ;
besides forty scholars in divinity to be maintained at

Oxford and Cambridge, form a part of the draft scheme which the king submitted to Cranmer.[1] It is strange that the latter, in his reply, suggests the omission of the prebendaries who were to form a part of the new foundation, and suggests twenty divines instead, so that the cathedral hardly escaped being turned into a great divinity college. It has now, (probably in order to obviate such a danger for the future), entirely excluded that teaching of divinity for the benefit of the diocese which constituted the principal feature of the king's design. It is to be hoped that the restoration of the study of divinity which has thus been eliminated, will be among the earliest of those reforms which the Cathedral Commissioners may propose, and that the great foundation which now has a solitary existence, though in the midst of a populous city, and a life apart from the diocese (if that can indeed be called a life which is rather a close captivity in the chains of obsolete statutes and in the ceaseless routine of perfunctory obligations), will resume its ancient place in the Church and in the diocese. But while the laity appear to have acquiesced in the change which was now being gradually brought upon the Church, the higher clergy by no means so readily submitted to it.   Nicholas de Harpsfield, Pole's energetic and influential archdeacon, " in a sermon at Canterbury, in February, 1559, stirred the people much to sedition ; and the members of that cathedral had openly said that religion should not and could not be altered.   The council also had. heard that the

---

[1] See Burnet's " Hist. of the Reformation," Appendix.

prebendaries there had bought up many arms; so a letter was written to Sir Thomas Smith, to examine into that matter. Harpsfield was not put in prison, but received only a rebuke."[1]

The process of transition from the Roman system, as reintroduced by Mary, went on very slowly and with prudent stages during the year 1559. The queen's injunction at length came out, not without great hesitation, in regard to the destruction or removal of images, for which she herself, probably more on æsthetical than theological grounds, had a strong predilection. The restoration of the right of marriage to the clergy; the ordering the public worship of the Church according to the Edwardian liturgy, now again substituted for the mass; the ordering of communion-tables instead of altars for the church, where altars had been removed; the licensing of preachers, and the various observances required by the restored ritual, were the chief features of these injunctions, to whose authority Archbishop Laud appealed in his argument against Prynne and his colleagues in the Star Chamber. Parker, who, on account of feeble health and failing energies had vainly endeavoured to escape from the anxious and exalted position which was in a manner thrust upon him, foretold too well the dangers to which the Church was exposed through the inevitable renewal of those bitter conflicts which the exiles from England in the Marian persecution had opened so painfully at Geneva and Zurich. "The whole strength of the Church," he

---

[1] Burnet, "Hist. of the Reformation," p. ii. book iii. (1559).

said in his letter to the Lord Keeper, "depended on the unity of the brethren in doctrine, but if there should be heartburnings among them and the private quarrels that had been beyond sea should be brought home, the peace of the Church would be lost, and the success of all their plan would be blasted."[1] Unhappily, the fears of the primate were too fully realized. The same heats which had arisen among the exiled clergy in regard to vestments, ceremonies, and Church government, were now transferred to the very centre of the Church, and were even more virulent in the day of her re-establishment than in that of her persecution and exile. It is impossible to look back upon such a conflict without grief and shame, and yet it has been so often renewed in times of greater enlightenment that at least we cannot reflect upon it with wonder. This fatal controversy, which, from the necessity attached to the ceremonies on the one side, and the equally superstitious belief in their sinfulness which prevailed on the other, grew on insensibly to such a degree of implacability as to admit of no pacification, brought about at last that open nonconformity whose development in so many forms meets us everywhere in this as in every other diocese of England. The fallacies which were alleged on the side of those who opposed the ceremonies might have been easily exposed and refuted, had not the other party in the heat of the conflict attached a kind of necessity to them which deprived them of the character of things indifferent. Milton's rule would,

[1] Burnet, l.c.

if carried out, reduce the whole Church to a state of anarchy such as no human society could tolerate and which certainly none could survive. "He is wont to say," are his words, "he enjoins only things indifferent. Let them be so still; who gave him authority to change their nature by enjoining them?"[1] The answer is obvious, that by enjoining them as useful and orderly helps to devotion and discipline, we do not "change their nature." The mere injunction of them does not affect their indifferent character, but leaves it where it was, as would be the case with any human law regulating public order or decency. But, unfortunately, the zealots of the Jacobean period instead of apologizing for them and commending them with such arguments as Hooker afterwards alleged, insisted on Episcopacy, and the ceremonies connected with it, as matters of necessity, which provoked that just observation in the "Letter of the Synod of Zeeland to the Church of Scotland," "As for such ceremonies and rites as have their original from minds arrogant and not contented with divine institution, *and to which an opinion of necessity is added*, as if without these holy things could not be decently gone about and the worship but coldly performed, *truly we cannot see how such ceremonies can be called indifferent*."[2] It is at this point that the controversy became so inveterate and almost irreconcilable.

During the first ten years of Elizabeth's reign, the

[1] Milton on Heresy, &c.
[2] "Letter of the Synod of Zeeland," Edinb. 1643.

X

Roman Catholics came to our churches, and until the excommunication of that queen by Pius V. (whose conspiracy with Ridolfi to murder her has lately been so thoroughly established as to add to his title of saint that of regicide), the loyalty of the adherents of the Papacy to the Crown was marked by their union with the National Church in her public worship. This general conformity appears to have been but little disturbed by the bull itself; but, on the accession of James I., and the exaction of the oath of allegiance and fidelity, the communion between the members of the two Churches was violently interrupted by the brief of Paul V., addressed to the " English Catholics" in 1604. In this the faithful are specially forbidden to attend the churches, services, or sermons of the Church of England, or to hold any communion with its members in religious rites or duties. At the same time they are strictly forbidden to take the oath of allegiance prescribed by the Government. It seems that up to this period the attendance of the Roman Catholics at the churches, whether freely or by compulsion, had been in great measure carried on, but it would appear at the same time that a large portion of our clergy had not improved the good opportunity which was thus given them of conciliating all classes to the Government, which was the great object of the queen, and too many of the preachers had made their pulpits the means of carrying on a continual warfare against Popery both in its civil and ecclesiastical aspect. These, as they affected a far higher degree of moral and doctrinal purity than the clergy of the more moderate party, went

by the name of *Puritans* or *Precisians*, a title
which, like that of the Methodists, whose separation
from the Church began in much the same manner
and on not dissimilar grounds, has adhered to them
ever since.

The friends of this great movement derived its
origin from the coldness and worldliness of the
national clergy, their dislike to preaching, and their ·
general idleness and insufficiency. Sir Robert Cotton
thus describes the fatal results which were occasioned by that cold fit which followed "the zeal
begotten in the time of the Marian persecution."
"In those days," he writes, "there was an emula-
tion between the clergy and the laity, and a strife
arose whether of them should show themselves
most affectionate to the Gospel. Ministers haunted
the houses of worthiest men, where Jesuits now
build their tabernacles, and poor country churches
were frequented with the best of the shire ; the
Word of God was precious, prayer and preaching went hand-in-hand together until Archbishop
Grindal's disgrace and Hatfield's hard conceit of
prophesying brought the flowing of those good graces
to a still water." Thus "most men grew to be
frozen in zeal and benumbed, that whosoever (as the
worthy Lord Keeper Bacon observed in those days)
pretended a little spark of earnestness, he seemed no
less than red-fire hot in comparison of the other.
And as some fare the worse for an ill neighbour's
sake dwelling beside them, so did it betide the
Protestants, who, seeking to curb the Papists, or
reprove an idle drone, were incontinently branded

with the ignominious note of *Precisian*."[1]　The real
origin of the division was not unlike that which was
opened between the secular and regular clergy of
an earlier age, and was simply the rivalry between a
preaching and a non-preaching ministry.　The
Puritans had secured the pulpits, very much as the
regulars contrived to supplant the seculars and to
become the popular preachers in an age which was
eminently a hearing and not a reading one, when the
monasteries were the sole repositories of learning,
and the seculars were in outer darkness.　To the
Court and Government (and the Court was then
the Government) the great object of uniting the
recusants with the Church was completely frustrated by those who "sought to curb the Papists;"
while the "reproof of the idle drones" (*i.e.*, the non-
preaching clergy) only opened a fatal chasm in the
ranks of the Church itself.　As late as the Canons of
1603, the distinction between the preaching and the
non-preaching minister is distinctly drawn, and the
rivalry between them most clearly indicated.[2]

The "prophesyings" authorized by Grindal, whose
inclination towards the Geneva doctrine and discipline
was very marked, had brought him into serious disgrace with the queen, who, in 1588, put forth a
proclamation against the attempts which were then
being made to discredit the form of government by
bishops and the present settlement of the English
Church.　In 1573, a similar proclamation had been

---

[1] See the "Healing Attempt," Lond. 1689, p. 3.
[2] Cann. 49, 56, 57.

directed against those who met together in private houses or public places to use any other rites or prayers than those of the Liturgy, followed by another against the "sectaries" of what was termed the "Family of Love." At the same time the most severe restraints were laid upon preachers in regard to their licenses, and the bishops were invested with an absolute power, even in the case of incumbents ; a power which by Grindal and Abbot would have been used in a very different manner from that in which Bancroft and Laud would have exercised it.

Besides, therefore, the original division which arose between the preaching and the non-preaching ministers,—those who relied rather on the prayers and sacraments than on the efficacy of preaching, in which Puritanism originated,—an impulse of a still stronger nature was given to it at a later period by the growth of two schools of preaching, one Calvinistic, or more properly Augustinian, and the other adapted to the principles of a still earlier and simpler system, that upon which the creeds themselves were built for every age and race. The diocese of Canterbury, for many obvious reasons, and not least of all from the larger element of foreign Protestantism which was so early introduced into it, and the almost entire elimination from it of the papal element, had a strong and growing tendency towards Puritanism. Some of its greatest divines and preachers were of this school, notably the celebrated Edward Dering, of the ancient family of Surrenden, who held at one time the rectory of Pluckley, and was chaplain to the queen at the Tower. He was also Lady Margaret Professor of

Divinity at Cambridge and a prebendary of Salisbury. He was a man of fearless boldness, and "in a sermon preached before the queen in 1569 he warned her lest she who had been (" tanquam ovis ") as a sheep appointed to be slain (Ps. xliv. 22) should come to be chastised (" tanquam indomita juvenca ") as an untamed and unruly heifer (Jerem. xxxi. 18). Her Majesty deemed the allusion a little too forcible, and Edward Dering was forbidden to preach any more before the Court. Some time afterwards he was prosecuted for Puritanism before the High Commissioners, and after a long suit was suspended from all his clerical functions.[1] Of the terrible Nemesis which followed up the High Church party of a later day in the person of his great-nephew, the famous Sir Edward Dering, of the Long Parliament, we shall have occasion to speak in a later chapter. The Puritan divine is said to have "strengthened the foundations of Protestantism in the hearts of thousands who listened with rapture whenever he preached, and bought up with eagerness large editions of his published sermons." His influence in his native county was doubtless as great as it was in London ; and his " Catechism," printed by Jugge, the first printer of the plays of Shakespeare, has the strong Calvinistic character of the early Elizabethan divines. His prayers were of singular beauty, and his " Commentary on the Hebrews " has passages of great interest and value.

But while there were many men of learning and eminence adorning the diocese, and even gaining a just celebrity throughout the Church of England

[1] " Proceedings in Kent," (Camden Society), preface p. vii.

at the opening of the reign of Elizabeth, the state of the diocese itself at that period was one of confusion and darkness which can hardly be well exaggerated. Two of the visitation books of Archbishop Parker, one dated in 1561 and another in 1573, have just been rescued from the obscurity in which they have lain ever since that day, and the latter of them (which has a clear and orderly arrangement) gives us a picture of the state of the parishes in Kent which may safely be said to have been never equalled in any earlier age. The former of them is drawn up in so slovenly and imperfect a form as to appear to be simply the rough draft of some more finished document. It only leaves us to conjecture from the visitation held twelve years after what must have been the condition of the churches throughout the diocese at the opening of Parker's primacy. As the visitation in September and October, 1573, was held only a year and a half before the archbishop's death, it proves how slow was the progress of the Reformation during his episcopate, notwithstanding the advantages it enjoyed from the settlement of the throne under Elizabeth. In thirty-eight important parishes the clergy were absolutely non-resident. In six there was either no minister whatever or the churches were vacant. In four the clergy maintained a kind of half-residence. In several there were only deacons, in others only readers. In some cases two, in one even three parishes had a single minister between them. Other churches had only occasional services, and thus about sixty parishes either suffered an entire " famine of the word of God," or received their spiritual food so irregularly as to make one feel but little surprise that the spirit of the Reformation flagged so soon in that scene where it had been so triumphant at first. The rarity of preaching, of which this visitation gives us remarkable proof, has been already suggested as the main cause of that great Puritan movement which this fatal departure from the practice of all the reformed churches so naturally provoked. Four sermons a year might satisfy the statutable requirement, but certainly did not satisfy the people, who required something more than a quarterly disproof of the pope's supremacy, or a quarterly defence of the queen's. But even this scant measure was often denied them. In Goodneston (near Wingham) it is complained that "they have not their *ordinary* sermons." In Crundall there is the same complaint, and also at Ickham and at Whitstable. At Tilmanstone the parishioners only had three sermons since the previous visitation. At Worth they had had no sermons for two years; at Seasalter none for a twelvemonth, and at Westbere none for the same period. At Ewell they were somewhat more fortunate, for they had one during the year; the same liberal measure was given also at Capel-le-Ferne. Even Saltwood was destitute of its quarterly sermons, while Wootton was fortunate in having two. Stanford had had none for a twelvemonth; while Paddlesworth had one during the same period, a privation which is charged to the farmer of the rectory, as it is in several other places. At Leysdowne they had one sermon a-year; while Bapchild, more fortunate, could boast

of three. Kingsdown had no sermons all the year
round, and was only served by a reader. Bobbing
and Stockbury, Badlesmere and Sheldwich, had but
one sermon in the year ; Debtling, again, none.
Brasted remembered none since the last visitation ;
while at Marden the zealous parishioners, being
deprived of preaching through the absenteeism of
the vicar, procured a preacher for themselves. At
Newenden the people could not get their "ordinary
sermons" because "the vicar could get none to
preach them." Other parishes make like complaints,
and the form in which they are made indicates
clearly the sense their inhabitants felt of this great
privation. To add to the destitution in regard to
their public worship we find the complaint made in
the important parish of Milton-next-Sittingbourne that
"the vicar will not allow the singing of psalms or
other things, and he will not suffer us to sing or say
with him" (i.e., to repeat the responses) "as before
he was wont to do, which is a great hindrance to
our youth and others, who being shut from the saying
and singing with him, they spend their time in service
lewdly or evil." Still more serious is the charge
against William Lovell, minister of St. Margaret's, Canterbury. He is said to be "suspected in religion, for
that he goeth suspiciously mumbling undecent prayers
to himself,"&c. On this account the parishioners allege
that they "cannot with safe conscience receive the
communion from him." Poor Mr. Lovell had doubtless been used to recite the prayers from his breviary
in the days of Cardinal Pole, and unconsciously
extended his work of repetition into the days of

Archbishop Parker. Truly the clergy of that day were more worthy of our pity than of our blame in all that they did or failed to do. To change their religion with every reign, and their ritual with every new injunction of the queen, required a degree of aptitude and versatility of character which few but a Vicar of Bray could claim.

A singular feature of this visitation is the constant complaint that the clergy use " common " instead of " wafer bread." The latter appears to have continued in use up to the middle of the reign of Charles I., and to have been, perhaps, from early habit, a very important point in Archbishop Parker's ritual system. The "lack of the Paraphrase of Erasmus," which is here constantly complained of, leads to the inquiry what could have become of the numerous copies which filled the churches in the earlier days of the Reformation? Were they destroyed in Mary's reign or sold? If the latter, the book would assuredly be a more common one in England, and would still be found in many parish churches. Images and " blasphemous windows " are discovered in some churches, the latter in the chapel of Mr. Roper, at St. Dunstan's, in Canterbury, probably a relative of the great Sir Thomas More. The curate at Wye is charged with " not coming down to read the Bible in the middle of the church according to the injunctions," while at Stodmarsh the chancel is said to be " destitute of pews and seats, both for the minister and preacher." The duties of the sidesmen are curiously illustrated at Birchington, where a person is found in an " alehouse in service-time, whereupon, he being admonished for the same by the sidesmen, he bade them scornfully go shake their ears." But if the state of the clergy is discovered to be so unsatisfactory, that of the laity is no less severely noted by the implacable churchwardens. If their "charges" and "suspicions" are true, the general state of morality must have been as lax as that of the churches was dilapidated; and, indeed, the picture of the diocese at this time makes us look with natural sympathy upon the noble but unsuccessful efforts of the good Archbishop Grindal to atone for the laxity of his predecessor by encouraging the revival of preaching, and restoring to the Church a learned and a faithful ministry. We have already seen the just remarks of Sir Robert Cotton on the fatal and irretrievable error into which Elizabeth was led in removing Grindal from her councils and depriving him of her favour. His meetings for " prophesyings," in other words, for the study of the Scriptures, might, if encouraged, have created a preaching ministry such as would have given life and fervour to the Church, and prevented the Puritan movement from developing itself into one of open enmity to the Established Church. But the golden opportunity was lost, and the troubles of a later day were the fatal and inevitable result. The influence of Grindal, as Bishop of London, had been employed to unite the friends of the Reformation both among the English and foreign Churches, and to enable them to disprove the calumnies of their adversaries by a conversation worthy of their higher religious privileges. Nicholas Gallars, an eminent

French divine, who was at the conference of Poissy, addresses him thus in his dedication to him of the works of Irenæus : " I am able myself to testify as I was myself present, saw and experienced with what care and vigilance you consulted the peace of the Churches over which you presided ; with how great zeal you purged them not only from impious rites, but from the errors of the Anabaptists which had then crept in ; with what diligence you appeased the tumults and discords which had arisen, either among your own people or among those without. For as far as you were able you did not merely preserve the outward fabric of the foreign Churches which were gathered together in London through the favour of Queen Elizabeth, but preserved them internally from fear, discord, and division. You kept the rash and innovating within bounds, repressed the insolent and refractory, humbled the proud, protected the innocent, appeased quarrels and disputes, and made yourself, in fine, a veritable Irenæus, and peace-maker."[1] Such was the character of Grindal when he was Bishop of London, and it was unchanged in any of its features when he attained to the primacy on the death of Parker, in 1575. Of the first Elizabethan archbishop we may truly affirm on a careful examination of his visitation book in the fourteenth year of his primacy, that however great he was as a divine, an historian, a munificent benefactor of his university, and a magnificent host of royalty, both at Croydon and Canterbury, he failed in his

---

[1] Ep. ad Edm. Grindal, Gen. 1570.

duty as a diocesan, and left his see to the devoted
and unfortunate Grindal in a state which was a disgrace to the Reformation, and a miserable contrast
to that which it presented in the days of Archbishop
Warham. During a period of unexampled prosperity
church-building and church-reparation seem to have
ceased altogether. The chancels and parsonages are
constantly reported as being in a state of disrepair,
and often falling down. Surplices are wanting in
many churches, and the charges against non-com-
municants are frequent. At Sturry there is the
curious entry that Elizabeth Saunders is faulty (fautie)
in the XVIIth Article. Perhaps her views on predestination may have been as obscure as the Article
itself, or did not quite agree with those of the churchwardens. It is curious that they present the vicar
for "receiving at the communion some that were not
in charity, *as we suppose*," a rather doubtful proof of
their own. The vicar is also accused for "not calling the youth to be instructed, nor yet doth nothing
contained in the Xth Article." The former portion
of the charge would merely involve a failure to teach
them the doctrine of original sin and prevenient
grace; but the latter one is much more perplexing,
as though there is much scope for faith, there is none
at all for action in the Article in question. From an
entry under Wye it would appear that copes were
still in use; while so lax was the practice on the
other side that even the surplice was in some cases
not used during the service. It is almost unaccountable that fourteen years of religious settlement, both
in doctrine and rite, should have left the diocese in

so disorganized a state; and the only reason which
can be assigned is that Parker was wholly a primate,
and hardly in any sense a diocesan. His princely
entertainment of Elizabeth at Canterbury, whose full
details are given us in Dr. Hook's life of him, proved
that he had not forgotten the "*stylus curiæ*" of his
predecessors, however he may have affected a simpler
ritual and a purer faith. No doubt this strange
combination suited well the taste of the queen and
her court, though it must have prevented that extension of the charity of the archbishop to his own diocese which the continuous plunder of the see, carried
on by the queen as by her father under the specious
pretext of exchanges with the Crown, still more fatally
contracted.[1] Her only quarrel with Parker appears
to have been his marriage, and his predilection for a
married clergy. At this time, and on this account,
the Elizabethan bishops were not accustomed to
live with their wives and families under the same
roof, Parker himself purchasing a house at Beakes-
bourne for his wife and family to reside in when he
took up his abode there, and also a house near the
Palace at Lambeth, called Duke's-place, during their
stay at that residence.[2]

---

[1] He left many legacies to his numerous friends from the
queen downward—while to the city of Canterbury he left the
miserable sum of £100 to be lent out to the wool manufacturers
of the place, to enable them to employ the poor in that industry.
Poor as he was, after leaving all that he had besides for
charitable purposes, Archbishop Grindal left the same sum to
the Metropolitical city.

Battcley's "Somner," ii. p. 80, Hasted's "Kent," vol. xii.
p. 455.

It was at Lambeth that the archbishop gave the grand entertainment to the queen, which is described in his "Antiquities of the British Church" (ed. Drake, p. 557). "The queen removing from Hampton Court to Greenwich visited the archbishop at Lambeth, where she staid all night. That day was Tuesday—the next day being Wednesday it was usual, as it was the season of Lent, that a sermon should be preached before the queen. A pulpit was therefore placed in the quadrangle near the pump, and a sermon was delivered by Dr. Pearce. The queen heard it from the upper gallery that looks towards the Thames; the nobility and the courtiers stood in the other galleries which formed the quadrangle. The people from below divided their attention between Her Majesty and the preacher. When the sermon was over they went to dinner. The other parts of the house being occupied by the queen and her attendants, the archbishop received his guests in the great room next to the garden below stairs. Here on Tuesday he invited a large party of the inferior courtiers. In the same room on the Wednesday he made a great dinner; at his own table sate down nine earls and seven barons: at the other table the comptroller of the queen's household, her secretary, and many other knights and esquires—besides the usual table for the great officers of state, where sate the Lord Treasurer, the Lord Admiral, the Chamberlain, and others. The whole of their charge was borne by the archbishop. At four of the clock on the Wednesday afternoon, the queen and her court removed to Greenwich."

Poor Archbishop Grindal, it would appear, having less courtly tastes and a clearer eye to his spiritual duties, was never honoured with a Royal visit; while his successor, Whitgift, who made such extravagant attempts to recal the mediæval grandeur of the primacy (once entering Canterbury with a train of 500 horsemen, of whom a hundred were his own domestics) received no less than fourteen recorded visits from Elizabeth, who sometimes stayed two and sometimes three days with the archbishop. Whitgift succeeded Grindal in 1583. He was in some respects the greatest benefactor the diocese has ever had, from the days of the Reformation to our time.

Having recovered many of the possessions of the archbishopric, which had been unjustly held in lay hands, and reduced the over-taxation from which it had suffered, he made use of the means he had thus acquired for the endowments of vicarages and stipends of curates, even abating for this purpose the fines on the renewals of his leases. He endowed in his life-time the hospital which goes under his name at Croydon, the building of which alone cost £2,700, while the endowment added to it was £184 a year. There can be no question that the new development of the episcopate under the reign of Elizabeth, and its return to that "lordly prelating" which Latimer so sternly rebuked, was one of the chief causes of the great outbreak of the Puritan faction, whose distinctive name is assigned by Heylyn to the seventh year of Elizabeth. The great apostle of the new party which triumphed so completely, somewhat more than half a century after, was Dr. Cartwright, Professor of Divinity at Cambridge, who took up in the course of his public teaching the question of Church discipline and government while Whitgift himself was Vice-Chancellor. The propositions which he advanced, and which formed the main principles of later Puritanism, were (I.) that, the names and offices of archbishops and archdeacons ought to be abolished ; (II.) that those of bishops and deacons ought to be reduced to their first apostolic institution—the deacons serving the tables of the poor, the bishops giving themselves to the Word and prayer ; (III.) that the government of the Church by chancellors or officers of archdeacons ought to be restored to the ministers and presbytery of every church ; (IV.) that every minister ought to have a fixed and definite place in the Church ; (V.) that no ministers ought to be appointed by Royal or other patronage ; (VI.) nor made by the bishops only, but by the Church itself. Whitgift procured the expulsion of Cartwright from the University, but the influence of a man of learning and high character, of whom Beza wrote that " the sun never shone upon a more learned man," was by no means so easily repressed.

King James sent to him, offering him the Professorship of Divinity at St. Andrew's, and the Archbishop of Dublin offered him preferment in Ireland. But his appointment by the Earl of Leicester as Master of the Hospital at Warwick kept him in England. Here he was urged by Sir Thomas Walsingham and the learned of both Universities to answer the authors of the Rhemish Testament and its pestilent doctrines ; but Whitgift, like an evil genius, again in-

terposed, fearing (as Fuller affirms) lest any of the
arrows shot against Rome might glance at Canterbury.
And here we may observe the fact, too little borne in
mind, that there were two distinct periods of Puritanism, one arising out of mere questions of Church
order and discipline, and another involving also doctrine.   At the period of Whitgift the doctrine of the
Church of England represented a fully-developed
system of Calvinistic, or, more properly, Augustinian
teaching on the doctrines of grace, and on the more
mysterious questions of predestination, election, and
reprobation, which were defined with almost legal
precision in what are known as the Lambeth Articles.[1]
Here, therefore, there was no scope for any controversy with the Puritan party, whose Calvinism was of
course unimpeachable.   But at a later day, and
during the milder reign of Abbot, a system of doctrine
more nearly approaching that of Arminius was gaining
ground in the Church, and this, brought out fully
by Archbishop Laud, fixed "a great gulf" of doctrine
as well as ritual and disciplinary controversy between
the High Church party and the Puritans of the
Laudian period.   Up to the time of Charles I., the
doctrines of Arminius, though they undoubtedly represent the teaching of the Western Church up to the
period of St. Augustine, and of the Eastern Church

---

[1] For a further proof of this statement we may refer to a
remarkable treatise published in 1696 "by J. Gailhard, Gent,"
called a "Plea for Free Grace against Freewill," in which the
evidence of the early Calvinism of the Church of England is
forcibly stated.

uninterruptedly to our own day, were regarded with
a degree of horror which we can hardly account for.
On the accession of Charles I. the increasing learning
of the age broke away from the restraints of the
Augustinian teaching, and vindicated for the first time
the truth that Christianity, as a universal religion,
could not do less than propose to its converts a universal salvation. It was on this ground that the
struggle between Puritanism and the Church became
a conflict of life and death; and rites and ceremonies, a preaching ministry, and even Church government itself, which gave the first impulse to Puritanism,
became as dust in the balance against the great and
fundamental truth that God, who would have none to
perish, but all men to come to the knowledge of the
truth, could not possibly have withdrawn by a secret
decree the salvation he had published by an open
proclamation to all alike. Accordingly, in the later
period of Puritanism, towards which our history is
hastening on, we shall find that the main charge
against the clergy in Kent was their Arminianism,
which was held to be next akin to Popery. Few of
them, indeed, could have had any idea of the meaning
of such a term—who Arminius was, and where and
when he lived; like the equally celebrated Erastus,
he gave name to a great theory, and a still greater
party, but few who employed it had any very clear
apprehension of the meaning they attached to it, and
it had no sooner become a reproach than it easily
fastened itself upon the very best and most faithful of
the clergy. There can be no question, however, that
if Parker had encouraged a preaching ministry, and

enabled the mind of the people to have been educated
and enlightened during his long primacy, the violent
reaction of the men of Kent against a Church which
they had so devotedly adhered to might have
never occurred, and the "root and branch" Reformation, to which their impulsive and eccentric
leader, Sir Edward Dering, hurried them on,
would not have ended as it did in the temporary
destruction of the national Church, and the disper-
sion of its ministry.   Nor was the habitual negligence
in matters of ritual less dangerous in its results, as it
prepared the way for the great conflict on ceremonies
which opened the religious troubles in Kent and
in the country generally.   If the apostolic precept
of doing all things, and especially the things per-
taining to divine worship, "decently and in order,"
had been carried out by Parker and his successors
the communion tables would have been duly railed
in, the services conducted with reverence, and
nothing would have been left for the zeal of Laud,
unhappily ever vehement and overbearing, to exercise
itself upon.   A preaching ministry would have
satisfied the just requirements of the age, and the
people would have been taught how light and in-
significant in the presence of the great realities of
religion were those bitter conflicts on the merest
trifles of ritual observance which formed the keynote
of the Laudian controversies.   Roman advocates,
wiser in their generation than those of our own
Church, took advantage of this laxity of practice, and
encouraged it in order to bring in the Roman doctrines
and usages, and by leading the people to brand with

the stigma of Popery even the modest rites of Anglican
Episcopacy, in order to bring on the reaction in their
own direction which was certain to follow the excesses
of their extreme opponents. It is a curious fact that
the Jesuit Contzen, who died in 1635, had in his
"Politics," laid down the most approved rules of
bringing in again the Roman system in countries
which had cast it out. These rules, which the famous
Puritan preacher, Matthew Newcomen, cited at large
before the House of Commons[1] against Laud, would
have been obviated altogether, had Parker, Whitgift,
and Abbot brought up the ritual of our Church to
that decent and comely form into which it so naturally
settled itself on the Restoration as to have never since
provoked any general remonstrance from either clergy
or laity. Read in the light of what were assumed to
be positive innovations, the rules of the Jesuit had
too apparent a bearing upon the Laudian changes.
Had the decent order of the Church of the Reformation been retained from the time of Parker, the sixth
rule of the Jesuit would have been superfluous, which
is to "foment the quarrels that are among the Protestants, and strengthen the party that is in nearest
compliance with Rome." Had the Puritans and the
Episcopalians never quarrelled there would have been
little room for this direction. In order, however, to
sow the seed of discord more completely between
them, he adds, " For who might not easily reduce the
Puritans of England into order, if he could extort

---

[1] "The Craft and Cruelty of the Church's Adversaries Discovered." A Sermon preached before the H. of C., 1643, p. 36.

from them an approbation of the bishops?" by which two-edged sword of Jesuitry he inflicts a wound upon the bishops, by enabling the Puritans to charge them with Romanising tendencies, and upon the Puritans by rendering them still more hateful to their Episcopalian fellow-subjects, and pointing out how they might be imperceptibly beguiled into the hated bondage of Rome. The first rule, which is the key to the rest, is " to proceed as musicians do in tuning their instruments; who strain their strings with a gentle hand, and set them up by little and little." It is clear that no such tuning would have been needed if the Church's practice had been raised to its natural pitch in the earlier days of the Reformation.

The character of Archbishop Whitgift presented perhaps the most singular combination of conflicting elements that could be conceived. A rigid Calvinist in doctrine, a high-churchman in matters of government, and a prince-bishop almost after the fashion of his greatest Roman predecessors, a munificent patron of learning, and the head of a family of domestics who were trained to military discipline as in feudal times, and ever prepared to assist in the defence of the country, so often threatened with invasion—we see him under such a variety of aspects as makes it difficult for us to judge of his life by the ordinary standard of opinion. His successor, Richard Bancroft, was translated from the bishopric of London,—a man of far more definite character, a high-churchman and energetic opponent of the Genevan and Scottish discipline. The character of Bancroft, like that of many of his predecessors, is drawn with such dark colours on the one side, and with such brilliant tints on the other, that it is not easy to fix its true value, or to determine how far he was fitted for the very anxious charge which he filled but for six years. We have, however, his picture as one of the memorable group of bishops and Puritan divines in the Hampton Court Conference, drawn by the hand of his devoted friend, Bishop Barlow, and are constrained to admit that Lord Clarendon's panegyric upon his character and lamentation over his irreparable loss are by no means justified by the representation of him as he lived and talked at that scene of Royal buffoonery and episcopal flattery which Barlow has so faithfully depicted—apparently in perfect unconsciousness of the impression it would make upon the reader in other days. This memorable conference—in which the king, instead of acting as a wise moderator, and preserving the impartiality of such a position without compromising the dignity of royalty, exhibited his skill merely in dreary witticisms and in an affected pedantry ; while the bishops contended for the prize in a competition of fulsome adulation, which Barlow himself crowns by attributing to the king the title of "a living library and a walking study"—presents the most humiliating picture which the Church of England has ever yet exhibited before the world. It must be noted, however, that the account given of the conference by Dr. Reynolds and the Puritan party represented the king as altogether on their side, and some described him as using language amounting even to obscenity. Bishop Barlow in setting before us the " true version," as he affirms it to be, though he clothes his narrative in courtly language, by no means produces a picture less humiliating in its view of the bishops or more dignified in its portrait of the king. The part which Archbishops Whitgift and Bancroft (then Bishop of London) took in this abortive colloquy tended to alienate the Puritans more than ever from the Church of England, or rather from that high-church party which had with so fatal and short-sighted a policy made use of this golden opportunity in order to crush its opponents. The accession of James had given the greatest hope to the party of progress, which believed that as he was brought up in the still severer Puritanism of the north, he would not turn a deaf ear to the more moderate Puritans of the southern kingdom. But the cry, "No bishop, no king," had acted as a charm upon the weak mind of James, and the disappointment of the Puritans must have been great indeed when at the close of the first day's conference "his Majesty professed," that "howsoever he lived among Puritans and was kept for the most part as a ward under them, yet since he was of the age of his son, ten years old, he ever disliked their opinions; as the Saviour of the world said, 'Though he lived among them, he was not of them.'" According to the narrative of Bishop Barlow, Bancroft lost his temper in the second day's conference. "His Majesty, observing my Lord of London to speak in some passion, said that there was in it something which he might excuse, something that he did mislike." In such hands as these it was that the interests of the Church of England and the care of the diocese of

Canterbury, then one of its most important divisions, was placed in these anxious times. The careful reader of the history of the Hampton Court Conference cannot fail to regard it as the seed-plot of that harvest of sorrow and violence which forty years after was reaped by other hands, and brought to a terrible death the "noble young prince who was sitting by upon a stool" while the king was making his "short but pithy and sweet speech, to the same purpose which the first day he made."[1]

Whitgift lived but a short time after his appearance at Hampton Court, and his decease was among the causes which delayed Bishop Barlow's pen. He is described in the preface to the bishop's narrative as "a man happy in his life and death, loved of the best while he lived, and heard of God for his decease ; most earnestly desiring, not many days before he was stricken, that he might not yet live to see this Parliament, near as it was." The fear of the conflict with Puritanism in which he had been so actively engaged, and which was now threatening to be more urgent than ever, doubtless inspired this prayer. Bancroft, his successor, carried on the warfare during his brief primacy ; and, according to Clarendon's very doubtful estimate, would have carried it on with much greater success had he not been succeeded by the milder Abbot, who, according to the view of the great historian of the Rebellion, prepared the way for the Puritan triumph and the fatal campaign of Laud. The twenty-

---

[1] Barlow, "Summe and Substance of the Conference at Hampton Court, Jan. 14, 1603 ;" London, 1604, p. 22.

two years of Archbishop Abbot's primacy were years of comparative peace to the diocese, but whether these years of peace were years of real progress, or rather of laxity of discipline too well preparing both the clergy and laity for the terrible conflict under the reign of his successor, must be left to the judgment of the reader rather than for the decision of the extreme historians on either side. Between Lord Clarendon's estimate and that of the Puritan writers it is hard indeed to draw a reasonable mean. But later writers have done more justice to the character and rule of the archbishop than his heated contemporaries, and it is no little credit to his name that without compromising the rights or interests of the Church he gained the respect, and even affection of all parties in it, at a moment when the religious troubles, which culminated in the Great Rebellion, were growing on to a fatal maturity.

His successor was the famous Laud, who, after a series of preferments, ending in the bishopric of London, was elevated to the primatial see in August, 1633. Of his primacy, and the part which the diocese of Canterbury took in the great events with which it was so mournfully connected, we shall have to speak in the ensuing chapter.

CHAPTER IX.

FROM LAUD TO SANCROFT.

WE have already directed attention to the peculiar causes which facilitated the progress of the Reformation in the diocese of Canterbury, and left in it so small a residue of those who were devoted to the Roman see.[1] The vast extent of the estates of the Church in Kent, and the fact that all those which were surrendered to the Crown passed into the hands of the greater nobility, or of those immediately attached to the Court,—the extreme danger incurred by those disaffected to the new order of things by remaining in a county which, from its position between the metropolis and the Continent, was under the most rigid and inquisitorial inspection on the part of the Government,—the vast number of foreign Protestants who were received and tolerated in all the ports and towns of Kent, and who tended to leaven the population with which they intermarried and held daily intercourse—these causes, added to the characteristic independence of the Kentish

---

[1] The list of Popish recusants in Kent, as late as 1641, numbered only sixteen names, of which only those of Guldeford Finch, Hawkins and Roper represent the older county families.— "Proceedings in Kent," Camden Society's Publ. 1861, p. 65.

yeomanry, and of those who had established other industries among them—the clothiers of the Weald, the iron-workers of the district bordering upon Sussex, and the gardening population of Sandwich and south-eastern Kent—all contributed to the signal and almost unparalleled success of a movement which brought at the same time temporal prosperity and spiritual freedom. But the same causes which led to this sudden and perfect change led on, at a later period, to those divisions which culminated in the overthrow of Episcopacy and the successive triumphs of Presbyterianism and Independency. The same energetic spirit which had led the people of Kent to throw off the yoke of Rome with so strange a unanimity, gave to every one of the divisions which the new state of freedom had induced, an independent and antagonistic force. Even in the days of Elizabeth, and far more in those of her successors, James I. and Charles I., every diocese, and most especially this of Canterbury, was divided into three great parties, which might be termed the parties of rest, of movement, and of reaction. The first represented those earlier reformers who believed that they had arrived at a *via media*, equally removed from Roman error and from the excesses of doctrine and nakedness of rite which marked the Presbyterian system of the Continent. These have their type in the divines who flourished in the earlier years of James I., in Archbishop Abbot, Dean Boys, and the Casaubons; men of as much moderation as erudition, and who defended the middle ground which the higher churchmen had then assumed against their adversaries on either side. Opposed to these was the party of movement, which held that the settlement effected by Edward VI. and Elizabeth was only a halting-place, and believed it to have been merely a wise expedient for making the Reformation more gradual and progressive. Thus Fuller compares our first reformers to the Patriarch Jacob, who would not overdrive his tender flock, saying, " I dare not march my Lord Esau's pace." Of these men of movement there were again two classes, those who, like Lord Bacon,[1] contended for gradual changes tending to assimilate the Church of England more closely to the other Churches of the Reformation ; and those who, like the more active and turbulent members of the Long Parliament (led on in the beginning by the famous Sir Edward Dering, who deserted them so timidly in the end), were termed the " Root and Branch " party, whose object it was to destroy Episcopacy, and with it all those distinctive features which made the Church of England the envy and admiration of the most learned of the French and German reformers. Lastly, there was a party of reaction, whose almost avowed object it was to bring back the Church into a sufficient degree of conformity to Rome to enable it to accomplish at a future time that plan of reunion, which, however impracticable it has been made by the infatuated policy of the Court of Rome at a later period, was naturally entertained by those who were not content to pray for the

---

[1] " Reasonable Consideration for the Better Establishment of the Church."

unity of the Church without in some degree contributing actively to the object of their prayers.[1]

The party of movement was naturally identified with those Calvinistic views which the Elizabethan reformers held in a modified form, and was bent on carrying them to their extreme results;[2] while the party of rest adopted a system which avoided at once the extremes of Calvinism, and what was denounced as Arminianism, and believed to be the inevitable forerunner of Popery. Those of the clergy, however, who tended towards the reaction which began to set in towards Rome held doctrines on grace, freewill, and other kindred subjects which so far harmonized with the Roman views as to expose them to an hostility even more violent than that to which the open profession of the former faith would have made them liable. The state of the diocese of Canterbury at the opening of that troubled

---

[1] The most prominent of the charges against Laud were those which related to his correspondence with Romish priests, and to his sympathies and endeavours for an accommodation with the Church of Rome. Although the statements of Prynne must be received with great caution, there is enough in his work to show that an influential party existed having the reactionary tendency here described.

[2] In proof of the extreme views which this party sought to enforce we need only refer to the larger draft of the "Petition of the County of Kent," which reckons among the "truths of God," which the ministers were too "fainthearted to preach, the doctrines of predestination, of free grace, of perseverance, of original sin remaining after baptism, of the Sabbath, the doctrines against universal grace, election for faith foreseen, and free will."—"Proceedings in Kent," p. 30.

period upon which we are now entering can hardly
be clearly understood without keeping in view the
fact, that while the higher clergy and most of the
great county families belonged to what we have here
termed the party of rest, the mass of the population
had everywhere the strongest tendency towards the
party of movement, and to that kind of " Root and
Branch " reformation whose first apostle was the
famous Dr. Cartwright, and whose most powerful
advocate in Parliament was the popular Sir Edward
Dering, whose near relative, Dr. Edward Dering, the
chaplain to Queen Elizabeth at the Tower, was one
of the most eminent among the Calvinistic
preachers of his age. During the primacy of Archbishop Abbot, and while Dean Boys was not only
influential at Canterbury but powerful at Lambeth,
the Protestantism of the Church of England was so
vigorously maintained, that the Puritans (as they were
termed from the seventh year of Elizabeth) did not
come into direct collision with the conforming clergy.
Although they had given out that " there were but
four profitable preachers in the greater part of Kent,"
as Dean Boys tells us, " their spite is now vented in
corners, and all their light is under a bed or bushel,
but our clergy shine as lights in the world in the
midst of a wicked and crooked nation."[1] Words like
these were certainly not unprovoked after the petition
of the Millenarians to the king, in 1603, in which
the established clergy were denounced as " a dumb

[1] " Expos. of the Epistles and Gospels," part I. p. 183, ed.
Lond. 1610.

and insufficient ministry." But it is much to be deplored that the Church was not represented at this time by an Usher instead of a Laud, and the Puritans by a Baxter or Herle instead of an Owen or a Dering. Then, to use the words of Herle, "Our differences would rather have ruffled the fringe than rent the garment of Christ. . . . . We should have rather prayed them less, than argued them more." But the temper of Laud in the first years of this embittered conflict brought about so violent a re-action in his diocese, that all attempts at union or compromise were hopeless.

The valuable collection of papers relating to the "Proceedings in Kent," published by the Camden Society from the MSS. at Surrenden Dering, discloses a picture of the state of the Church throughout the county which must at once prepare us for the cata-strophe then so near. In the notes of the proceedings taken by the "Sub-Committee on Religion, appointed Nov. 23, 1640"—a body delegated by the "Grand Committee" (or Committee of the whole House) on the subject,[1] we have a portrait of Laud as he was in his diocese—the only view of that many-sided character, so grand in some of its features and yet so mean in others, which the scope of our narrative permits us to take. It represents the case of a Mr. Snelling, Vicar of Paul's Cray, and the deposition of the facts of it by "John Sedgewick, clarke :"—

"Dr. Wood (Chancellor of Rochester) came up,

---

[1] These are comprised in a MS. in the handwriting of Sir Edward Dering himself.

staring and chafing, halfe out of breath, saying, 'For
Jesus' sake—for God's sake—for the king's sake—
somebody helpe me against this Puritan, Snelling.
I demand justice against this dunce.' Wood's
fury continuing, Bishop White asked, 'What's the
matter?' Wood said that Snelling would not read
the Book for Sportes, therefore he had suspended
him. The Bishop sayd he had not done so much,
and going on in his discourse, Sir John Lambe interrupted, saying, 'Hold, my Lord.' Mr. Snelling
presented two answers, a large one, that was rejected;
then a shorter one was exhibited, which was received.
And Dr. Ryves said it was an answer for theire turne,
but it was first defaced (as Mr. Snelling says) by Sir
John Lambe on his appointment. After the day of
sentence of deprivation the archbishop asked Mr.
Snelling, saying, 'Are you conformable?' Mr. Snelling: 'Yes, as far as is by law established.' Archbishop: 'Are you conformable to the new conformity?' Then turning to the company, said,
"There is no more believing this kinde of men then
of a dogge.' Then Bishop Wren said, 'You may
know him by his band that he has a wonderful tender
conscience,' and so said Sir John Lambe." Mr.
Snelling was suspended *ab officio et beneficio* for not
reading the " Book of Sports." He was finally excommunicated for the same offence. And though it
appears that no authority was found in the book itself
for the suspension and excommunication of ministers
refusing, yet Dr. Wood, in his great zeal upon a mere
verbal command of the late Bishop of Rochester,
and " upon another verbal direction from the arch-

z

bishop in his garden at Croydon," did "suspend Mr. Snelling, for he saith that my lord of Canterbury expressing his pleasure to be such, he did take that pleasure soe expressed to be as a command, and accordingly enforced it."[1] Poor Mr. Snelling meanwhile was allowed only a moiety of his benefice, and was obliged to borrow money for his support, and " is never likely," continues Sir Edward Dering, "to be recovered from his debts." This was but one out of a number of Laud's severities in the diocese. Richard Culmer, writing to Sir Edward to announce the preparation of a petition from Canterbury against the archbishop, writes : " I have had very ungracious dealings with the Lambeth patriarch, by whom I have been deprived of my ministry, and all the profits of my living, three years and seven months, having myself, my wife, and seven children to provide for ; such is the prelate's tyranny for not consenting to morris-dancing on the Lord's Day."[2] The cause of this persecution for disobedience to what the archbishop significantly termed the " new conformity," was the republication of the "Book of Sports" by Charles I. on Oct. 18th, 1633, the year of Laud's accession. The shibboleth of orthodoxy and the determination of the qualification for orders in that day were involved in the three questions—Whether the " Book of Sports" be allowable? whether bowing towards the altar be superstitious? and whether the Church have power to determine matters of faith ? On the failure to answer the first and third in the affirmative, and the

---

[1] " Proceedings in Kent," pp. 91–93. [2] Id. p. 120.

second in the negative, numbers of faithful ministers were suspended or silenced, and the Church lost the services of some of the most valuable and efficient of her teachers. From the authentic documents which are collected in the volume here referred to, it is difficult to imagine a condition more helpless, and even hopeless, than that of the clergy of the diocese of Canterbury. The primate and the Crown exercised, the one actually and the other virtually, and by a kind of connivance, an authority both spiritual and temporal that had no precedent in the worst periods of the Roman usurpation, and certainly has had no example in more recent times. On a mere suspicion of disaffection to the " Book of Sports " and the Laudian conformity, the unfortunate clergyman was made a prisoner in his own house, watched over by a pursuivant of the primate's, and treated almost as an outlaw. The case of Mr. Thomas Wilson, the rector of Otham, was one of a hundred. A pursuivant had been despatched for him, whose clutches he had contrived to escape. Sir Edward Dering took him with him to London, and presented a petition to the House in his behalf. His words on this occasion were interesting and significant :—" Now, Mr. Speaker . . . I will present unto you the petition of a poor oppressed minister in the county of Kent, a man orthodox in his doctrine, conformable in his life, laborious in his ministry as any we have or I do know. He is now a sufferer (as all good men are) under the general obloquy of a Puritan. . . . The pursuivant watches his door, and divides him and his cure asunder, to both their griefs. . . . About a week since I went over to Lambeth to move that great bishop (too great indeed) to take this danger off from this minister and to recall the pursuivant. And withal I did undertake for Master Wilson . . . that he should answer his accusers in any of the king's courts at Westminster. The bishop made me answer (as near as I can remember) in hæc verba, 'I am sure that he will not be absent from his cure a twelve-month together, and then (I doubt not) but once in a year we shall have him.' This was all I could obtain, but I hope (by the help of this house) before this year of threats runs round, his Grace will either have more grace or no grace at all. For our manifold griefs do fill a mighty and vast circumference, yet so that from every part our lives of sorrow do lead unto him, and point at him, the centre from whence our miseries in this Church, and many of them in the Common-wealth, do flow."[1] It is deeply to be deplored that words like these, spoken in the ears of the excited members of the Long Parliament, and contributing so largely to the terrible fate of the primate, were occa-sioned by a series of cruelties and persecutions which made his earlier history so sad a contrast to its clos-ing scene. They seem to contain the prophecy of his terrible destiny, while they give the reasons which hardened the hearts of his judges. The famous peti-tion from the county of Kent which the committee on religion had evoked hastened on the fatal consum-mation. This, as it is one of the most important of the documents which belong to our diocesan history,

---

[1] "Proceedings in Kent," p. 39, note.

cannot be fully appreciated unless we present it to the
reader *in extenso*. A much larger version of it was
sent to Sir Edward Dering in the first instance, but
the petition, as it was actually presented, runs thus :

"The humble petition of many of the inhabitants
within his Majesty's county of Kent.

"Most humbly showing that by sad experience we
do daily find the government in the Church of England by archbishops, &c. . . . to be very dangerous
both in Church and Commonwealth, and to be the
occasion of manifold grievances unto his Majesty's
subjects in their consciences, liberties, and estates,
likely to be fatal to us in the continuance thereof.
The dangerous effects of which lordly power in them
have appeared in these particulars following.

"They do with a hard hand overrule all other
ministers, subjecting them to their cruel authority.[1]

"They do suspend, punish, and deprive many
godly, religious, and painful ministers upon slight and
do upon no grounds ; whilst in the meantime few of
them preach the Word of God themselves, and that
but seldom ; but they do restrain the painful preaching
of others both for lectures and for afternoon sermons on the Sabbath Day. They do countenance,
and have of late encouraged papists, priests, and
Arminian, both books and persons.

"They hinder good and godly books to be printed ;

---

[1] This alludes to the charge against Laud of having "suppressed and abrogated the privileges and immunities granted by
his Majesty and his Royal ancestors to the Dutch and French
Churches " as Pym's speech before the House of Lords in 1641
expresses it.

yet they do license to be published many Popish, Arminian, and other dangerous tenets.

"They have deformed our churches with Popish pictures, and suited them with Romish altars.

"They have of late extolled and commended much the Church of Rome, denying the pope to be Antichrist, affirming the Church of Rome to be a true Church in fundamentals.

"They have practised and enforced antiquated and obsolete ceremonies, as standing at the hymns, at Gloria Patri, and turning to the east at several parts of the Divine Service; bowing to the altar, which they term the place of God's residence upon earth; the reading of a second service at the altar, and denying the Holy Sacrament of the Eucharist to such as have not come up to a new-set rail before the altar.

"They have made and contrived illegal canons and constitutions, and framed a most pernicious and desperate oath—an oath of covenant and confederacy for their own hierarchical greatness, besides many other dangerous and pernicious passages in the said canons.

"They do dispense with plurality of benefices; they do both prohibit and grant marriages, neither of them by the rule of law or conscience; but do prohibit that they may grant, and grant that they may have money.

"They have procured a licentious liberty for the Lord's Day, but have pressed the strict observation of saints' holidays; and do punish, suspend, degrade, deprive godly ministers for not publishing a book for liberty of sports on the Sabbath Day.

"They do generally abuse the great ordinance of excommunication, making sometimes a gain of it, to the great discomfort of many poor souls who, for want of money, can get no absolution.

"They claim their office and jurisdiction to be *jure divino*, and do exercise the same (contrary to law) in their own names and under their own seals.

"They receive and take upon them temporal honours, dignities, places and offices in the Commonwealth as if it were lawful for them to use both swords.

"They take cognisance in their courts and elsewhere of matters determinable at the common law.

"They put ministers upon parishes without the patron and the people's consent.

"They do yearly impose oaths upon churchwardens to the most apparent damage of filling the land with perjury.

"They do exercise oaths, *ex officio*, in the nature of an inquisition even into the thoughts of men.

"They have apprehended men by poursuivants without citation or missives first sent; they break up men's houses and studies, taking away what they please.

"They do awe the judges of the land with their greatness, to the inhibiting of prohibitions and hindering of habeas corpus when it is due.

"They are strongly suspected to be confederate with the Roman party in this land[1] and with them to be

---

[1] Richard Carpenter, a convert from Rome, was advised by Dr. Baker (the licenser) not to publish his sermon in vindication of his change "because the Church of Rome and we are in a

the authors, contrivers, or consenters to the present commotions in the North; and the rather because of contribution by the clergy and by the papists in the last year, 1639, and because of an ill-named bene-volence of six subsidies intended to be granted this present year 1640, thereby and with these moneys to engage (as much as in them lay) the two nations into blood.

" It is therefore humbly and earnestly prayed that this hierarchical power may be totally abrogated, if the wisdom of this honourable House shall find that it cannot be maintained by God's Word and to His glory.

" And your petitioners shall ever pray, &c."[1]

This remarkable document gives the key to the entire position of the diocese at this eventful period, and is illustrated and cleared up by the numerous petitions to the committee from various parishes in all parts of the county appended to the narrative of Sir Edward Dering. We observe, first, that the whole diocese, excepting only those parishes which were occupied by the chaplains and nominees of the arch-bishop, had fallen into a laxity of rite and observance which almost exactly resembled those of the Pres-byterian Churches which since the toleration edicts of Edward VI. and Elizabeth had been established at Canterbury, Sandwich, and the other principal centres

peaceful way, and therefore not fit to augment controversies." He was "advised therefore to say as little as might be (some-thing must be said) against the Church of Rome." ("Pro-ceedings," &c., p. 85.)

[1] "Proceedings in Kent," pp. 29-32, note. The larger peti-tion is given in the text.

of population in Kent. The primacy of Archbishop
Abbot had brought about a state of negligence in the
diocese both in doctrine and rite, which sowed the
seeds of those fatal disorders which were developed
during the government of his successor. Lord Clarendon describes him as a man "totally ignorant of
the true constitution of the Church of England; and
the state and interest of the clergy," as " having made
very little progress in the ancient and solid study of
divinity, but adhering to the doctrine of Calvin, whose
discipline he did not think so ill of as he ought to
have done." He is charged with having been
extremely remiss in regard to churches and chapels,
and the neglected state both of these and of the
services which were held in them rendered the
government and re-organization of the diocese a most
difficult work. Unfortunately, these were left to a
man whose vehemence of temper and extreme impru-
dence precipitated a conflict which a gentler and
more forbearing spirit might have averted, or at least
delayed, until a period in which more moderate
counsels prevailed on both sides. The immense and
hitherto latent powers of the archbishopric were now
wielded with a vigour and energy which had been
never witnessed since the days of Becket or Langton ;
and the almost autocratic power which was exercised
in the diocese is sadly illustrated in the petitions of
the clergy and the depositions both of clergy and
laity before the "Committee of Religion." In the
days of Abbot it was enough that the clergy should
hold the Augustinian views on grace, election, predestination, and such "higher doctrines," and should

denounce the Church of Rome on every available
occasion as the Antichrist; it signified little how far
the directions of the ritual, the canons and orders of
the Church were neglected or thrown into abeyance.
We must read, therefore, both the general petition
and the individual addresses by which it was supported with caution and reserve, while at the same
time we give full value to the facts which they detail
—remembering always, however, that we have only in
a few cases the counter-statements of the accused,
and that where we have them they generally explain
away the more startling charges of the accuser.

The summary jurisdiction exercised by the archbishop in the way of suspension, deprivation, and even
excommunication for the most trivial causes; the
disturbance of the clergy by pursuivants and other
officers; their dispensations in the case of pluralities
and marriages, and the other charges against Laud of
violating the rights of the subject and perverting the
course of justice, have too great a weight of proof to
enable us to resist the plea of the petitioners. But
the denunciation of "standing at the hymns," "bowing
at the altar," "turning to the east," as "antiquated
and obsolete ceremonies," shows that the memory
of the petitioners was not much older than the days
of Abbot, and that they had adopted the bare and
irreverent usages of the Presbyterian Churches which
had been found among them, and which seemed (as
Dr. Heylin says) but the "setting up Presbytery to
confront Episcopacy, and a commonwealth in the
midst of a monarchy." The excesses which the
neglect of "decency and order" in the Church had

occasioned induced Laud to order the railing-in of
the communion-tables, and the disuse of the prevailing
practice of bringing the table into the body of the
church at the time of the celebration, or of carrying
the elements down into the church and handing them
from pew to pew. Complaints against this new
arrangement, and the manner it which it was carried
out, came up to the committee from Woodchurch,
East Peckham, Yalding, Capel, Leysdown, Boughton-
under-Blean, Horsmonden, Sturry, Lyminge, Tonbridge, Chatham, Rolvenden, and other places,—all
of them very suggestive as indications of the pre-
Laudian practice—all of them proofs of the violence
and extreme indiscretion with which the change was
introduced and enforced. Of the Vicar of Woodchurch it is complained, "He is a man superstitiously
affected, by his actions manifested in his exalting
the communion-table, and violently compelling the
churchwardens to rail in the same." The Vicar of
East Peckham had gone further by "setting up our
communion-table at the east end of the chancel, close
to the wall, altarwise, the said table there railed in,
and a new wainscot at the east side of the said table,
made with the picture of angels therein carved."
The Vicar of Yalding is charged with the same inno-
vation, his rail having "two ascents thereto." From
Capel the complaint is made of the vicar, "He is so
ceremonial, that if he come out of the rails he saith
he shall offend God," and did "dismise some five or
sixe of us when we presented ourselfes one our knees
in the chansell to receive the sachrament, because we
did not come to the raiels wheare he doth cringe and

bowe." At Horsmonden the communion-table was
set "up unto the walle ;" and upon the said wall was
written these words, "Wee have an altar," &c. The
rector is charged further with going up to the table to
read great part of the service (i.e., the "Communion"
portion), an indication of the general practice of
reading the entire service from the desk. Not only
the arbitrary refusal of the Communion to all who did
not come up to the rails to receive (as in these previous cases), but the most unseemly and violent
conduct to the communicants is charged against the
Rector of Sturry ; while, in addition to the altar-rail
complaint, the Vicar of Lyminge is accused of being
a defender of image-worship, affirming that the papists
were in a righter way than we. And being asked by
Richard Cozins of the same parish, "Why Shadrak,
Mesach, and Abednigo would not worshipp the King's
Image, hee answered, that it was a ffable."

In consequence of these innovations the Tonbridge
petitioners complain that "divers of the best-minded
families there have removed their dwellings into other
parishes, and some gone out of the kingdom." The
same depopulation is described as threatening the
town of Tenterden, but in that case arising from the
non-residence and neglect of the vicar. The curate
of Chatham, in the neighbouring diocese of Rochester,
is denounced for "complaining how he is abased in
administering the sacrament, going from pew to pew,
as one that dealeth alms, or a dole to the people."
When urged by the Apostle's words (on his saying
that seldom-preaching was that he looked for), "that
his duty did consist in preaching, and to be instant

in season and out of season, ' In season,' he saith, ' is
to preach upon Sundaies in the forenoones, and out
of season in the afternoones.' "

Among the evils of the Church which Laud had
rather inherited than provoked were those of the
non-residence of the clergy, insufficiency of their
maintenance, pluralities, doctrinal excesses, and irregular and oppressive exactions in the matter of tithes.
Complaints against non-resident clergymen came in
from Little Chart, Smarden, Sutton Valence, Minster,
Goudhurst, Ivychurch, Hucking, Maidstone, and
Tenterden. The poverty of their ministers is alleged
by the parishioners of Walmer, Brabourne, Oare,
Whitstable, Folkestone, and Waltham. These were
probably mere typical cases of a much larger class of
necessitous cures. Of pluralities we have the cases
of Minster and Sutton Valence. Chislet, Molash,
Stourmouth, Rolvenden, and other places complain
of the life or doctrine of their ministers, or of both ;
while St. Mary Cray, Shoreham and Otford, Fairfield,
Promhill and Midley, represent cases of hardship and
oppression in the matter of tithes. If the time of
Laud had been spent in his diocese instead of in the
Star Chamber or in the Council,—at Canterbury instead of at Lambeth, and if, instead of delegating his
authority to his officials, he had exercised it in his own
person—in other words, had substituted his pastoral
for his judicial office, the petition of the county of Kent
had never been drawn up, nor its sad corroborative
evidences set before the Committee of Religion. But
the fatal die was cast. The death-struggle between
the archbishop and his Puritan clergy was entered

upon without the slightest effort at mediation or reconciliation, and a war *à outrance* was the result.

To the spiritual misery and destitution occasioned
by this continual warfare, were added the temporal
evils so necessarily associated with them. The Weald
of Kent and the Marsh appear, from many indications of these papers, to have presented a sad contrast to that which they exhibited in the earlier days
of the Reformation. The petition from Ruckinge
discloses the attempt of the farmers there to establish
paupers in the farm-houses of the parish, "not able
to give relief, but to receive," by which the people
became unable to contribute either to the Church or
poor, or to find arms to serve his Majesty. This plan
doubtless led on to the depopulation of the Marsh,
and to the non-residence of its clergy, evils which
survived even to our own day, and which have in
many cases been only recently remedied. The poverty
of some of the principal livings offered a melancholy
contrast to the pluralities which united some of the
richest benefices, and often added to them a cathedral
dignity besides. These occurred chiefly in the livings
in the archbishop's own gift, Dr. Meric Casaubon,
Laud's chaplain, holding the vicarages of Minster,
Monkton, and Birchington, together with a prebendal
stall at Canterbury, while Maidstone, even then numbering 6,000 inhabitants, was left to a poor curate,
the archbishop himself receiving the tithes, which
amounted to "at least £400 a year." It had been
well if the zeal and influence of Laud had been exercised in redressing these practical grievances, instead
of being exhausted in efforts to force the inhabitants

of the diocese into a more reverent observance of
ritual matters. As it was, they gave additional weight
to the heavy charges which became so fatal to him,
and prepared the way for that great revolution which
involved destruction rather than reformation. An
anonymous writer, fifty years after, thus judiciously
summarized the case between Laud and his adversaries :—" Many, to avoid the superfluous and superstitious rites whereby the worship of God was in the
Church of Rome corrupted and obscured, have run
into a contrary superstition, avoiding and neglecting
even natural expressions of reverence and decency in
it. This justly moved some of our bishops, and Dr.
Laud especially, to labour (as he saith), that the
external worship of God (so much slighted in many
parts) might be preserved, and that with as much
decency and uniformity as might be. But it was
pressed too far, in unnecessary matters, in a kind of
arbitrary manner, without an equal concern for the
promotion of real and internal piety ; nay, with obsti-
nate refusal and opposition of reformation of other
great abuses in discipline, non-residence, pluralities,
&c., and with opposition even of some means of the
promotion of religion, the observation of the Lord's
Day, lectures,[1] and the purchase of impropriations, as

---

[1] The undue elevation of preaching was the characteristic of
the Puritan movement which Laud so energetically opposed—
the undue depression of it was the error of the Laudian system.
Dean Boys said well, " Preaching may not thrust out of the
church common prayer, for it is an *oratory*—neither may prayer
shuffle preaching out of the church, for it is an *auditory*." (" On
the Epistles, &c., Summer Portion," p. 230.)

if it were the only thing necessary, and that it and absolute subjection to the will of the prince under the notion of loyalty was the sum of all religion. And this again, on the other side, made it to be looked upon as mere formality, and a project to prepare us for the readmission of Popery, and so raised a greater antipathy against it, which at last cast all out, but in its place brought in indecency, profaneness, and confusion."[1]

Notwithstanding the evils which afflicted both the diocese and the Church at large during this fatal period, we may rejoice that the best results of the zeal of Laud remain, and that the restoration of the ritual of our Church to its first estate, which certainly was his great design, was not retarded or neutralized in the day of her re-establishment. The revulsion of feeling which succeeded his cruel death brought the higher features of his life into prominence, and his earlier errors and severities, so bitterly felt in his own diocese, and made conspicuous by the "Committee of Religion," were gradually forgotten. The proverb seemed, in his case at least, to be reversed, "*qualis vita, finis ita*," for the fidelity he declared to the doctrines of the Reformation on the scaffold rather contrasted with than completed the testimony of his primatial reign. The altar-rails, which were his work, the coming up to the table to receive, the reading of the Communion Service from the altar instead of at the desk, these and many other

[1] "The Spirit of the Church-Faction Detected." London, 1691, pref.

results of his zeal for the reverential observances of the Church still survive in the diocese and in the Church at large. Many of the altar-rails and tables of the rural churches in Kent belong either to this period, or to the revived and very doubtful taste of the epoch of the Restoration. Yet it would be ill to forget at how dear a price the forced uniformity of Laud was obtained, and the immense injury it inflicted upon the diocese. These are partly set forth in the larger petition of the county, which alleges its immediate results to have been "the discouragement and distraction of all good subjects, of whom multitudes, both clothiers, merchants, and others being deprived of their ministers, and overburdened with their pressures, have departed the kingdom to Holland and other parts, and have drawn with them a great part of the manufacture of cloth and trading out of the land into the place where they reside, whereby wool (the great staple of the kingdom) is become of small value, and vends not; trading is decayed, many poor people want work, seamen less employed, and the whole land much impoverished, to the great dishonour of the kingdom and blemish of the government thereof."[1] It will be observed that the principal complaints against the Laudian changes came from the Weald of Kent and the places adjacent, where these industries were specially established. In the rural parishes of East Kent the complaints relate chiefly to the inadequate stipends of the ministers, to non-residence, and the disputes which had arisen in regard to tithes.

[1] "Proceedings in Kent," p. 37.

2 A

The first effort of Laud for the better observation
of the ritual in the diocese was put forth at Canterbury. He drew up a body of new statutes for the
cathedral, in which, among many injunctions for the
greater solemnity to be observed in the services, he
equired all the clergy " summâ reverentiâ adorare
Deum versus altare." He next ordered the removal
of what the chapter, in their letter of reply, describe as
the " exorbitant seats within our quire," reminding the
archbishop of the "extraordinary expenses " they had
been involved in "for the ornaments of the altar."[1]
The archbishop had already written to his vicar-
general, Sir Nathaniel Brent, requiring him to command the " Communion Table at Maidstone to be
placed at the upper or east end of the chancel, and
there railed in, and that the communicants there
shall come up to the rail to receive the Blessed
Sacrament ; and the like you are required to do in
all other places where you are to visit metro-
politically."[2] This was in 1633, the year of his
accession.

His next act was much more questionable, and is
incapable of any reasonable defence. The Dutch
and French congregations at Canterbury, Maidstone,
and Sandwich, had enjoyed the most complete toleration, under special grants of the Crown, from the
time of Edward VI., every succeeding sovereign
either confirming or enlarging them. Laud appears,
from the opening of his primacy, to have resolved to
limit these privileges to the persons of the then

---

[1] Prynne, " Canterburies Doom." p. 79.   [2] Id. p. 89.

existing ministers and their congregations, and by
enjoining upon them the observance of the English
Liturgy in its French and Dutch translations, to
bring them into a perfect conformity with the Church
of England and an entire subordination to himself.
By this very doubtful policy he hoped to remove the
anomaly which his devoted chaplain and biographer,
Heylin, describes as the "setting up Presbytery to
confront Episcopacy, and a commonwealth in the
midst of a monarchy." He believed, doubtless, that
by the gradual removal of the model by which too
many of the churches of the diocese had adjusted
their ritual, he should be enabled to raise the
standard of religious observance in his diocese, and
destroy an influence whose results we have already
seen in the laxity which prevailed almost everywhere.
Accordingly, he issued injunctions to the Dutch and
Walloon congregations in his diocese "to hear divine
service *in their parish churches ;*" and "required
their ministers and other strangers that may come
over to them to have the English Liturgy translated into French and Dutch, *for the better settling
of their children to the English Government.*"[1]
He denied them the exercise of any ecclesiastical
jurisdiction, and enjoined on them the use of the

---

[1] Prynne, p. 402 (ed. fol. 1646). This was a direct con-
travention of the orders in Council by which the foreign Churches
were protected, and which in every case permitted their members.
"*though born in the kingdom,* to belong to their congregations.
and extended the privileges to *their children.*" (See Philip
Nye's "Discourse on the King's Authority in dispensing with
Eccl. Laws." Lond. 1687, p. 26.)

English Liturgy, and obedience to the laws of the Church of England.

This edict, which was issued in 1637, was a flagrant infraction of the liberties enjoyed for a century by the foreign Churches, and was a high derogation of the authority of the Crown, justifying the charges brought against the bishop in the Kentish petition. The case of the foreign Churches was fully laid before the world in 1645, in "A Relation of the Troubles of the Three Foreign Churches in Kent, caused by the Injunctions of William Laud, Archbishop of Canterbury; by John Bulteel, Minister of the Walloon Church at Canterbury."

In 1642, the county of Kent was in a state of rebellion, and the proclamation of the king was issued, promising pardon to all who were implicated in this open resistance of his authority; an exception being made in the case of Sir Michael Lively, Bart., and Thomas Blount, Esq.

In 1643, the Parliament, more interested (it would appear) in the religious than in the civil disputes of the age, passed several acts of the most "Root and Branch" character, which they sent on to the king at Oxford, but which he naturally refused to sanction. The first was for the suppression of divers innovations in churches and chapels, for the due observance of the Lord's day, for the better advancement of preaching, &c. The second was an act for abolishing archbishops, bishops, deans, and all the episcopal platform, carrying out the "Root and Branch" reformation in its most radical sense. The third was an act for the punishment of scandalous clergymen ; the fourth, an act against pluralities ; and the fifth, an act for calling together the assembly of divines. Meantime the popular resentment against Laud was increasing in violence and vindictiveness, and the strange transition of his character from the persecutor to the martyr became daily more marked and impressive. It must have been difficult to those who witnessed such scenes as that which his interview with Snelling presented, to have realized the fact that the same character stood before them in that day of humiliation and suffering, in which the heartless Sir John Clotworthy, in reply to the aspiration of Laud, "Cupio dissolvi et esse cum Christo," rejoined, "That is a good desire, but there must be a foundation for that desire, as assurance." "No man," said the archbishop, "can express it ; it is to be found within." "It is founded upon a word though," added the cold-blooded controversialist, "and that word would be known." "That word," replied the archbishop, "is the knowledge of Jesus Christ, and that alone."[1] Truly, the zeal which was "not according to knowledge" of his earlier history was atoned for by that practical knowledge of the Saviour in his closing life which was witnessed in this hour of his last conflict. Those in whose minds the earlier memories of his life survived the later, must have been few indeed in comparison with those who forgot in the touching incidents of the final scene, the errors which had led on to so terrible a destiny. With the

[1] See the original tract describing the last words of the archbishop, 4to. p. 18.

death of Laud began those fifteen years of anarchy, during which Presbyterianism and Congregationalism (or Independency) were successively established in the diocese.

At this fatal period began also those " sufferings of the clergy," described by Walker in his famous narrative, and those endless divisions which, when they had worn out the very life of the Church, left it weak and powerless in the day of the Restoration. The death of Laud in the opening of the year 1645 left the whole Church in a state of anarchy, and the bonds of diocesan government were dissolved. The abolition of Episcopacy, already effected in 1643, was now completed by the cruel fate of the primate ; and the meeting of the assembly of divines at Westminster, in 1647, inaugurated a new system, both of doctrine and government, in agreement with that of the Churches of the Calvinistic confession on the Continent, a system which is now represented by the Scottish Kirk. It must, however, be carefully observed that this " advice of the assembly of divines concerning a confession of faith," is so broad, and even vague, in regard to the matter of Church government, that ample room was left for the great controversy between the advocates of the Presbyterian and Congregational (or Independent) methods, which so soon broke out in the midst of the general anarchy. This omission of any clear direction in so grave a matter was doubtless occasioned by the order of Parliament of Nov. 6, 1645, which empowered the committee to act, and instructed them " to endeavour an union, if possible, of the different opinions of the assembly in point of Church government ; and in case that cannot be done, to find out some way that tender consciences, not submitting in all things, might be borne with," &c.   There were many eminent peace-makers in the assembly who endeavoured to bring about a *modus vivendi*, and even a virtual reconciliation between the two parties.   Eminent among these was Mr. Herle, the prolocutor, and Mr. Coleman, one of the members of the assembly.[1]   But the attempts to give to the Presbyterian government an organiza-tion as complex and elaborate as that which had grown up during the process of centuries in the Epi-scopal Church, and the example which the Scottish Presbyteries presented of the state of spiritual bond-age into which a Church might fall under such a system, hastened the triumph of Congregationalism, for which the churches in Kent were far better pre-pared than for the transfer of an absolute power from an individual to a synodical organization.   In the rare and remarkable treatise of William Dell, called "The Way of Peace," addressed to "Lieutenant-General Cromwell, and to the Lord-General Fairfax,"[2] the writer observes, "Most evident then it is, that during the time of the apostasie, the Church hath been most miserably lorded even amongst us ; for the priest he lorded it over the people, the arch-deacon over the priest, the dean over the archdeacon, the bishop over the dean, and the archbishop over the bishop ; under which woful bondage the Church

---

[1] "Brief History of Presbytery and Independency," London, 1691, pp. 25, 26.

[2] London, 1647, pp. 33-35.

cried out, as Isa. xxvi., 'O Lord our God, other lords beside Thee have had dominion over us.' And is this bondage of the Church now eased by casting off those strange lords? Yea, do not men seek rather to increase it, by setting yet stranger over it, whose names are so full of mystery that the common people cannot understand them? For now they would have the *Classical Presbytery* set over the *Congregational*, and the *Provincial* over the *Classical*, and the *National* over the *Provincial*, for so it is voted, 'that it is lawful and agreeable to the word of God that there be a subordination of Congregational, Classical, Provincial, and National assemblies for the government of the Church.' Now here is *mystery*, and nothing but a certain rising up into the old power under a new name. . . . . If this might be brought about, which they design, the Church would be so far from being eased of its strange lords that it should have them exceedingly multiplied. For what is a national assembly but an archbishop multiplied? and what a provincial assembly but a bishop multiplied? and a classical but a dean and archdeacon multiplied?"

The controversy thus awakened became more and more embittered, notwithstanding the efforts of the best and wisest men on either side, and indeed the only bond of union that remained was the obligation, rather political than religious, of the "Solemn League and Covenant," taken by the House of Commons and the assembly of divines on Sept. 25, 1643, on which occasion a vigorous and not ineloquent address was delivered by the famous Puritan divine, Mr. Philip Nye, whose "thanksgiving beard" is cele-

brated in "Hudibras." It does not appear that the
elaborate organization enjoined by the assembly was
ever established in Kent, where indeed from the character of the clergy and people it would have been
perhaps more difficult to carry out than in most other
counties. The foreign Churches in Kent had become from necessity, if not also from choice, more
Congregational than Presbyterian, so that the only
model for the new Church system was of the later
rather than the earlier type. Essex had already, in
great part, followed her eloquent teacher, Dr. Owen,
in his transition from the Presbyterian to the Independent views ; and it would seem that the "Country
Essay for the Practice of Church Government there "
of Cromwell's favourite chaplain was as much followed
in Kent as in Essex, whose inhabitants and fortunes
were so closely connected with those of the metropolitical diocese.

Among the most fatal of the results which this
long-protracted religious conflict produced throughout the country, those who were living within memory of it have noted the origin and progress of
Deism among the higher and more influential classes.
" In the time of King Charles I. (which confineth my
longest acquaintance with men)," observes the writer
of " An Account of the Growth of Deism in England, in 1696," "'twas usual for gentlemen to send
their sons abroad into Italy, Spain, France, Germany,
&c., to accomplish themselves by travel. But lest
they should be prevailed upon to change their religion, care was taken that their tutor or governor
who travelled with them should show them the idola-

try and superstition of the Roman religion, and also let them see that Popery in all its branches was only a device of the priesthood to carry on a particular interest of their own; to increase their wealth, honours, and power over the lay-people. . . . . Now the young gentleman being thoroughly convinced of this, returneth to Old England, where he meets with zealous contests about religion (as was pretended) between the Church of England, headed by Archbishop Laud, on the one part, and the Presbyterian Kirk on the other, and having carefully read the debate on both sides, with those very eyes which he had so lately cleared up in Italy or France, he could not forbear to see that both these Protestant parties, under the pretence of religion, were only grasping at power, and that the controversy at bottom was not whose religion was best, but only what sect of the clergy should make the best market of the mere laymen. And as this young gentleman had before resolved with himself not to become a property to the Popish priesthood, no longer now will he be such to the Protestant clergy of any denomination, since both pursue the same ends."[1] Perhaps on no other grounds than these can the suddenness of the outburst of Socinianism and Deism in the day of the Restoration be accounted for, and to scarcely any other can we attribute the fact (though nothing can supply the justification) of the chilling contrast which the pulpits of that period present to the fervid teaching

[1] "An Account of the Growth of Deism in England;" London, printed for the author, 1696, p. 5.

of the Puritan divines, and the rich stores of both patristic and later divinity which fill their discourses and make the long series of their sermons before the House of Commons so valuable and interesting.[1]

Although the fifteen years which were interposed between the death of Laud and the Restoration formed, in a certain sense, a blank in the history of the diocese, for all the limits and landmarks of episcopal jurisdiction were obliterated in a moment by the Act of the Long Parliament already referred to, and the diocese merged in the country, the Church history of the period is not altogether lost to us, and the biographical notices of those who succeeded to the ejected clergy give us a clear view of the state of the diocese in all its principal towns and villages during this lapse of its episcopal history. On the accession of the Protector to the supreme power, he appointed a committee to examine the parish ministers with a view to the removal of those who were (according to the new standard) incompetent. Of this committee the eminent Mr. Caryl was president. "For the eleven years which succeeded the death of Charles I., no system of Church government was fully established. The Presbyterians, if any, enjoyed this distinction; but the ministers, though agreed, with scarcely an exception, in evangelical doctrine, held different opinions on

[1] In two collections of sermons possessed by the writer, one of Puritan divines from the library of the late Duke of Sussex, in five volumes, the other formed by Hooper, bishop of Gloucester, extending from the Restoration to the time of George I., in twenty volumes, this contrast is very conspicuous.

ecclesiastical polity. Many of them were adherents
of the old episcopacy and the liturgy, many were
desirous of a reformed episcopal system like the plan
proposed by Archbishop Usher, others were Presbyterians, some were Independents, and a few were
Baptists. Cromwell's policy encouraged this diversity,
as he dreaded the ascendency of any one party."[1]

The limits of the present work prevent us from
noticing more than a few of the most eminent among
the eighty who were ejected from the parishes of
Kent on the ground of Nonconformity, from whose
unhappy and forced separation from their conforming
brethren the older Nonconformist Churches in Kent
derive their origin. Many of them were on terms of
intimate friendship with the more learned and liberal
of the bishops (as Stillingfleet), many continued
devoted to the liturgy and offices of the Church of
England, attending her services as well as their own
special meetings, and thus laid the foundation for
that "occasional conformity" which awakened such
bitter controversies at a later period. The cathedral
pulpit was filled by Mr. John Durant and Mr. John
Player ; the former a practical preacher and author of
some note, the latter a man of higher education, who
had been a scholar in the King's School, and was a
brother of Sir Thomas Player, the chamberlain of
London. At St. Margaret's, in the same city, a native

[1] Timpson's "Church (Nonconformist) History of Kent"
(London, 1859, p. 152), a work of an Independent minister of
moderation and judgment, to which the writer is indebted for
the notices of the principal Kentish ministers here given. His
authority is that of Dr. Calamy.

of Canterbury, also a King's scholar, and a graduate
of Cambridge, Mr. Thomas Ventress, was appointed
the minister. He had been ordained by Laud, and
was curate to Archdeacon Kingsley; he had so
conducted himself in these difficult times that he
found more favour with the gentry and clergy than
most of his brethren. He was, however, ejected in
1662, but continuing to labour in his ministry,
suffered much oppression, and finally imprisonment.
His death was touching, and worthy of his peaceful
and holy life; laying himself down on his bed,
dressed as he was, and taking his Greek Testament in
his hand, he kissed it and placed it on his heart, and
presently fell asleep in Christ, in the seventy-fourth
year of his age. Barham was fortunate in the ministry
of Mr. John Barton, who, after his ejectment, held
religious meetings which were attended by several
members of Parliament and other persons from the
adjacent parishes. At Benenden, Mr. John Osborne,
though appointed by Cromwell's committee, was so
beloved by the people that the patron, Sir John
Henden, desired him to continue his ministry after
the Restoration, but his scruples against the Act of
Uniformity prevented him from remaining. He lived
in friendship with the conforming clergy, and is said
to have been greatly beloved. Chatham was filled by
an excellent scholar, Mr. Thomas Carter, a friend of
Bishop Stillingfleet, who assisted him until his death.
After his ejection, he practised physic near London,
and died in 1685. At Chatham Dock, an equally
eminent man was minister, Mr. Laurence Wise, who
was sufficiently influential to be one of the five seni

for by Charles II. when he proposed to grant liberty
to the Dissenters. He was imprisoned in Newgate as
a Nonconformist, and died in 1692. At Chilham
Mr. Sampson Horne was supported by Sir John Fagge
at his house of Mystole after his ejectment, and died
there. At Cranbrook, an early seat of Nonconformity
no less than ten ministers were ejected ; while Goud
hurst lost the ministry of Mr. Edward Bright, "a
good man and endowed with a great deal of patience
which indeed he needed, having the affliction of a
very froward and clamorous wife ; on this account
as many thought, it was his happiness to be dull o
hearing." The ejected minister of Ickham became
like some others, a physician ; while Maidstone had
so moderate a teacher that after his ejectment the
minister of the neighbouring parish of Boxley ofter
admitted him into his pulpit. Some of those who
were thus silenced (as Mr. French, of Malling) entered
into trade ; six of them, having been commissioners
for ejecting " scandalous ministers," were themselves
ejected in turn. Among these was Mr. Robert
Webber, of Sandwich. Mr. Poyntel, of Staplehurst
was a singular instance of one whose learning and
moderation enabled the archbishop, with whom he
was very intimate, to license him to preach in his old
pulpit if the incumbent should allow him. Very dif
ferent were the conduct and character of Mr. Richard
Culmer, who succeeded the learned Dr. Meric Casau
bon at Minster. The reader will remember his bitter
complaints to Sir Edward Dering on the severities
exercised against him by Laud. His revenge, how
ever, upon the " Lambeth patriarch " was strangely

manifested in an attack upon the great window of
the cathedral. Perhaps, as the reparation of the
stained glass at Lambeth was one of the charges
against Laud at his trial, the fanatical destroyer of
the magnificent window at Canterbury might have
regarded his act as the greatest injury he could inflict
upon his memory. On Dr. Casaubon's restitution,
Culmer removed to Monckton. Mr. Thoroughgood,
of the latter place, was very eminent as a Nonconformist divine, and left a diary which throws much
light on the persecutions of this period. At Wootton,
Mr. Edward Coppin, after first conforming, became
uneasy in his conscience, and retired to his native
village of Beaksbourne, where "when liberty was given
he preached in his own house to all who would come,
but he frequented the established worship," another
early example of "occasional conformity in Kent."
The touching account given us of the last discourse
of Mr. William Lock, the minister of Loose, near
Maidstone, may well close the brief notice of the
more conspicuous of those who filled the pulpits of
the diocese in the day of the Protectorate. " Just
before his ejection in 1662, he preached his last
sermon to his people from Acts xx. 32, telling them
in his introduction that 'Those words, which were
part of Paul's farewell sermon to the Ephesian elders,
he had chosen for the subject of his to them, but
with this sad difference, that Paul was but called by
Providence to service elsewhere, but he and a considerable number of his brethren must be laid by in
silence. The Ephesians, it is true, were no longer to
hear him, but,' said he, ' our mouths must be stopped

from speaking in a ministerial way any more as we have done.' In these circumstances he declared that he knew nothing that he could do better for them than to 'commend them to God, and to the word of His grace.' And now since his public ministry must end, he 'commended them to God who takes care of His Church and children as they had heard,' and to the word of His grace, which through mercy they had in their hands, and which, studied and used aright, would build them up and give them an inheritance among all them that are sanctified." It must be the cause of ceaseless, though unavailing, regret to every pious member of the Church of England, that men of such a spirit and such a life as this were lost to her so painfully in the day when they were more than ever needed. The mutual recriminations of Walker in his "Sufferings of the Clergy," and of Neale in his "History of the Puritans," must ever jar painfully on the ears of all who regard with grief and humiliation the results of intolerance and persecution, from whatever side they come. They sprang from political, rather than religious passions, and from impulses which have long died out ; and above all, from a theory of the actual identity of the Church with the State. This renders it an interesting subject of inquiry how far the Church of England, as a Church, was involved in excesses which every one of her members now so deeply deplores. Even in the day when the remembrance of them was the freshest and the passions they had evoked had hardly cooled down, Bishop Burnet says of the ejected ministers of that day, " Many of these were distinguished by their abilities and zeal. They cast themselves upon the providence of God and the charity of their friends, which had a fair appearance as of men that were ready to suffer for their consciences. This begat esteem and raised compassion, whereas the old clergy, now much enriched, were as much despised."[1] Was then the Church, *as a Church*, responsible for these great evils? In a letter addressed to the late Mr. Goulburn in 1850, the writer observed, "the State in its first adoption of the Reformed Church recognised no other form of Christianity within its jurisdiction, and by a severe compulsion fulfilled its acknowledged obligation to provide for the religious instruction of its people. The Church and State were thus made conterminous and even identical. . . . . Our reformers (as Dean Tucker remarks) considered nonconformity to the external mode of public worship, and nonconformity to the civil laws of the country, as one and the same thing, and therefore they punished both actions on the same principle," and this notwithstanding the tolerant doctrines of the 20th and 34th Articles, in which, he observes, "they came within sight of toleration and yet could not see it."

Unfortunately, the bishops, as sharing in the civil government, took too large a part in those corrosive measures which belonged rather to the temporal than to the spiritual power. The mild reign of Archbishop Juxon was too soon succeeded by the arbitrary and impolitic government of Sheldon, and the last opportunity of so conciliating Nonconformity, as to prevent

---

[1] "Letters to Dr. Kippis," p. 62.

2 B

it from turning into the open, and even virulent hostility of dissent, was irretrievably lost. We cannot read the words of the Roman Catholic courtier of that day, Lord Castlemaine, without feeling painfully conscious of the justice of them in too many points :—" It was never known that Roman Catholics persecuted, as the bishops do those who adhere to the same faith with themselves, and established an inquisition among the professors of the strictest piety among themselves; and however bloody the persecution of Queen Mary, it is manifest that their persecution exceeds it, for under her there were not more than two or three hundred put to death, whereas under their persecution above treble that number have been rifled, destroyed, and ruined in their estates, lives, and liberties—being, as is most remarkable, men of this same spirit for the most part with those Protestants who suffered under the prelates of Queen Mary's time."

The writer was evidently less acquainted with the history of his own Church than with that of the Church he censures, and failed to observe that the claim of an unlimited supremacy and the supposed duty of a passive obedience under every circumstance was the real cause of both these persecutions. Yet let it not be supposed that the Puritan party were in any degree more tolerant in the day of their power. Toleration has been, indeed, a plant of very slow growth and very difficult culture, even in the most enlightened periods of our history. The cruelties inflicted by the Parliamentary party in the ejectment of the conforming clergy were merely retaliated upon their Puritan successors in the day of the Restoration. The unifor-

mity for which Laud so violently contended as the
only means of bringing up to the same standard the
public observances of the Church, which had fallen,
under Abbot, into a state of universal irregularity and
confusion, was taken up by the State in the day of the
restored Monarchy as a political engine, and a test
of loyalty to the doctrines of Divine right and passive
obedience, which form almost the key-note of the
sermons of this period of spiritual darkness and decadence. The pulpits were attuned by the Court.
The constant dread of Popery on the one side, and
Nonconformity on the other, led to a state of disquiet
and suspicion which affected society throughout. In
a sermon of Dean Sherlock's before the Court, which
traces all the misfortunes of the country to the death of
Charles I., which, "however we may not answer for
it in another world, we may suffer for in this," he
observes, "these terrible convulsions of State, like
a sharp fit of the gout when the pain is gone, leave a
great weakness upon the Government, and make it
very unquiet and liable to relapses." [1]

Archbishop Sheldon, who succeeded the gentle and
pious Juxon in 1663, had suffered so severely from the
Parliamentary party in his earlier life that he appears
never to have forgiven his sequestrations and imprisonment, and to have regarded Nonconformity as an inex-
piable crime. He opposed all efforts for a comprehen-
sion and wrote to all the bishops of his province to put
the laws into execution against the Nonconformists.
The description given of him by Bishop Burnet, even

---

[1] Sermon before the House of Commons, 1692.

when deprived of its extreme, and perhaps exaggerated features, indicates him as a man least of all
qualified to govern a diocese which was suffering from
the severe and corrective remedy of the Act of Uniformity, as it had been applied at the Restoration.
" He seemed," writes Burnet, " not to have a deep
sense of religion, if any at all ; and spoke of it most
commonly as an engine of government and a matter
of policy."[1]

The blame of the severity of the Act of Uniformity,
which was (as Burnet, an eye-witness, affirms) the
inevitable and real cause of the dissent which has
separated so many thousands from the Church of
England, rested with Sheldon.   He was the one who
moved the Privy Council for the punctual fulfilment
of the Act, and he himself undertook to fill all the
vacant pulpits in London.   It was he who procured
the promotion of Archbishop Sharp to the Chancellorship of Scotland, and was in great measure responsible for the results of that fatal appointment.
He was the chief advocate of the cruel and deplorable
" Five-mile Act," which by placing the Dissenters in
a state of the most barbarous persecution, rendered
their separation inveterate, and furthered more than
any other measure the progress of the Romish party,
whose policy it was to complete the severance between
the sectaries and the Church of England, and to make
the former their allies, as they attempted to do (but
fortunately without success) in the subsequent reign.

[1] " History of his Own Times ; " Ed. fol. 1724, tom. i. p.
177.

It had been well for the Church if the pious and
gentle Juxon had survived to prevent these sad excesses. Of their course in the diocese of Canterbury
we have already spoken ; their results are before us
in the vast influence of Nonconformity both in East
and West Kent, in almost every parish of which some
early martyr to this fatal severity became the " seed "
of a separate congregation. Among the most singular
of the results of this policy was the fear of Sheldon in
regard to the creation of a county militia. He alleged
that " the Commons, of whom the militia must be
composed, being generally ill-affected to the Church,
this would be a prejudice rather than a security."[1]
A sad and humiliating confession, which the perfect
toleration of a later day enables us to look back upon
with amazement.

The death of Sheldon took place at a moment when
the religious anxieties of the country had taken
another turn. The secret adherence to the Roman
Church of Charles II., whose leanings towards it had
been so long suspected, compelled the bishops to defend themselves from a far more urgent danger, and
Sheldon was appealed to by the king to prevent the
controversial treatment of Roman doctrines by the
clergy—a necessary prelude to the " toleration " which
was then contemplated, no longer as a means of
relieving Dissenters, but as an insidious method of
reintroducing Romanism.

This appeal was skilfully averted by the bishops
reminding the king that he was a Protestant, and that

---

[1] Burnet's " History of his Own Times," tom. i. p. 243.

the defence of Protestantism was therefore a natural and loyal course towards himself.

The primacy of Sheldon was succeeded by that of Sancroft, during which nothing of note occurred in relation to the diocese ; until the Revolution of 1688 (in whose opening scene he took so important a part), ushered in the modern history of the see of Canterbury, and brings us on to the last portion of our narrative.

CHAPTER X.

FROM THE REVOLUTION TO THE PRESENT DAY.

FROM the period of the great political change of 1688 to the present time the history of the diocese of Canterbury, like that of every other, especially those nearest to the great centre of religious and political life in England, ceases to have that distinctness of character and individuality, so to speak, which it had in earlier days, when it was identified with the history of the Primacy, and (during its fatal lapse) with that of the Parliamentary party in Kent. The new doctrines, both religious and political, which were now everywhere triumphant, tended to produce a uniformity very unlike that for which the Laudian party and the promoters of the Act of 1662 had contended. The conversion of the clergy generally to the principles of the new government was almost universal. "I am sufficiently assured," writes a dignitary of that period to another, "that much the greatest part of the clergy have come in to the government as you and I have done, out of a prospect to preserve the Church. For. . . we did dreadfully apprehend . . . that if we had not taken the oaths the whole Church might have been overturned all at once, and Presbytery or something like it set up in the Church."[1]

[1] "Querela Temporum, or, the Danger of the Church of England ; in a Letter from the Dean of —— to —— Prebend of —— ;" London, 1695, pp. 1, 2.

The "Divine right of episcopacy," which so soon after came on the scene, eclipsed at this critical juncture the "Divine right of kings" and that passive obedience to legitimate monarchy which Bishop Lake in his famous dying declaration affirmed that "he had been brought up in and had also taught others," looking upon the doctrine of Passive Obedience "as the distinguishing character of the Church of England."[1] Lake was one of the four bishops who refused the oath of allegiance to William and Mary, and had also been of the seven who had immortalized their names as the subscribers of the petition which led to their imprisonment in the Tower, and precipitated the very results from which he, in company with Sancroft, Ken, and Turner, recoiled with so great a dread. It is impossible not to regard with the profoundest respect the course of the four non-juring bishops and those of the clergy who followed them into what was at once temporal ruin and spiritual exile. Their accession placed those who held with them the political doctrines of the old high-church party in a position of considerable rebuke and of no little perplexity. The dignitary already cited describes somewhat pathetically the situation of himself and his friends. After a melancholy review of the past he proceeds :—" Add to this a very fatal dilemma in which the Dissenters have caught us, and have improved it amongst the people to our no small prejudice. For if we stick to 'pas-

---

[1] "Letter to a Person of Quality on Bishop Lake's Declaration;" London, 1689, pp. 1, 2.

sive obedience ' in the high sense, as it is contained
in the Homily against Rebellion, we must condemn
what we have done, and what we still continue to do.
But if we call that an error, then we own that our
Church has been all along, before this revolution, a
false guide, and that the Dissenters have taught the
truth in this point of doctrine. And then the people
make the application that it is safer trusting to them
than to us in other doctrines. . . How shall we
retract all the hard words we have given them for
opposing that doctrine which we now profess? for
using those same distinctions which we now set up?
. . . and though you and I can vindicate ourselves
as to the preaching of ' passive obedience ' in former
times, what is this to all that generality of the clergy
who were never weary, nor would give over, upon that
subject? who found it in every text they could
meet with, and pressed it oftener and more pathetically than any article of the Creed."[1] He might
well conclude, " Indeed our case here is very
difficult." The dilemma had been put in another
form by the Court party in the previous reign, in a
pamphlet which was greatly circulated among the
advocates of the so-called indulgence.[2] On the
other hand, the defenders of the Revolution somewhat
naïvely reminded their adversaries that the verse,
"'Touch not mine Anointed," on which they so
greatly relied ought never to be wrested from its

---

[1] "Querela Temporum," pp. 21, 22.
[2] "A Layman's Opinion in a Letter to a Considerable
Divine ;" London, 1687.

context, "Yea, He reproved even kings for their
sakes."[1]   By the secession of the learned and excellent Sancroft and the gentle and pious Ken, the
Church of England and the diocese of Canterbury
experienced a loss which was in some sense irreparable.   A schism was thus opened which, though it
had rather a political than a religious origin, resulted
from the assertion of principles which had been unfortunately bound up with the outer life of the Church,
and were almost identified with her spiritual system.
Sancroft, in his defence, published the famous Convocation Book of Bishop Overall, which was a kind
of historical introduction to the canons of 1603,
though it had never received any public sanction.
Unfortunately for his own cause, it provided a way of
escape for those who had taken the oath of allegiance
to the new Government ; for it declared that whenever a great change of government had been effected
which was succeeded by a general acquiescence and
a peaceful settlement of the kingdom, it must be regarded as the work of Providence, and submitted to
without resistance.   Bishop Lloyd, one of the king's
chaplains, gave timely aid to this reasonable conclusion in his " Discourse of God's Ways of Disposing of
Kingdoms."   He seems, however, to assert the king's
title rather on the ground of deliverance by conquest
than on that of popular acquiescence—a theory
doubtless better suited to the martial character of
William III.—and refers us to the case of Constantine,

---

[1] " History of Self-defence, in requital to the ' History of
Passive Obedience ;' " London, 1680 (Qu. 1689 ?).

who (he affirms) though " he might have taken upon him the government of the countries he had gained as a conqueror, which title he seemed to affect upon other occasions, yet where he had declared his cause of war to be for the people's deliverance, this being so just and so honourable a title, himself used it, and would have no other in all his inscriptions."[1] As the *salus populi* is the root of all kingly power and of the " Divine right" itself, the bishop properly calls such a providential deliverance "God's transferring His power by way of justice." Upon this principle Tillotson may be accepted as a legitimate successor of the good Sancroft. There was simply a providential transfer of authority, arising out of a virtual if not actual surrender of the archiepiscopal throne. While every sound Churchman must mourn over the loss of Sancroft, he may well be thankful that he had a successor so far beyond the chilling age in which he lived in sound common sense and in practical religion and piety. We are tempted in an age of life and energy, both in spiritual and temporal matters, which has hardly had a precedent in earlier times, to depreciate the labours of men like Tillotson and Tenison, whose lot was cast in times of a loose morality and a practical infidelity which we can hardly realize, and still more hardly appreciate. If the light of their doctrine seems cold and dim, we should do well to remember the thickness of that darkness in which it shone. We are accustomed to read the sermons of Tillotson as

---

[1] " God's Way of Disposing of Kingdoms ; " London, 1691, p. 69.

beautiful specimens of the religious literature of a day of formality and coldness such as the Church o England had never before witnessed. We fail to see that they were also the day-star shining on to a more perfect dawn, and to realize the fact that their ligh has brightened the path of many indeed at a perioc when the most brilliant teaching might have dazzled and even misled. Yet the Church of England, and least of all the diocese of Canterbury, ought never to forget the debt it owes to Sancroft, or to regret the obstacle which his strong convictions had raisec against taking the new oath of allegiance. The London minister who wrote a " Vindication of thei Majesties' Wisdom in Nominating to the Vacant Arch bishoprics and Bishoprics,"[1] has these just observa tions hereupon : " I thank God I never think of some of these great men's stout defence of the nation': religion and laws, by petitioning King James agains reading the Declaration ; by an undaunted appearance at the Council table, and going in that unconcernec manner to the Tower with the spirits of noble and brave patriots and heroes; by standing a trial a Westminster Hall—further, I never reflect upon tha noble and almost unparalleled act of the late Arch bishop of Canterbury, Dr. Sandcroft,[2] with others o his brethren, addressing to King James and telling him to his face, with all modesty and becomingness yet with more than a Roman courage, all those fault of his whereby he had violated the laws and incensed

[1] London, 1691, p. 20.
[2] This was the ancient spelling of the archbishop's name.

his subjects against him, with a humble desire to rec-
tify those errors of his government from time to time—
I say I never think of these things without thoughts
of great honour and admiration." Great were the
efforts made in every diocese, and by all classes,
to prevent the final act of deprivation of the non-
juring bishops. Equally great were the efforts of their
friends to persuade them into such a submission as
might have been accepted by the Government. In
a dialogue published at the time,[1] the conforming
advocate, in reply to the question, "Was there no way
to have healed this rupture before it grew so wide?"
observes, "I cannot tell that; but the time assigned
by the law, and the king's long forbearance to fill
the sees after the day of deprivations, argues a willingness in the State to give men time to consider, and
to allay their prejudices, and to use means to come
under the public shelter. . . . But the recusants
seem, against all entreaties, wanting to themselves
and a happy coalition. They have made no offers,
no applications, but receded further from civil and
social communion than at first they did."

The shameful misrepresentation of Archbishop
Sancroft's primacy by Bishop Burnet is too well
refuted in his life by Dr. D'Oyley to need any refutation here. He is represented, in the same breath,
as dying in the poor and despicable manner in which
he had lived for some years and yet to have amassed
a large fortune. Both statements are absolutely false;

---

[1] "Solomon and Abiathar, or the Case of the Deprived
Bishop discussed;" London, 1692, p. 34.

for he died peacefully and happily on his own estate at Fresingfield, in Suffolk, which had descended to him from a long ancestry. Sancroft's refusal to con secrate Burnet might naturally have embittered him but cannot justify positive falsehoods. But one year elapsed between the deaths of Sancroft and Tillotson and it was hoped that the death of the former would have healed the breach between the conforming and the nonconforming clergy. It seemed, however rather to re-open the wound, and those who had clung so tenaciously to their oath in the face of events which had rendered its fulfilment impossible, rather became more confirmed in their opposition as the chances of its success became more desperate.

Not content with the mere passive state of resistance that kind of *vis inertiæ* which so well agreed with their cardinal doctrine, they set forth a form of prayer which was privately propagated,[1] and designed to foment those insurrections against the Government which so soon broke out in Ireland. The object o this devotional performance may well be discerned from the prayer, " Restore us again the public worship of Thy Name, the reverent administration of Thy sa craments ; raise up the former Government, both in Church and State, that we may be no longer withou king, without priest, without God in the world.' And again, " We beseech Thee to look compassion ately on this persecuted part of Thy Church, now

---

[1] It was entitled "A Form of Prayer and Humiliation fo God's Blessing upon His Majesty and his Dominions, and fo Removing and Averting of God's Judgments from this Church and State ; " London, 1690.

driven from Thy public altars into corners and secret closets. . . . . We pray Thee to be gracious to our Prince, who for the sins both of priest and people is now kept out, and that in Thy due time Thou wouldst deal with him according to the justice of his cause," with much more to the same purpose. That this invitation to disloyalty to the cause of the Revolution prepared the way for the rebellion in Scotland which broke out so soon after can hardly be doubted; while the fact that it proceeded from men who ought of all others to have submitted cheerfully to the will of the country is painful and humiliating. "There are no small grounds to believe," are the words of a contemporary critic, "that thousands of these prayer-books have been printed and dispersed at a charge more than private. In all probability they were cal-culated for the expected descent of the Highlanders with their officers from England and Ireland."[1]

Whatever success may have attended these sedi-tious efforts elsewhere, they do not appear to have had any appreciable influence on the diocese of Can-terbury. The conflicts of bishops and churches were now seen at a considerable distance, and the registers of the archbishops no longer give us that inner view of the life of the Church they represent, which they did in the days when the primates were not only living in the diocese but constantly passing from one to another of their many dwelling-places. Perhaps their silence is as suggestive as the more stirring events of

---

[1] "Reflections upon a Form of Prayer lately set forth by the Jacobites of the Church of England;" London, 1690, p. 24.

our earlier history are demonstrative. In any case it shows that the religious life of the diocese, though it was at this time destitute of that strong sentiment and vigorous energy which had inspired in earlier days the great Kentish petition, was too practical in its character to fall an easy prey to a reaction which threatened the safety of the Reformed Church, as well as the overthrow of a Government which exhibited so welcome a contrast to the tyranny and cruelty of that which it had superseded. The mild and moderate policy of Tillotson disarmed the hostility even of those who least admired the principles upon which he came in. His published works had no less general an influence for good than his private life and conversation, and it was indeed an influence greatly needed. For as his successor, Archbishop Tenison, wrote on the death of the good Queen Mary, "Great is our loss of a most pious queen, in an atheistical and profane age, the seeds of which impiety had been sowing for some years and now seem to spring up in greater plenty than ever ! Great is our loss of a most charitable queen, in an age which takes up the reverse of our Lord's saying, and declares that it is more blessed to receive than to give."[1] At this time, however, the feelings of the clergy throughout England took a very fatal and almost ruinous tendency. The Toleration Act, which had given freedom of worship to the Dissenters, had ever been to the mass of the clergy an unpopular, and even hated measure. The dignitary we have already quoted affirms that " it

---

[1] " Sermon preached at the Queen's Funeral, 1695 ;" p. 17.

shook and rent and almost overturned our Church.
The very next Sunday after it was known," he continues) "the churches in many places were almost
quite deserted, and the meeting-houses, which before
were neglected, ... were like trenches when the sea
hath broken the dykes, swollen and overflown in a
moment. Toleration upon toleration," he adds, "has
brought ruin upon ruin since, so that we are now
loose at the very roots, and at the mercy of every
wind and wave." [1] A humiliating confession that the
Church depended for her very life upon those penal
laws which were the true cause of her decadence and
spiritual death. She had leaned since the Restoration
on the secular arm, and identified her very existence
with the "divine right of Episcopacy." The one prop
had failed her in the deprivation of the non-juring
bishops, and the other in the sanction of the Toleration Act. Her clergy, destitute of spiritual influence
themselves, dreaded the introduction of any such
influence from without, and as their very *raison d'être*
was involved in the penal laws which had simply
restrained the outward action of the Nonconformists,
but had given their pent-up feelings an almost irresistible influence over the minds of their former
people, they began to devise schemes by which the
toleration would become, if not practically inoperative,
at least very seriously compromised. Among these
was the famous Bill against the "Occasional Con-

---

[1] "Querela Temporum, or, the Danger of the Church of
England ; in a Letter from the Dean of —— to —— Prebend
of —— ;" London, 1695, p. 5.

formity of the Dissenters," which was introduced, and was very nearly successful, at the close of the primacy of Archbishop Tenison. That excellent prelate (if we may believe Burnet, who here at least appears to speak from actual facts) was almost persecuted by the clergy even of his own diocese for the then unpardonable guilt of being a tolerant bishop and a calm moderator of the different factions which then were rending the Church. The object of the promoters of this fatal movement was to prevent all those who had taken the sacrament in the Church of England (under the Test and Corporation Acts) from ever attending any dissenting place of worship, or any religious assembly different from those of the Church under penalties which were of an almost ruinous character—the preamble of the Bill professing nevertheless an entire devotion to the Toleration Act which it was virtually destroying.[1] The Bill was in the end lost, but not so much on the grounds of its gross injustice and falsehood as through differences which arose between the two Houses in regard to its technical details.

It is strange that the extreme advocates both of the Church and of Dissent were engaged in the defence of this monstrous, but happily abortive, effort to undermine the great principles of the Toleration Act. Thus, a Dissenter who addressed the famous Mr. How under the initials D. F., described " Occa-

[1] See the tract called, "Contra Torrentem Brachia, or, A Vindication of our present English Liberty of going either to Church or to Meetings;" (London, 1703) where the case against the Bill is fairly stated.

sional Conformists " as like a workman " who builds
with one hand and pulls down with the other; like a
fisherman, who catches fish with one hand and
throws them into the sea with the other ; like everything which signifies nothing. To say a man can be
of two religions is a contradiction, unless there be
two gods to worship or he has two souls to save. . . .
There is in religion no neuter gender, no ambiguous
article—God or Baal—mediums are impossible." A
zealot, on the other side, quotes these views with
admiration ;[1] and thus it is that in every communion
and in every age the advocates of bigotry meet one
another with open arms. Yet those who know anything of Kentish diocesan history in later times would
know how important an element of spiritual life was
this "Occasional Conformity" then so greatly dreaded.
At the very darkest periods of Church of England
preaching, the doctrinal influences which the fatal
Act of 1662 had forced out of our Church reacted
upon it through the teaching of men who still loved
her, and even joined in her communion at stated
intervals ; and thus a spirit of union and charity was
preserved among the rival, but not then hostile
systems, which has left a legacy of peace to the
spiritually-minded of every denomination. The assertion of a Nonconformist of that earlier day, so little
admitted by the Church party then, would meet with
no denial from those of any party now : " A Dissenter
that is sound in all the articles of faith and orders

---

[1] " For God or Baal, or no Neutrality in Religion." Sermon
by Philip Stubs, M.A., preached at St. Alphage, London,
October 4, 1702, p. 10.

his conversation accordingly, is incomparably more
of the Church of England than the most exquisite
formalist that hath learnt all his gaits and postures,
but is neither sound in his head nor in his heart."[1]
The intolerant views of the clergy were a fatal result
of the loss of influence experienced by the primates
from their long non-residence in the diocese.   In all
the painful controversies since the Revolution the
bishops had almost invariably advocated the cause
of toleration, while the parochial and dignified clergy
had as systematically opposed it both in the Convocation and in their spheres of local influence.   The
attempt to make Episcopacy of divine right was
carried by the Lower House of Convocation, but the
fatal dowry was wisely declined by the bishops themselves.   In vain did the learned Dr. Isham preach
charity to the Convocation of 1701, and remind it
of the claims of the foreign reformed Churches upon
the affections of the Church of England, notwithstanding their failure in this feature of Church government.   The majority of the clergy seemed to hold
that the Church was created for the bishops, as
blindly as the Roman Catholics assume that the
Church exists for the sake of Peter, and the noble
and tolerant efforts of Tillotson and Tenison were
met with contumely and contempt.   It would have
been well therefore if the primates had lived more
among their clergy at this critical time.   Personal
intercourse would have tended greatly to remove

---

[1] "Notes on the Bishop of Salisbury's Discourses to his
Clergy ;" London, 1695, p. 28.

these dangerous illusions. As it was, however, Tillotson must have been better known even in Kent
by his published sermons than by any personal intercourse between himself and his clergy; and his
excellent successor, Tenison, rather from the active
part he took in the great literary movement against
the Roman aggression, and the admirable foundation in London which goes by his name, than for
any act which connects his name with the diocese.
Lambeth and Croydon, the favourite residences of
the primates, were also the recipients of their benefactions; though of Juxon and Tenison it may be
said that the claims of the poorer clergy of the diocese were not unremembered by them. The chari-
ties included in the will of Archbishop Tenison
were of an extensive and munificent character, among
which was the gift of £1,000 for the augmentation
of the smaller livings in his diocese. His successor,
Archbishop Wake, whose life also was spent between
Lambeth and Croydon, had been conspicuous in its
earlier period in the great controversy with Rome,
and especially in the refutation of the specious
writings of Bossuet and his celebrated "Exposition."
It is said that Clement XI. was heard to declare that
it was a pity that so profound a writer was not a
member of his Church. The same kind of compliment had been paid to Hooker and to the learned
Whitaker,—to the latter, by as great a controversialist as Bellarmine himself. The efforts which
Wake made to devise a plan of reunion between the
Churches of France and England have a special and
almost affecting interest to those who yearn after

the restoration of the unity of the Catholic Church, and are ready to exclaim almost in despair, " Alas ! who shall live when God doeth this ?" It is for Him alone to reply, who uttered those words of profound meaning, " This generation shall not pass away until all these things be fulfilled. " Archbishop Wake held the primacy somewhat more than ten years, during which time he amassed a large fortune, besides the great bequests he made to Christ Church, Oxford, and the large sums he spent upon the palaces of Lambeth and Croydon. Through the marriage of his daughter with Dean Lynch, of Canterbury, he is now represented by the ancient Kentish family of the Brockmans, of Beachborough, whose benefactions to Church purposes in East and West Kent have repaired in a later day the failure of the archbishop to make some provision for the needs of his diocese. Archbishop Potter, who succeeded him, was well qualified both by his learning and piety for so important a charge. At the age of nineteen he published a treatise of such learning as gave promise of his future powers. He is said to have devoted himself during the ten years of his primacy more exclusively than most of his predecessors to the spiritual duties of his high office. His recognition of the bishops and clergy of the Moravian Church, and of the great work of Count Zinzendorf, show how deeply he had at heart the interests of vital and spiritual Christianity wherever its real fruits were seen ; and there can be little doubt that had he lived to see the great awakening of religious life in the preaching of Wesley and Whitefield, he would have at least endeavoured to keep within the Church those earnest men whom the coldness and formalism of his successors so fatally detached from its ranks. Archbishop Potter was succeeded by the Bishop of Bangor, Thomas Herring, whose primacy filled another decennial period, a period of spiritual deadness and darkness both in the diocese and in the Church, which almost recalls the picture of the Church in the tenth century as it is drawn for us by Baronius.

The primacy of Archbishop Herring witnessed the origin of the greatest religious movement which has ever affected the Church in Kent, and which up to this day has retained its influence over large masses of the population both of the eastern and western divisions of the county.

Never were the words of Mordecai to Esther more strangely illustrated than in that great deliverance from spiritual deadness and almost death which was opened at this time: "If thou altogether hold thy peace at such a time, then shall there enlargement and deliverance arise to the Jews from another place." But the rulers of the Church in that day did not know that they were "come to the kingdom for such a time as this," and fell back upon the old remedy of obsolete Acts of Parliament and magisterial influence to resist the pressure of a movement they might themselves have guided. The rector of a neighbouring parish to that in which these lines were written was threatened with committal by the magistrates of the district, on account of his encouragement of meetings for religious purposes. His message in reply was, " Tell them, that if they commit me, they will only commit themselves."

It was in an age of formalism and coldness such as this that the great upheaving of the spiritual life of the Church under Wesley, Whitefield, Fletcher, Romaine, and countless other eminent and pious men began.

In order to estimate fully and impartially this great revival of spiritual life, which in the end so unfortunately separated, but can hardly be said to have alienated, so large a body of earnest and religious men from the Church of England, it is necessary that we should calmly and fearlessly view the state of utter secularity and deadness of religious sentiment and conduct, which brought about this great reaction. It is scarcely too much to say that at this period our Church had forgotten her divine origin, and was contented to be considered a mere department of State. The bishops were little more than great officers of the Court ; the clergy separated from them by an almost impassable gulf, were mixed up with secular plans and occupations which destroyed their influence with the poorer classes of their parishioners, and lowered their position among the higher members of their congregations. A remarkable letter, written by " A Country Clergyman " (probably of his own diocese) to Archbishop Herring, in the year 1754, gives a picture of the state of the Church by an eye-witness, so truthful and vivid that we cannot but exhibit it here, as giving at once the reason and the apology for that vigorous spiritual reaction to which it refers.

The occasion of it appears to have been the utter and ominous silence of the Episcopate on the great controversies upon the doctrine of the Trinity which were then convulsing the public mind, and enlisting all but those who were expected to be the most deeply interested in them, in the work of explanation or of defence. The writer, in an almost despairing tone, entreats the archbishop to contemplate the miserable and helpless state in which the clergy were left in the face of an almost infidel but educated laity, and the evils which they were experiencing through the neglect and indifference of those to whom they looked for advice and support. His complaints point with sad significance to the ignorance and incompetency which prevailed so generally among the clergy, and of which an appeal of this kind, *ad misericordiam*, to the bishops gave so humiliating a proof.

" In this situation, we naturally look towards our superiors for such aids and instructions as men of inferior talents and limited provinces do from time to time require. . . . And yet, alas ! so it is that very little of this instruction is to be had in proportion to our necessities. Our bishops' and archdeacons' charges when we are favoured with them, which is but seldom, are commonly short and general, consisting chiefly of declamatory adulations on our own system, and reflections on the principles of the adversary ; of political observations which we understand not, and allusions to facts we never heard of ; with, perhaps, some few gentle directions concerning our conduct, which, if they had the least experience of the condition, abilities, commerce and connections of the inferior clergy, their lordships would know to be impracticable. What reception at his bishop's palace a poor clergyman would meet with who should desire more explicit rules for his behaviour, on these critical occasions, I cannot guess, never having heard of any who applied for such rules, though I have known some who have earnestly desired and very much wanted them. Their lordships are not easy of access, nor fond of being interrupted by business which cannot be despatched by their officers. We have heard, indeed, that when their lordships think proper to open themselves to particular friends, it is generally in such maxims as these,—'That we ought to acquiesce in the wisdom of our superiors, to take no notice of petulant objectors, unless it be to refer them to the ancient worthies of the Church, who have on former occasions answered all cavils that can be brought against her to the satisfaction of all reasonable men.' I am afraid their lordships do not sufficiently consider the times we live in. The laity are grown more knowing, and consequently more inquisitive than heretofore. New books have afforded new lights. The circumstances that made these old answers go down with our ancestors are changed. The answers are found upon examination to be trifling and insufficient." But if the shortcomings of the bishops are boldly stated in this fearless letter, the state of the clergy is revealed with a still more unflinching courage. "The collective body of the clergy," he proceeds, "excepting a very inconsiderable number, consists of men whose lives and ordinary occupations are most foreign to their profession. We find among them all sorts of secular characters—courtiers, politicians, lawyers, merchants, usurers, civil magistrates, sportsmen, musicians, stewards of country squires . . . not to mention the ignorant herd of poor curates, to whom the instruction of our common people is committed, who are accordingly, in religious matters, the most ignorant common people that are in any Protestant, if not in any Christian society upon the face of the earth. There are to be found among the clergy of our Church geniuses who are fit for almost anything but the particular character and function they have undertaken, or rather into which they have been driven; and I am much mistaken if a college of the Apostles would not find a large majority of us much fitter for something else." The prevailing non-residence of the clergy is dwelt upon as rendering the regular ministry of the Church utterly fruitless, and being in effect a contradiction of their office; while the spiritual courts are alleged to be the "curse of the poor, the jest of the rich, and the abhorrence of the wise and good even among the clergy themselves." The writer then puts the significant question, "Is it astonishing that such a set of men as the Methodists should arise and attempt to awaken the drowsy heads and alarm the stupefied hearts of our people, immersed as they are in all the secular security into which the doctrines and examples of their own pastors may with too much probability be supposed to have thrown them?" These are not the words of an enemy of the Church, but of a zealous Churchman who deplored the state of spiritual ruin into which it had fallen, and who earnestly entreats the primate to begin that great work of reformation, which (like that of an earlier day) would be forced upon him from without unless initiated by him from within. But the appeal was made in vain. The hot fit of enthusiasm which had been the disease of the age of an almost antinomian spiritualism, had been succeeded since the Revolution by a cold fit of paralyzing apathy. The very idea that the Church was a divine institution, independent of any earthly head, would have been deemed in that day to savour of enthusiasm ; and the sermons of the age rather represent a half-Christianized philosophy than a dogmatic religion divinely revealed and authoritatively promulgated. The great work of Wesley and Whitefield shook this mere temporal structure to its very foundation ; and first from their place within the Church, and then unhappily from without the pale, inaugurated a revival which but for the fatal resistance of those in power would have restored without dividing the Church, and left in the diocese of Canterbury a single temple and a single altar.

No Church-reformer, from the time of Huss and Luther downwards, has ever predicted that the work which he began in the midst of the Church and under the influence of all its associations, would find him at its close far beyond its pale with new influences surrounding him and a new system of his own creation preventing him from re-entering the Church which he designed to reform, but never to desert. The sermon of Wesley on the laying the

foundation-stone of the Chapel in the City-road is a
singular illustration of this often-experienced truth.
Never was a more energetic determination more
energetically expressed of adherence to the Church of
England in all her sins and sorrows.   But the organization which he was introducing among his people
was utterly incompatible with the maintenance of
their position within a Church whose ancient and unchangeable constitution could admit of no such
empirical development.   This he believed to be
essential to the spiritual life of his followers, and
his natural and constantly asserted devotion to the
Church of England, weakened too naturally by the
bigotry and indifference which almost closed every
avenue of return against him, yielded to what
appeared to him a paramount and inevitable obligation.   But we should greatly err if we regarded the
religious awakening in England in the middle of the
last century as an influence standing alone and apart,
and not rather a result of that great spiritual revival
which was felt by Germany in the pietistic movement
under Spener, by which the cold dogmatism of
orthodox Lutheranism was broken down, and in the
far more extended and more lasting wave of religious
thought and conduct which passed over the Roman
Catholic world in Jansenism, which, although it was
crushed out by a persecution such as no power but
the Court of Rome could have devised or carried
out, has left results upon that Church which can
never be effaced.   The Cardinal de Cusa in the
fifteenth century strangely enough predicted an
eclipse of faith such as it had never before ex-

perienced, as coming over the Church in the first years
of the eighteenth century, that pope and bishop alike
would fall under the fatal influence of the universal
darkness, and the Word of God and its preachers
should fail. The state of Christianity throughout
Europe in the former half of the century seemed
everywhere to verify this prediction, which was
published at Rome itself in 1452. A great reaction
everywhere was the necessary result or rather the
Providential remedy for this general defection, and
the return of spiritual life, both in the Church and
beyond its pale in England, was worthy of the great
part which our country had filled from the earliest
period in the religious life of Europe. This profound re-awakening may be truly said to have begun
in the very bosom of the Church, and among those
who, like Wesley, were eminently the high-church-
men of the day. The two great leaders in the movement represented at once the Calvinism of Grindal
and Abbot, and the Arminianism of Laud and
Sancroft; and in this twofold reflection of the
religious mind of England lay the secret of its wonderful success. Instead of awakening a bitter controversy, such as that which had convulsed the nation
in an earlier day, these conflicting doctrines, having
as their sole aim the spiritual life of the masses of the
population, rather fell into a practical co-operation,
meeting and confronting one another, especially in
Kent, without any appearance even of rivalry, far less
of hostility. These remarks will serve to introduce
us to the following narrative of the introduction and
progress of Methodism in the diocese of Canterbury.

The writer is indebted for it to the learned and pious Dr. Osborn, the Principal of the Wesleyan College at Richmond, a divine as highly honoured in our own Church as in that of which he forms so distinguished an ornament. Through the kind intervention of a common friend, Dr. Rigg, the Principal of the Wesleyan Training College at Westminster, and late President of the Conference, he was enabled to obtain from Dr. Osborn the following account of the rise and progress of Wesleyanism in the diocese, of whose religious life it now forms so remarkable an element. He cannot but avail himself of the opportunity of expressing his obligation for this favour, enhanced as it is by the fact that Dr. Osborn's health was seriously tried at the moment he so kindly penned the following sketch.

The history of the rise and progress of Methodism in Kent has not been attempted, so far as I can learn, in any separate publication. But on examining the journals of Wesley and other contemporary documents we may find materials for a brief sketch, and trace some of the steps by which it has gained its present position.

Returning from Georgia, whither he had gone as a Missionary of the Society for the Promotion of Christian Knowledge, he landed at Deal. After a night's rest and morning prayer, said at his inn, he set out for London, and reached Feversham the same night, where he read evening prayers and expounded the Second Lesson to a people as savage as any he had seen on the other side of the Atlantic. From the date of his arrival, Feb. 3, 1738, until June of the

same year, when he went into Germany, he spent
much of his time in London, and it was here, at the
season of Whitsuntide, that he and his brother passed
through that great spiritual change of which he has
given so full an account in his journal, and which left
its stamp upon his whole future life. An earnest,
zealous, and laborious preacher he had been for many
years previous. But after May 24, 1738, he understood the duty and privilege of endeavouring " to
spread abroad the glad tidings of reconciliation by
Christ," and "to seek for the sheep of Christ dispersed in this naughty world" in a different sense;
and for the fifty-two years that followed he travelled
and preached incessantly, often averaging a thousand
sermons a year.

Kent being always a part of his " home circuit,"
even when it had a separate organization of its own,
neither his arrangements nor his actual movements
are traced as fully with regard to it as to some more
distant places. But we find him preaching at
Deptford in 1739. Here he speaks of finding "a
society" not unlikely one of Dr. Woodward's.

At Lewisham he had a friend to whom and to
whose family both he and his brother Charles were
much attached. Here, too, he preached frequently,
and especially in those seasons when he retired for a
week or more from the pressing duties of his London
life, to read, write, or examine in privacy some particular question. The country house and grounds of
Mr. Richard Blackwell, a banker in Lombard-street,
were understood to be at his disposal for this purpose.
To preach morning and evening and write all day was
his method of resting.

Possibly from this point Methodism proceeded to Greenwich, where if not actually introduced it was long sustained, and spread by the labours of a schoolmaster, named Bakewell, who, without abandoning his home or profession, preached continuously for more than seventy years, and died in a good old age full of honour. His memory will be preserved by a hymn which has found a place in many collections and is sometimes ascribed to Toplady,—" Hail ! thou once-despised Jesus." In the year 1796, chapels were built both at Greenwich and Woolwich, each of which has since been replaced by a much more capacious building.

Deptford and these adjacent places were formally separated from London, and organized as a distinct circuit in 1818 (a circuit, it should be here observed, once for all, being a group of preaching places arranged with a view to convenience of supply, as a district is a group of circuits arranged for economical and disciplinary purposes). From that period to the present many changes have passed over the neighbourhood, and the condition of some societies has fluctuated greatly. Sweet rural villages have become large towns, and all traces of the country are disappearing fast. In Methodistical buildings a corresponding change is observable. Small, obscure, and unsightly places of worship are now but few in number ; while several, which cannot be described by any of these epithets, have either taken the place of others, as at Greenwich, Lewisham, Blackheath, Sydenham, and Chislehurst, or as at Plumstead, Bromley, New Cross and Brockley, contribute some-

thing towards the needs of rapidly-increasing popu-
lations.

The aggregate cost of these chapels has not fallen
far short of £40,000.

Another notable place in the early history of
Methodism in Kent is Bexley. The Rev. Henry
Piers, vicar of that parish, invited Wesley and Whitefield to preach in his church, and gave all possible
countenance to their labours. So great was the interest excited in this quiet parish that it is said that
on one occasion more than six hundred attended at
the Lord's Supper.

In 1742, Piers was appointed to preach a Visitation
sermon at Sevenoaks, the visitation being held by the
Dean of Arches, who had jurisdiction over the peculiar of the Deanery of Shoreham. The discourse
turned on the duties and qualifications of the Christian
ministry, and the preacher was careful to substantiate
what he advanced by large citations from the formu-
laries of the Church. But the patience of his hearers
was soon exhausted. Twice the principal official sent
a message desiring the preacher to desist, and when
he still went on the great man walked out, followed
by most of the clergy, and left the preacher to finish
alone !

How far the preacher's reputation as a Methodist
had preceded him and conduced to such a result we
have no means of knowing. But two years after this
Piers introduced the Wesleys to the Vicar of Shoreham. John Wesley was not slow to perceive what
sort of person he had been made acquainted with,
and writes in his journal, Aug. 14, 1744,—" I hope to

have cause of blessing God for ever for the acquaintance begun this day ! "

The scholar and the gentleman would, of course, be at once appreciated, and the spiritual sympathies of the vicar were before long fully developed. He welcomed the Wesleys to his house and to his pulpit, opened a room on his premises for society purposes, and was always ready to assist with his advice and prayers those whom he believed to be labouring for the spiritual benefit of his parishioners and neighbours. For many years all labour appeared to be lost (or nearly lost) upon them, but about 1772 a great reformation took place, and the old man's heart was cheered by seeing some of the seed spring up, and even two out of the three public-houses in the place admitted visitors for religious conversation and prayer.

The Perronetts had property in and about Canterbury, and it seems highly probable that the first visit of Wesley to that city grew out of this connection. Here, as in most other places, the beginnings were small and discouragements many. Sometimes the mob was triumphant, sometimes friends were unfaithful, and even perverse ; but after sixteen years of trial and fluctuation, ground was obtained and a chapel built in 1764. For two years afterwards Canterbury appears on the " Minutes of Conference " as the name of a circuit ; but it was felt that the designation was scarcely appropriate, and Kent was substituted, under which all the " work" in what are now known as the Mid and West portions of the county were comprised. This designation continued in use as long as Wesley lived, and though not strictly accurate is sufficient for our purpose.

An account of all the societies composing the Kent circuit in 1773–4 has been preserved. Taking no notice of places visited in the itinerant's round, merely for preaching purposes, it shows societies gathered as follows :—

Canterbury	57	Faversham	16	Chatham	... 68
Sheerness...	46	Margate ...	34	Sittingbourne	8
Dover	... 34	Sandwich...	8	Ashford	... 11

At each of these places Wesley had preached before this time, at some of them frequently, *e.g.*, at Dover in 1756, where he had gathered a small society, but found the practice of smuggling most prejudicial to its spiritual welfare ; at Sheerness in 1767, at Margate in 1765, at Ramsgate in 1767, at Gravesend in 1771, thus opening out many chief places to the labours of his associates and successors.

At Chatham he began sooner than at any other place in the list, excepting Canterbury, preaching at Brompton in 1753. Many vicissitudes were observable here also. A room in a private house was occupied, and closed by the owner's removal, another by death ; a room in the barracks was first allowed, occupied, and then refused, and various other places were borrowed or hired until, in 1767, when the society consisted of twenty members, they resolved upon attempting to build, and three years afterwards opened the new chapel. Their faith and patience, long tried, were fully rewarded, and the society continued to grow morally and numerically until, in 1810, a new and much larger chapel was joyfully occupied. At Brompton, too, a good chapel, to accommodate more than 300 hearers, was opened by Mr. Wesley in 1789. From these have sprung many smaller chapels in the neighbouring towns and villages, as Frindsbury, Gillingham, New Brompton, Rainham, Hoo, and others.

Several preachers in the Methodist connection have been reared and trained in this neighbourhood, the most memorable of whom was John Baxter. Originally a shipwright in the Chatham dockyard, he received, in 1779, an appointment to the dockyard in Antigua, and found on his arrival a small company of pious negroes, gathered together by the benevolent care of Mr. N. Gilbert, the Speaker of the House of Assembly, who had become a Methodist in England several years previously. Baxter's labours were so welcome and so useful that he ultimately resigned his situation in the dockyard and employed himself wholly in teaching and preaching. In 1786, help was sent them from England, and thus the Methodist missions in the West Indies were commenced. Mr. Baxter's strength appears to have been most unusual. While at Chatham he is reported to have frequently walked more than twenty miles, after preaching thrice on Sunday, that he might present himself at six o'clock on Monday morning in the dockyard.

No very remarkable circumstances are recorded as attending the rise and growth of Methodism in the other places given in the list, except in connection with Feversham, where, finding a people disposed to be riotous, and magistrates not active in keeping the peace, Wesley was compelled to threaten them with legal proceedings if they failed in their duty any further. The little society held on their way, and in 1806 were able to open a chapel, which has since given place to one more in accordance with the needs of the town. We read of Wesley visiting Sevenoaks and Tunbridge, but cannot now trace the connection between his labours and the formation of societies there. Maidstone, though the county town, was never visited by him; and though a society was formed, and a chapel built before his decease, the place continued to be organically connected with Sevenoaks until 1814. The chapel erected in 1788 was replaced by a much larger one in 1823. Sevenoaks (1774), Tunbridge (1780), have both in like manner ceased to be occupied because larger and better structures have recently arisen, and Tunbridge Wells also.

And thus the advance of time has witnessed both material and numerical progress from one end of the county to the other.

The Kent members of the Society amount in the current year to 8,817.

On our return from this necessary digression to the path of our diocesan history, we may observe that the period included between the primacies of Wake and Herring is generally and justly regarded as the darkest and most lifeless age of all the history of our Church. A late writer has remarked, "Between contests for

power, thirst for riches, and inordinate love of pleasure, the nation sank down into corruption, and the
Church erected a feeble barrier against the fashion-
able pursuits. All its great preferments were bestowed
to secure friends to the Administration ; whatever
prime minister prevailed, the prelatical bench looked
up to their creator with devotion and assiduous attention."[1] This extremely low state of religion led the
Dissenters to make extraordinary efforts for its revival, and to extend their influence by church-building, religious publications, and every other means.
The exertions of Matthew Henry, Dr. Watts, Dr.
Doddridge, and numerous excellent men, have told
with incalculable benefit, not only on their own
religious communities, but also upon the Church
itself in her hour of darkness and spiritual trial. The
establishment of seminaries by them for the instruction of young men for the ministry dates from this
period. These efforts had their crowning success in
that great impulse which has been already described,
by which one of the most energetic religious bodies
in the world was called into existence. From the
sympathizers with these great religious movements
within the Church, the Fletchers, the Romaines, the
Cecils, and a host of spiritually-minded men, sprang
up that great "Evangelical" party within our pale whose
too limited views and imperfect learning led on to that
great counteracting force originating at Oxford which
is still fresh in the memory of the older readers of
these lines. We feel conscious that we are treading

---

[1] Haweis' "Impartial Church History," vol. iii. p. 228.

on difficult, and very delicate ground when we enter
upon the diocesan history of the close of the last
century, or even of the opening of that in which we
live. A series of archbishops, excellent in private
life, and of piety and learning unimpeached, pass
before our eye, who were as absolutely unable to
guide the spiritual life of their distant diocese as the
late Duke of York was to direct that of his secularized
bishopric of Osnaburg. Some idea of the infinite
distance between the archbishops and their clergy
may be formed by the panegyric which Hasted bestows upon Archbishop Cornwallis, in these terms :
" At his first residence at Lambeth he abolished that
disagreeable distinction of his chaplains dining at a
separate table, for however the parade and state of
the archbishop's household, as well as the manners
of the former times, might have made it consistent for
them to sit at table with his upper domestics, yet the
change of manners and the alteration of the times
had long made it odious, and complained of by
every one ; and it remained for an archbishop of Dr.
Cornwallis's noble birth to declare that they should
be seated at the same table with himself."[1] The *noblesse
oblige* of the archbishop is somewhat a reflection,
however unintentional, upon his less dignified predecessors. But we are led to ask, if the chaplains sat
with the higher domestics, where a curate could
have his place but in his Grace's kitchen? There
could be little sympathy where there was this great
distance, or even while the slightest memory of it

---

[1] Hasted's " Kent," vol. xii. p. 513.

remained. In those days of slow and perilous travelling, Lambeth was almost as difficult to reach as the Vatican, and even a chaplain as hard of access as a cardinal. When the archbishops travelled into Kent it was in a semi-regal style, and their courtly equipage was generally met by the mayor and corporation at Harbledown, a scene which is within the memory of persons still living. The attendants on the archbishop when he entered the cathedral were girt with swords, which might perhaps be intended to secure him from the fate of Becket.[1] The clergy who assembled at the visitations exhibited a still more suggestive contrast. The late Registrar of the diocese, Mr. Cullen, who, were he now living, would be more than a centenarian, remembered how at the early archidiaconal visitations the clergy sat down after the dinner smoking long white pipes, after the fashion of a farmer's gathering, and doubtless discussing the temporalities of their parishes far more than their spiritual incidents. Railway travelling and railway legislation, in the shape of successive inroads of the Ecclesiastical Commissioners upon the see of Canterbury,—realizing the remark of Thucydides, that the richest countries are always the most exposed to invasion,—have changed the state of the archbishopric and of the diocese to an extent which would in earlier days have been deemed revolutionary. Even the ancient diocese has been dealt with as a conquered country by the same autocratic power; its ancient

---

[1] The writer is indebted for these recollections to his friend John Starr, Esq., whose family had an almost hereditary connection with the chapter of Canterbury.

limits having been extended, its deaneries multiplied, its peculiars destroyed, and almost all its earlier landmarks effaced. It has been the misfortune of the Church of England to be afflicted with periodical fears that the Church is in danger, and the corruptions which abounded in its beneficiary system in the early part of the century awakened the too natural apprehension of some of its most devoted members that the searching reforms which had been already applied to the State would presently be extended to the Church, in a destructive rather than a conservative form. Hence, the fearless and eloquent letter of Lord Henley to the king, which was the first impulse in the movement which resulted in the Ecclesiastical Commission. The Church in her panic forgot, and surrendered entirely, her grand legal position of a combination or congeries of corporations rather than a single corporation, which was capable of being dealt with as a whole, and the result was a surrender by bishops, deans, chapters, and incumbents, representing a vast number of corporate bodies, collective or sole, into the hands of the Commissioners appointed under the new Act, who thenceforth dealt with the whole of the enormous property which fell into their hands, first, as a twofold, then as a single fund, leaving the bishops (until a recent enactment) mere stipendiaries, and the chapters absolutely dependent upon the same precarious support. The fatal surrender once made could never be cancelled, and the diocese of Canterbury has probably suffered more than any other by the merging into the common fund of a large portion of its ancient inheritance. It is not to be

denied that much benefit has accrued to many of the
smaller benefices in the diocese by this great change.
But the cathedral has suffered more, probably, than
any similar body in the kingdom. Its twelve prebendaries have given place to four residentiary canons,
the two archdeaconries being added as a kind of sup-
plement; forming six in all. The commutation of the
estates having been made with more financial skill
on the part of the Commissioners than on that of the
Chapter, the "great church" has been less fortunate
than her suffragan churches, and has probably contributed more in proportion to the common fund
than any other. The days of Archbishops Moore
and Manners-Sutton were days of great sinecures and
of pluralities worthy of the mediæval period; those of
the good Archbishop Howley formed the transition
period between the new and old *régime*, and closed
the princely days of the Archbishopric; while the
simple and almost Apostolic features of the rule of
Archbishop Sumner form the graceful link between a
past which can hardly be regretted and a present
which may well awaken the most sanguine hopes and
recall the most pleasing remembrances. One of the
last links of a past which is fast fading from memory
falls within the recollection of the writer, and is here
gratefully recorded. The late Archdeacon Croft, the
son-in-law of Archbishop Manners-Sutton, however
he may have fallen short of a spiritual standard which
was unknown in his time, was conspicuous for that
kindliness of heart and graceful hospitality which commended and "magnified his office" so greatly to the
clergy with whom he was connected. He had sur-

vived long enough to be the colleague of Archbishop
Sumner, whose singularly beautiful character has left
an image never to be effaced in the memory of
all who witnessed it, and that character seemed
to have made an impression on his later life.
Few will fail to remember the energy and devotion
with which up to the very last the archbishop entered
upon all the duties which the care of the diocese
devolved upon him. Up to his latest years he carried
on his progresses in the diocese, every part of which
was personally known to him ; and when he was
urged to intermit in some degree this active oversight,
he was accustomed to say that the time would come
when he might be unequal to it, but till then he was
anxious to continue his personal knowledge of his
diocese. Travelling in the simplest manner with a
single servant, and only distinguished by that graceful
dignity which was ever conspicuous in him, he is
remembered everywhere as realizing that ideal of the
Apostolic ministry which he had traced in his earliest
and most popular work. Nor is his successor remembered with less affection, though in many respects so
different from him. In him the title of " Father in
God " seemed less a conventional term than a picture
of that paternal character which was read even in his
countenance, and exemplified to all his clergy so
affectionately and so invariably. Of his successor,
who still has been spared to the diocese after a series
of afflictions which are too fresh in the memory of all
his clergy to permit the writer to do more than
allude to them here, it would be unbecoming to
speak in this place. One only remark may here be

made on his primacy, which, as it less conveys an eulogy than a fact, can hardly be held to violate that reserve which is justly required of an historian of his own time.   It is, that without compromising his own religious opinions the present primate has conciliated the respect and affection of the representatives of every school of religious thought and sentiment in his diocese ; a result to which the long history of the primacy, which is here so briefly sketched, can hardly present a parallel.

In closing this faint and hurried retrospect of a history extending over nearly fourteen centuries, we cannot but turn our eyes towards that future which may yet be reserved for the diocese of Canterbury in the life of our National Church.   It is obvious, from the very position which it occupies on the map of England, that it can never, even apart from its metro-political character and venerable historical claims, fail to take a leading part in the future history of our Church.   Standing as it does on the great highway to the Continent, filled with towns of considerable size and importance, whose increase has been more rapid and remarkable than that of any other, except those in the great manufacturing and mining districts, it cannot but take a very conspicuous place in the future history of our country.   We may well rejoice to recognise a consciousness of this great destiny in the active and zealous labours of both clergy and laity in church-building, church-restoration, national education, and in every plan of spiritual advancement and influence which this age of religious activity has everywhere developed.

Perhaps the most important of these labours has
been that in the direction of the education of the
labouring population, in which the voluntary efforts
of the inhabitants of the diocese have been so energetic, as to have rendered the intrusion of Board-
schools less frequent than in many other places.
How long the unequal struggle can continue is a
problem yet unsolved; but it may be safely conjectured, that between the great Church of England and
Wesleyan influences in Kent, the attempt to bring
about a mere secular education will be a more signal
failure here than in any other county in England.

The great religious movements which gave such
varied and often conflicting influences to the spiritual
life of our Church through the rise of the Evangelical
party and the counteracting force of the great Oxford
school, have perhaps less affected the diocese of
Canterbury than many others.   The traditions of the
diocese had been from the period of the Revolution
of a strongly Protestant character, yet blended with a
political conservatism which gave it ever a tendency
towards what would be called moderate high-church
doctrine and practice.   The cathedral city itself has
for generations been distinguished by an Evangelical
tone of preaching and sentiment, which was the
natural result of the vigorous element of foreign
Protestantism which was so early engrafted upon
the native stock.   The numerous surnames of purely
French origin which there meet the eye in every
direction and may be found in every directory, prove
that a large proportion of the inhabitants of the city
are the descendants of the settlers from France and

Flanders in the time of Edward VI., and some of the most eminent of the prebendaries of the cathedral have had a similar foreign origin.[1]

Within the present century and notably in the last forty years, which witnessed the great revival of church architecture, not only the cathedral but also most of the parish churches of the diocese have undergone restorations of various degrees and kinds, from the work of actual rebuilding, which was in too many cases necessary through the prolonged neglect and failures of the previous century, down to that of a reverent and conservative preservation of the failing structure, the best and truest of all restorations. Of this latter work the precious and unique Church of Barfrestone presents a laudable instance ; while that of Minster, in Thanet, exhibits an excess of reproductive power, detracting materially from the impressive effect which it produced on the observer in an earlier day. The Diocesan Society for Church-building, originated by Archbishop Longley, has been a most important agent in this work of architectural progress.

Church extension in the larger towns, as in Maidstone, Ashford, Folkestone, Dover, and other increasing towns, has been carried on with an energy and success which is too well-known to their numerous visitors to need here any special description. In all the larger communities there are churches and ritual forms suited to every spiritual need or religious

[1] As Isaac and Meric Casaubon, Adrian Saravia, Peter du Moulin, and his son of the same name, Bernardinus Ochinus, Gerard Vossius, and others whose names are evidently French or Italian.

taste ; and though the breaking-up of the iron uniformity of an earlier age has left an excess of variety which might well give a pretext to some future Bossuet to write a history of the variations of the Protestant Churches in ritual as well as doctrine, we may yet entertain the hope that the prudence of those who are most tempted to exceed the limits of a wise moderation may be enabled to prove that "though every piece of the building cannot be of one form, ... its perfection consists in this, that out of many moderate varieties and brotherly dissimilitudes that are not vastly disproportional, arises the goodly and graceful symmetry that commends the whole pile and structure." The diocese of Canterbury as filling the place in regard to our English primacy which the "suburbicary churches" did to the great Roman patriarchate, ought to maintain its vantage-ground among the dioceses of England, and to prove itself not unworthy of its ancient name and glory. It cannot afford to live upon the memories of the past, or to remain inactive and unprogressive at a period when every power and influence in Church and State is moving on so rapidly, and with an almost irresistible impulse. Without attempting to reopen those efforts after a union with distant Churches in which so much of the zeal of Archbishop Wake was wasted and lost ; without entering into vain endeavours after a reunion with the Churches which have sprung from herself, and should rather constitute the subject of her deepest thanksgivings than the object of her fruitless regrets, our Church ought to address herself to that first principle of all

real unity, an ardent faith and an active charity.
For "though there may be no immediate hope of
the reunion of Churches or sects, we ought to look
to the future and sow such useful seeds as may produce fruit in the end; and if we merely succeed in
diminishing hatred among Christians, and in rendering them more social in their intercourse, we shall be
amply rewarded for all our troubles and disquie-
tudes." Then "we may safely leave to the providence of God the work of bringing them into a
nearer and more perfect union through the confession of the same faith, when the moment determined
in the secret counsels of Him who overrules all
things shall have arrived."[1]   The assembly of the
Anglican bishops from every part of the world at
Canterbury on the occasion of the recent Conference
at Lambeth, set forth with a touching and inspiring
force the increasing union between the members of
that world - wide communion which looks towards
Canterbury, as Canterbury once looked towards
Rome, and recognises her as still the faithful depo-
sitory of those truths which the great St. Gregory
proclaimed to his Saxon converts.   To this great
tradition we may still fearlessly appeal.   That absolute devotion to the Scriptures, and vindication of
the study of them by the laity which involves the
distinctive principle of the Reformation, as it was
inculcated in the teaching of St. Gregory, so finds
still its fullest development among ourselves.   It was
left for the Gregorys and the Clements of a much

---

[1] Tabaraud, "De la réunion des Communions Chrétiennes,"
pp. 314, 528.

later and degenerate age to denounce the reading
of the Scriptures, in the bull "Unigenitus," and
in periodical maledictions pronounced on those
noble societies whose object is to spread everywhere that great "Epistle of the Heavenly Emperor" as Gregory the Great termed them in his
entreaty to the layman Theodore to read them with
unintermitting diligence.[1] "Study, I entreat you,"
are the words of the great teacher of the Anglo-Saxon
Church, "and daily meditate upon the words of
your Creator. Learn the heart of God from the
words of God."[2] May the Church of England and
the diocese of Canterbury ever hold fast to this first
principle of her ancient teacher, and illustrate their
truth by such an exercise of faith and charity as
may make her a light and an example to those many
and distant Churches which have been now brought,
through the influence of our two last archbishops,
into so close an intercommunion with one another
through the bond of their union with herself. We
have traced in these brief pages the outline of the
Church of England as she was in the days of her
union with Rome—perplexed between many obe-

---

[1] On the strength of the denunciations of the Bull
"Unigenitus" a priest in the diocese of Arezzo, threatened to
refuse absolution to a lady whose custom it was to read the
Scriptures constantly. The Bishop, Mgr. Marcacci, a worthy
successor of the great Gregory, from whose doctrine Clement
XI. had so fatally apostatized, appealed at once to the noble
words of our English apostle and rebuked the follower of his
degenerate successor. — ("Atti dell' Assemblea tenuta in
Firenze, 1787," tom. iv. p. 661.)

[2] Reg. Epp. l. iv. Ind. xiii. Ep. xi.

diences, cumbered with much serving, plundered like the traveller from Jerusalem to Jericho, and in the days preceding her reformation in such a state as to be half-dead, like him. We have seen her revival in the season of the Reformation, its partial eclipse, the return of her liberty and strength, and the afflictions which followed when she leaned upon the arm of flesh, and sought for support rather in the idea that she was a national institution than a Divine incorporation. Few who read these pages can ever believe that she will be led to return to that "obedience" which her stern stepmother imposed upon her in an earlier day, or that she will ever again make Rome "the centre of all her hopes and all her fears, and the pole-star to which all her teaching points."[1] Fortunately, she has a better centre both for her hopes and fears, and may rest her eye upon a "more sure word of prophecy" than any which can be inspired by the illusive dream of infallibility, "taking heed unto it as unto a light that shineth in a dark place" until the judgment of all that exalts itself against the true and only Head of the Church shall be proclaimed amid the joys and terrors of the "great and terrible day of the Lord."

---

[1] "Roma ch'è il centro di tutti i loro timori e di tutte le loro speranze è la stella polare che gli dirige."—The Abate Tanzini, in his sketch of the degraded state of the Tuscan clergy in 1787.—"Istoria dell' Assemblea," pref. p. viii.

SUCCESSION OF THE ARCHBISHOPS OF CANTERBURY,

FROM THE

CONSECRATION OF ST. AUGUSTINE.

With a few exceptions, it may be considered that the date of the death of an Archbishop is contemporary with the date of the accession of his successor.

Names of Archbishops.	Year of Consecr.	Acc. or Trans.
	A. D.	A. D.
1 Augustine	597	597
2 Laurentius	604	604
3 Mellitus	604	619
4 Justus	604	624
5 Honorius	627	627
6 Deusdedit	655	655
7 Theodore	668	668
8 Berhtwald	693	693
9 Tatwin	731	731
10 Nothelm	735	735
11 Cuthbert	736	741
12 Bregwin	759	759
13 Jaenberht	766	766
14 Ethelhard	793	793
15 Wlfred	805	805
16 Feologild	832	832
17 Ceolnoth	833	833
18 Ethelred	870	870
19 Plegmund	890	890
20 Athelm	909	914
21 Wulfhelm	914	923
22 Odo	926	942
23 Alfsin	951	959
24 Dunstan	957	960
25 Ethelgar	980	988

Names of Archbishops.	Year of Consecr.	Acc. or Trans.
	A.D.	A.D.
26 Sigeric	985	990
27 Elfric	990	995
28 Elphege	984	1005
29 Living..	999	1013
30 Ethelnoth	1020	1020
31 Eadsi	1035	1038
32 Robert	1044	1051
33 Stigand (*dep.* 1070)	1043	1052
34 Lanfranc.....................................	1070	1070
35 Anselm	1093	1093
36 Ralph d'Escures	1108	1114
37 William de Corbeuil...................	1123	1123
38 Theobald	1139	1139
39 Thomas Becket	1162	1162
40 Richard	1174	1174
41 Baldwin	1180	1185
42 Hubert Fitz Walter	1189	1193
43 Stephen Langton	1207	1207
44 Richard Grant	1229	1229
45 Edmund Rich	1234	1234
46 Boniface.....................................	1245	1245
47 Robert Kilwardby........................	1273	1273
48 John Peckham	1279	1279
49 Robert Winchelsey	1294	1294
50 Walter Reynolds	1308	1313
51 Simon Meopham	1328	1328
52 John Stratford	1323	1333
53 Thomas Bradwardine	1349	1349
54 Simon Islip	1349	1346
55 Simon Langham	1366	1369
56 William Whittlesey	......	1368
57 Simon Sudbury...........................	1362	1375
58 William Courtenay	1370	1381
59 Thomas Arundel	1374	1396
60 Henry Chicheley	1408	1414
61 John Stafford.............................	1425	1443
62 John Kemp	1419	1452
63 Thomas Bourgchier	1435	1454
64 John Morton	1479	1486
65 Henry Dene	1496	1502
66 William Warham	1502	1503

Names of Archbishops.	Year of Consecr	Acc. or Trans.
	A. D.	A. D.
67 Thomas Cranmer	1533	1533
68 Reginald Pole	1556	1556
69 Matthew Parker	1559	1559
70 Edmund Grindal	1559	1575
71 John Whitgift	1577	1583
72 Richard Bancroft	1597	1604
73 George Abbott	1609	1610
74 William Laud	1621	1633
75 William Juxon	1633	1660
76 Gilbert Sheldon.........................	1669	1663
77 William Sancroft	1678	1677
(*deprived in* 1690)		
78 John Tillotson	1691	1691
79 Thomas Tenison	1692	1695
80 William Wake	1705	1715
81 John Potter	1715	1736
82 Thomas Herring	1738	1747
83 Matthew Hutton	1743	1757
84 Thomas Secker..........................	1735	1758
85 Frederick Cornwallis	1750	1768
86 John Moore	1775	1783
87 Charles Manners Sutton	1792	1805
88 William Howley	1813	1828
89 John Bird Sumner	1828	1848
90 Charles Thomas Longley...............	1836	1862
91 Archibald Campbell Tait	1856	1868

DEANS AND PRIORS OF CANTERBURY.

BEFORE ARCHBISHOP LANFRANC.

	Names.	Date of Installation.	Date of Death.
		A. D.	A. D.
1	Aegelwine	......	......
2	Chilnoth	......	870
3	Alfric	......	......
4	Kinsyn	......	......
5	Maurice	......	......
6	Alsine	......	......
7	Aelfwine	......	......
8	Athelsine	......	......
9	Aelfwine II.	......	......
10	Athelsine II.	......	......
11	Ægelnoth or Ethelnoth	......	1008
12	Godrich	......	......

PRIORS.

		Date of Installation.	Date of Death.
1	Henry	......	1102
2	Ernulphus or Arnulphus	1096	1123-4
3	Conrad	......	1127
4	Gosfridus or Goffride	......	1154
5	Elmerus	1123	1137
6	Jeremiah (deposed)	1143	......
7	Walter, surnamed Durdens	......	1161
8	Walter (Parvus) deposed	1153	......
9	Wybert	......	1167
10	[Oliver]	......	......
11	Richard	......	......
12	Odo	......	1199
13	Benedict	1175	1194
14	Harlewine	1177	......
	(resigned)	1179	......
15	Alanus	1179	1202

Names.—Priors continued.	Date of Installation.	Date of Death.
	A. D.	A. D.
16 Honorius	1186-7	1188
17 Roger Norris	1189	......
18 Osbern de Bristo	1190	......
19 Galfridus	1191	1205-6
20 John de Chatham	1206	......
21 Walter III.	......	......
22 John II. (de Sittingburn)	1222	1234
23 Roger de la Lee	1232	1244
24 Nicholas de Sandwich	1244	1289
25 Roger de St. Elphege	1258	1263
26 Adam de Chillenden	......	1274
27 Thomas Ryngmere	1274	......
28 Henry de Estria	1285	1331
29 Richard de Oxinden	1331	1338
30 Robert Hathbrand	......	1370
31 Richard Gillingham	......	1376
32 Stephen Mongeham	1376	1377
33 John Finch (Winch) of Winchilsea...	1377	1391
34 Thomas Chillenden	1391	1411
35 John Woodnesborough	1411	1427
36 William Molash	1428	1437
37 John Salisbury	1437	1445
38 John Elham	1446	1448
39 Thomas Goldston I.	1449	1468
40 John Oxney or Oxne	1468	1471
41 William Petham	1471	1471
42 William Sellynge	1472	1494
43 Thomas Goldston II.	......	1517
44 Thomas Goldwell (resigned)	......	......

DEANS.

1 Nicholas Wootton	1541	1567
2 Thomas Goodwin	1567	1590
3 Richard Rogers	1584	1597
4 Thomas Nevil	1597	1615
5 Charles Fotherby	1615	1619
6 John Boys	1619	1625
7 Isaac Bargrave	1625	1643
8 George Aglionby	...	1643
9 Thomas Turner	1660	1672
10 John Tillotson	1672	1694

Names.—Deans continued.	Date of Installation.	Date of Death.
	A. D.	A. D.
11 John Sharp	1689	1714
12 George Hooper	1691	1721
13 George Stanhope	1704	1728
14 Elias Sydall	1728	1733
15 John Lynch	1734	1760
16 William Friend	1760	1766
17 John Potter	1766	1770
18 Hon. Brownlow North	1770	......
19 John Moore	1771	1805
20 Hon. James Cornwallis	1775	......
21 George Horne	1781	1792
22 William Buller	1790	......
23 Folliot Herbert Walker Cornewall	1793	......
24 Thomas Powis	1797	......
25 Gerard Andrews	1809	1825
26 Hon. Hugh Percy	1825	1857
27 Hon. Richard Bagot	1827	1854
28 William Rowe Lyall	1845	1857
29 Henry Alford	1857	1871
30 Robert Payne Smith	1871	......

INDEX.

WYMAN AND SONS, PRINTERS, GREAT QUEEN STREET, LONDON.

PUBLICATIONS

OF THE

Society for Promoting Christian Knowledge

THE FATHERS FOR ENGLISH READERS.

A Series of Monographs on the Chief Fathers of the Church.
Fcap. 8vo., cloth boards, 2s. each.

Boniface. By the Rev. Canon GREGORY SMITH, M.A.

Clement of Alexandria. By the Rev. F. R. MONTGOMERY HITCHCOCK, B.D. (3s.)

Gregory the Great. By the late Rev. J. BARMBY, B.D.

Leo the Great. By the Rev. Canon GORE, M.A.

Saint Ambrose: his Life, Times, and Teaching. By the Ven. Archdeacon THORNTON, D.D.

Saint Athanasius: his Life and Times. By the Rev. R. WHELER BUSH. (2s. 6d.)

Saint Augustine. By the Rev. E. L. CUTTS, D.D.

Saint Basil the Great. By the Rev. RICHARD T. SMITH, B.D.

Saint Bernard, Abbot of Clairvaux, A.D. 1091—1153. By the Rev. S. J. EALES, M.A., D.C.L. (2s. 6d.)

Saint Hilary of Poitiers, and Saint Martin of Tours. By the Rev. J. GIBSON CAZENOVE, D.D.

Saint Jerome. By the Rev. EDWARD L. CUTTS, D.D.

Saint John of Damascus. By the Rev. J. H. LUPTON, M.A.

Saint Patrick: his Life and Teaching. By the Rev. E. J. NEWELL, M.A. (2s. 6d.)

Synesius of Cyrene, Philosopher and Bishop. By ALICE GARDNER.

The Apostolic Fathers. By the Rev. Canon SCOTT-HOLLAND.

The Defenders of the Faith; or, The Christian Apologists of the Second and Third Centuries. By the Rev. F. WATSON, D.D.

The Venerable Bede. By the Right Rev. G. F. BROWNE, D.D.

NON-CHRISTIAN RELIGIOUS SYSTEMS.

Fcap. 8vo., cloth boards, 2s. 6d. each.

Buddhism : Being a Sketch of the Life and Teachings of Gautama, the Buddha. A New and Revised Edition (18th Thousand). By T. W. RHYS DAVIDS, M.A. With Map.

Buddhism in China. By the late Rev. S. BEAL. With Map.

Christianity and Buddhism : a Comparison and a Contrast. By the Rev. T. STERLING BERRY, D.D.

Confucianism and Taouism. By Professor DOUGLAS, of the British Museum. With Map.

Hinduism. By the late Sir M. MONIER WILLIAMS, M.A., D.C.L. A New and Revised Edition. With Map.

Islam and its Founder. By J. W. H. STOBART. With Map.

Islam as a Missionary Religion. By CHARLES R. HAINES. (2s.)

Studies of Non-Christian Religions. By ELIOT HOWARD.

The Coran : its Composition and Teaching, and the Testimony it bears to the Holy Scriptures. By Sir WILLIAM MUIR, K.C.S.I., LL.D., D.C.L., Ph.D. A New and Revised Edition.

The Religion of the Crescent ; or Islam : its Strength, its Weakness, **its Origin, its** Influence. By the Rev. W. ST. CLAIR TISDALL. (4s.)

THE HEATHEN WORLD AND ST. PAUL.

Fcap. 8vo., cloth boards, 2s. each.

St. Paul in Damascus and Arabia. By the Rev. GEORGE RAWLINSON, M.A., Canon of Canterbury. With Map.

St. Paul at Rome. By the late Very Rev. CHARLES MERIVALE, D.D., D.C.L., Dean of Ely. With Map.

St. Paul in Asia Minor and at the Syrian Antioch. By the late Rev. E. II. PLUMPTRE, D.D. With Map.

THE HOME LIBRARY.

Crown 8vo., cloth boards, 3s. 6d. each.

Black and White. Mission Stories. By the late H. FORDE.

Charlemagne. By the Rev. E. L. CUTTS, D.D. With Map.

Constantine the Great : the Union of Church and State. By the Rev. EDWARD L. CUTTS, D.D.

John Hus : the Commencement of Resistance to Papal Authority on the part of the Inferior Clergy. By the Rev. A. H. WRATISLAW.

Judæa and her Rulers, from Nebuchadnezzar **to Vespasian.** By M. BRAMSTON. With Map.

Mazarin. By the late GUSTAVE MASSON.

Military Religious Orders of the Middle Ages : the Hospitallers, the Templars, the Teutonic Knights, and others. By the Rev. F. C. WOODHOUSE.

Mitslav ; or, the Conversion of Pomerania. By the late Right Rev. R. MILMAN, D.D.

Narcissus. A Tale of Early Christian Times. By the Right Rev. W. BOYD CARPENTER.

Richelieu. By the late GUSTAVE MASSON.

Sketches of the Women of Christendom. By the late Mrs. RUNDLE CHARLES.

The Churchman's Life of Wesley. By R. DENNY URLIN, Esq.

The Church in Roman Gaul. By the Rev. R. T. SMITH. With Map

The Inner Life, as Revealed in the Correspondence of Celebrated Christians. Edited by the late Rev. T. ERSKINE.

The Life of the Soul in the World : its Nature, Needs, Dangers, Sorrows, Aids, and Joys. By the Rev. F. C. WOODHOUSE.

The North African Church. By the late Rev. J. LLOYD. With Map.

Thoughts and Characters : being Selections from the Writings of the late Mrs. RUNDLE CHARLES.

EARLY CHURCH CLASSICS.

Small post 8vo., cloth boards, 1s. each.

Bishop Sarapion's Prayer Book. An Egyptian Pontifical (dated probably about A.D. 350-356). Translated from the Edition of Dr. G. WOBBERMIN, with Introduction, Notes, and Indices, by the Right Rev. JOHN WORDSWORTH, D.D., Bishop of Salisbury. (1s. 6d.)

St. Augustine's Treatise on the City of God. By the Rev. F. R. M. HITCHCOCK, M.A., B.D. (1s. 6d.)

St. Polycarp, Bishop of Smyrna. By the Rev. BLOMFIELD JACKSON, M.A.

The Doctrine of the Twelve Apostles. Translated into English, with Introduction and Notes, by Rev. C. BIGG, D.D.

The Epistle of St. Clement, Bishop of Rome. By the Rev. JOHN A. F. GREGG, M.A.

The Epistle of the Gallican Churches: Lugdunum and Vienna. With an Appendix containing Tertullian's Address to Martyrs, and the Passion of St. Perpetua. Translated, with Introduction and Notes, by the Rev. T. HERBERT BINDLEY, B.D.

The Epistles of St. Ignatius, Bishop of Antioch. By the Rev. J. H. SRAWLEY, M.A. In two volumes. (1s. each.)

The Liturgy of the Eighth Book of "the Apostolic Constitutions," commonly called "The Clementine Liturgy." Translated into English, with Introduction and Notes, by the Rev. R. H. CRESSWELL, M.A. (1s. 6d.)

ANCIENT HISTORY FROM THE MONUMENTS.

Fcap. 8vo., cloth boards, 2s. each.

Assyria, from the Earliest Times to the Fall of Nineveh. By the late GEORGE SMITH, of the British Museum. New and Revised Edition by the Rev. Professor SAYCE.

Babylonia, The History of. By the late GEORGE SMITH. Edited by the Rev. Professor SAYCE.

Persia, from the Earliest Period to the Arab Conquest. By the late W. S. W. VAUX, M.A., F.R.S. A New and Revised Edition, by the Rev. Professor SAYCE.

Sinai, from the Fourth Egyptian Dynasty to the Present Day. By the late H. SPENCER PALMER. A New Edition, revised throughout by the Rev. Professor SAYCE.

DIOCESAN HISTORIES.

Bath and Wells. By the Rev. W. HUNT. With Map. Fcap. 8vo. Cloth boards. 2s. 6d.

Canterbury. By the late Rev. R. C. JENKINS. With Map. Fcap. 8vo. Cloth boards. 3s. 6d.

Carlisle. By the late RICHARD S. FERGUSON. With Map. Fcap. 8vo. Cloth boards. 2s. 6d.

Chester. By the Rev. RUPERT H. MORRIS, D.D. With Map. Fcap. 8vo. Cloth boards. 3s.

Chichester. By the Rev. W. R. W. STEPHENS. With Map and Plan of the Cathedral. Fcap. 8vo. Cloth boards. 2s. 6d.

Durham. By the Rev. J. L. Low. With Map and Plan. Fcap. 8vo. Cloth boards. 2s. 6d.

Hereford. By the late Rev. Canon PHILLOTT. With Map. Fcap. 8vo. Cloth boards. 3s.

Lichfield. By the Rev. W. BERESFORD. With Map. Fcap. 8vo. Cloth boards. 2s. 6d.

Lincoln. By the late Rev. Canon E. VENABLES, and the late Ven. Archdeacon PERRY. With Map. Fcap. 8vo. Cloth boards. 4s.

Norwich. By the Rev. A. JESSOPP, D.D. With Map. Fcap. 8vo. Cloth boards. 2s. 6d.

Oxford. By the Rev. E. MARSHALL, M.A. With Map. Fcap. 8vo. Cloth boards. 2s. 6d.

Peterborough. By the Rev. G. A. POOLE, M.A. With Map. Fcap. 8vo. Cloth boards. 2s. 6d.

Rochester. By the Rev. A. J. PEARMAN. With Map. Fcap. 8vo. Cloth boards. 4s.

Salisbury. By the Rev. W. H. JONES. With Map and Plan. Fcap. 8vo. Cloth boards. 2s. 6d.

Sodor and Man. By A. W. MOORE, M.A. With Map. Fcap. 8vo. Cloth boards. 3s.

St. Asaph. By the Venerable Archdeacon THOMAS. With Map. Fcap. 8vo. Cloth boards 2s.

St. David's. By the Rev. Canon BEVAN. With Map. Fcap. 8vo. Cloth boards. 2s. 6d.

Winchester. By the Rev. Canon BENHAM, B.D. With Map. Fcap. 8vo. Cloth boards. 3s.

Worcester. By Rev. I. GREGORY SMITH and Rev. PHIPPS ONSLOW. With Map. Fcap. 8vo. Cloth boards. 3s. 6d.

York. By the Rev. Canon ORNSBY, M.A. With Map. Fcap. 8vo. Cloth boards. 3s. 6d.

MISCELLANEOUS PUBLICATIONS.

"A Glad Service." By Lady HAMMICK, Author of " Hearts and Lives given to Christ." A series of Lessons for Girls. Post 8vo., cloth boards, 1s. 6d.

Bible Places; or, the Topography of the Holy Land: a Succinct Account of all the Places, Rivers, and Mountains of the Land of Israel mentioned in the Bible, so far as they have been identified. Together with their Modern Names and Historical References. By the Rev. Canon TRISTRAM, D.D., LL.D., F.R.S. New Edition. Crown 8vo. With Map and numerous Woodcuts. Cloth boards, 5s.

Cheerful Christianity. Having to do with the Lesser Beauties and Blemishes of the Christian Life. By L. B. WALFORD. Printed in red and black. Post 8vo., cloth boards, 1s. 6d.

China. By Professor R. K. DOUGLAS, of the British Museum. With Map, and eight full-page Illustrations, and several Vignettes. Post 8vo., cloth boards, 5s.

Christians under the Crescent in Asia. By the Rev. E. L. CUTTS, D.D., Author of "Turning Points of Church History," etc. With numerous Illustrations. Post 8vo., cloth boards, 5s.

Gospel of Suffering, The. By Mrs. COLIN G. CAMPBELL, Author of "Bible Thoughts for Daily Life." Post 8vo., cloth boards, 1s.

Illustrated Notes on English Church History. Vol. I. From the Earliest Times to the Dawn of the Reformation. Vol. II. The Reformation and Modern Church Work. By the Rev. C. A. LANE. New and Revised Edition, with numerous Illustrations. Crown 8vo., cloth boards, each 1s. The two parts in one volume, 2s. 6d.

Israel, The Land of. A Journal of Travels in Palestine, undertaken with Special Reference to its Physical Character. Fourth Edition, revised. By Rev. Canon TRISTRAM, D.D., LL.D., F.R.S. With numerous Illustrations. Cloth boards, 10s. 6d.

Jewish Nation, A History of the. From the Earliest Times to the Present Day. By the late E. H. PALMER. Crown 8vo. With Map and numerous Illustrations. Cloth boards, 4s.

Lesser Lights; or, Some **of** the Minor Characters of Scripture traced with **a** View **to** Instruction and Example **in** Daily Life. By the Rev. F. BOURDILLON, M.A. Post 8vo., cloth boards. First and Second Series, each 2s. 6d. Third Series, 2s.

Magic **of Sympathy, The.** By EMILY C. ORR. Small post 8vo., cloth boards, 1s.

Natural **History of the Bible,** The: being a Review of the Physical Geography, Geology, and Meteorology of the Holy Land, with a Description of every Animal and Plant mentioned in Holy Scripture. By the Rev. Canon TRISTRAM, D.D., LL.D., F.R.S. Crown 8vo. With numerous Illustrations. Cloth boards, 5s.

Official Year-Book of the Church of England. Demy 8vo., paper boards, 3s. ; limp cloth, 4s.

Our Own Book. Very plain reading for people in humble life. By the Rev. F. BOURDILLON, M.A., Author of "Bedside Readings," etc. Post 8vo., cloth boards, 1s.

Parish Priests and Their **People in** the Middle Ages in England. By the Rev. E. L. CUTTS, D.D. With numerous Illustrations. Demy 8vo., cloth boards, 7s. 6d.

Pictorial Architecture **of the British Isles.** By Rev. H. H. BISHOP. With 150 illustrations. Royal 4to., cloth boards, 4s.

Pictorial Architecture of Greece and Italy. By the Rev. H. H. BISHOP. With numerous Illustrations. Royal 4to., cloth boards, 3s. 6d.

Pictorial Geography **of the British Isles.** By MARY E. PALGRAVE. With numerous Illustrations. Royal 4to., cloth boards, 3s. 6d.

Plain **Words for Christ.** By the late Rev. R. G. DUTTON. Being a series of Readings for Working Men. Post 8vo., 1s.

Russia, Past and Present. Adapted from the German of Lankenau and Oelnitz. By Mrs. CHESTER. With Map and three page Woodcuts and Vignettes. Post 8vo., cloth boards, 5s.

Scripture Manners and Customs : being an Account of the Domestic Habits, Arts, etc., of Eastern Nations mentioned in Holy Scripture. Twenty-second Edition. Crown 8vo. With numerous Woodcuts. Cloth boards, 4*s.*

Spiritual Counsels ; or, Helps and Hindrances to Holy Living. By the late Rev. R. G. DUTTON, M.A. Post 8vo., cloth boards, 1*s.*

Thoughts for Men and Women. The Lord's Prayer. By EMILY C. ORR. Post 8vo., 1*s.*

Thoughts for Working Days. Daily Readings for a month, original and selected. By EMILY C. ORR. Post 8vo., 1*s.*

The True Vine. By the late Mrs. RUNDLE CHARLES. With border-lines in red. Post 8vo., cloth boards, 1*s.* 6*d.*

Turning Points of English Church History. By the Rev. E. L. CUTTS, D.D. New and Revised Edition. Crown 8vo., cloth boards, 3*s.* 6*d.*

Turning Points of General Church History. By the Rev. E. L. CUTTS, D.D. Crown 8vo., cloth boards, 4*s.*

Verses. By the late CHRISTINA G. ROSSETTI. Small post 8vo., cloth boards. 3*s.* 6*d.*

SOCIETY FOR PROMOTING CHRISTIAN KNOWLEDGE

LONDON : NORTHUMBERLAND AVENUE, W.C.

43, QUEEN VICTORIA STREET, E.C.